THE PROMISE OF THE FOREIGN

THE PROMISE OF THE FOREIGN

NATIONALISM AND THE TECHNICS OF TRANSLATION IN THE SPANISH PHILIPPINES

Vicente L. Rafael

Duke University Press DURHAM AND LONDON 2005

© 2005 Duke University Press

All rights reserved

Printed in the United States of America

on acid-free paper ∞

Typeset in Scala and Othello types by

Keystone Typesetting, Inc.

Library of Congress Cataloging-in-Publication Data

appear on the last printed page of this book.

For Leila, Carlos, and Aliaha

*To redeem in his own tongue that pure language exiled in
the foreign tongue, to liberate by transposing this pure language
captive in the work, such is the task of the translator.*

WALTER BENJAMIN

*Each time I open my mouth, each time I speak or write,
I* promise. *Whether I like it or not. This promise heralds the
uniqueness of a language yet to come. It . . . precedes all language,
summons all speech and already belongs to each language as it
does to all speech. . . . It is not possible to speak outside of this
promise that gives a language, the uniqueness of the idiom,
but only by promising to give it.*

JACQUES DERRIDA

CONTENTS

ACKNOWLEDGMENTS

This book has grown out of the tangled legacies of several writers who have come to shape my thinking about nationalism, translation, and related topics. John Schumacher, sj, introduced me to the serious study of nationalism in the Philippines. His careful and precise work on the first generation of Filipino nationalists is still unsurpassed. On Schumacher's evidentiary grounds, many other scholars have set up their own interpretive forays into Philippine history. James T. Siegel's political ethnography of Indonesian nationalism and his more recent work on sorcery have been inspired acts of deconstructive thinking set amid colonial and postcolonial contexts. The strength and generosity of his work is such that I find myself often compelled to translate what he has written about Indonesia (and what lies outside of it) in terms that might make sense in the different context of the Philippines. No one today writing about nationalism, whether in Southeast Asia or beyond, can do so without consulting the work of Benedict Anderson. Several sections of this book bear the ineluctable traces of his thinking, though in ways that will seem sufficiently displaced and distorted, and so even more telling of his influence. I am also indebted to Jacques Derrida, Martin Heidegger, and Walter Benjamin whose inquiries into language, technology, and futurity have helped me engage the aporias of colonialism and nationalism. The marks of these authors are dispersed and unevenly distributed throughout this book, registered in endnotes rather than in more explicit theoretical distractions.

Michael Meeker read earlier drafts of several chapters and patiently pointed out parts that seemed problematic while prodding me to pursue other interpretive possibilities. Francisco Benitez and John Sidel also shared with me many astute comments and criticisms of the manuscript. Two anonymous readers for Duke University Press offered strong and detailed readings of subsequent drafts that proved extremely beneficial for revising the manuscript. As he had with my earlier books,

Ken Wissoker provided keen editorial advice and was enthusiastically supportive of this project from its inception.

I must thank many other colleagues who gave me time and tools with which to shape this book. Reynaldo Ileto was always patient and attentive to the questions I raised in relation to nationalism and the vernacular. Time and time again, Ambeth Ocampo shared with me many of the Philippine sources for this study and clarified some of my questions about Rizal. Nicanor Tiongson saved me from several errors relating to the section on vernacular theater. Others in Manila who have generously supported me in my work include Karina Bolasco of Anvil Publishing; Filomeno Aguilar Jr., Maricor Baytion, Eduardo José Calasanz, the late Doreen Fernandez, Lulu Reyes, Soledad Reyes, and Bennie Santos of Ateneo de Manila University; Virgilio Almario, José Buenconsejo, Nita Churchill, Neil Garcia, Preachy Legasto, and Bienvenido Lumbera of the University of the Philippines; and writers Tina Cuyugan, Rayvi Sunico, Krip Yuson, and Jessica Zafra.

Portions of this book were given as talks in various venues, and I thank those who provided me with receptive audiences and helpful comments: Itty Abraham, Emily Apter, Pheng Cheah, Carol Gluck, Monica Fagioli, Jeff Handler, Susan Harding, Carol Hau, Lotta Hedman, Marilyn Ivy, Jo Labanyi, Christian Lammerts, Rosalind Morris, Yoshiko Nagano, John Pemberton, Craig Reynolds, Geoff Robinson, Florentino Rodao, Michael Salman, Doris Sommer, Mary Steedly, Karen Strassler, Neferti Tadiar, Ricardo Trimillios, Anna Tsing, Sarah Zambotti, and Peter Zinoman. It is with great fondness that I acknowledge the support of my colleagues at the University of California, San Diego, where earlier sections of this book were written: Suzanne Brenner, Yen Espiritu, Steve Fagin, Val Hartouni, Robert Hortwitz, Ramon Gutierrez, George Lipsitz, Richard Madsen, Chandra Mukerji, Carol Padden, Michael Schudson, and Kit Woolard. My colleagues at the department of history and the Southeast Asian Studies Center at the University of Washington have also been generous with their support of the later stages of this work, and I am especially grateful to Ann Anagnost, Tani Barlow, Gillian Harkins, John Findlay, Judith Henchy, Susan Jeffords, Chandan Reddy, Laurie Sears, Nikhil Singh, Bob Stacey, Kathleen Woodward, and the fellows at the Society of Scholars, Simpson Center for the Humanities. I also thank Michael Cullinane and Glenn May for responding to queries I had about the Katipunan.

A John Simon Guggenheim Fellowship enabled me to carry out

much of the research for this book, and support from the following institutions allowed me to complete the writing of the manuscript: the University of California Humanities Research Institute; the Asian Studies Department at the University of Hawai'i, Manoa; the Committee on Research and the Department of Communication, University of California, San Diego; the Department of History and the Simpson Humanities Center at the University of Washington.

A version of chapter 1 appeared in Doris Sommer, ed., *The Places of History: Regionalism Revisited in Latin America* (Durham: Duke University Press, 1999) and part of chapter 2 was published in James T. Siegel and Audrey Kahin, eds., *Southeast Asia Over Three Generations: Essays Presented to Benedict R. O'G. Anderson* (Ithaca, N.Y.: Cornell Southeast Asia Program Publications, 2003). I thank the respective editors for permission to reprint the revised versions here.

As in the past, the care of and for my extended family was crucial in every way to the writing of this book and I thank them all: Carol Dahl (who, even now, reminds me to listen); Craig and Cristi Rasmussen; Gregory Rand; Yoshiko, Daudi, and Dana Harden-Abe; and Catalina, José, David, Enrique, Rosemary, and Menchie Rafael. I am especially grateful to the youngest ones, who will be left with the impossible task of bearing witness to a future yet to come: Leila Dahl-Abe, Carlos Rafael, and Aliaha Rafael. It is to them that I dedicate this book.

PREFACE

"Forgetting, and I would even go so far as to say historical error, forms an essential factor in the creation of a nation," writes Ernest Renan in his classic essay "Que'est-ce qu'une nation?" (1882). Indeed, "the essence of a nation," he says in a much-cited passage, "is that all of its individual members should have many things in common; and also that all of them should have forgotten many things. . . . Every French citizen ought to have already forgotten St. Bartholomew, and the massacres of the Midi in the thirteenth century."[1] This imperative to cultivate a shared amnesia has to do with the fact that every nation is founded on violence borne by political and cultural differences. Constitutionally hybrid, nations are made up of peoples with divergent ethnic, racial, religious, economic, and linguistic origins. To arrive at what Renan calls a "fusion" necessary for nationhood, such differences must be set aside. Overcoming them allows for assimilation into a new community. Such overcoming requires forgetting one's origins. "It is good for all to know how to forget," he writes.[2] In place of a heterogenous and conflict-ridden past, one takes on a common legacy that marks out a shared destiny.

What does this common legacy—what Renan calls the "spiritual principle" that animates nations—consist of? It has to do with inheritance and commemoration. Renan argues that the nation's "soul" resides in the sacrifices of those who have suffered and died for its sake. Such sacrificial deaths call out to the living, whose responsibility is to mourn those who have passed on.[3] Mourning means caring for this inheritance of death. By commemorating the suffering of the dead, we, whoever we are, recall not their individual lives in all their contingency and particularity, but the cumulative effect of their end. In this way, we come to regard them as ancestors whose deaths form a collective gift. Reconceptualizing death as a gift makes possible the emergence and survival of the nation. The calculated and ritualized act of forgetting thus produces a new genealogy. Mourning the dead, which is to say, remembering to forget them, we lay claim to what Renan calls their "glory." We pass on their, and our, passing on to future generations.[4]

If Renan is right—that the forgetting of origins comprises the essence of nationhood—such a task entails two things: substitution and estrangement. From the recent scholarship on nationalism, we learn that in fact the real origins of the nation lie outside of the national. These include but are not limited to the violent and revolutionary breakup of dynastic, religious, and colonial orders; the expansion of capitalist markets in general and print capitalism in particular; the rise of new technologies of transportation and communication; the vernacularization of languages of power; the spread of the serial, mechanical temporality of clock and calendar alongside modern modes of publicity such as newspapers and novels producing new publics populated by emergent social types; and the compulsion, especially among emergent elites, to comparative thinking.[5] Such historical events comprise the leading features of modernity and furnished the conditions of possibility for the rise of the nation-form. These developments, as uneven as they were overdetermined, were global in scope and therefore beyond and before the national. They make up a kind of historical excess of which the nation is but an effect. While they properly belong to the study of the formation of nations, there is nothing about them that is proper or native to the nation as such.

In Renan, however, we see how the historical and technical conditions for nationhood are humanized and domesticated. The notion of sacrifice—of death as a gift to the living that creates among them a filial bond—comes to substitute for all those forces that came before and continue to come beyond the nation. Nationalist discourses replace the violent heterogeneity of the historical and the nonhuman agency of the technological with unifying narratives about "our glorious past," and "our obligations to the future." Meant to spur assimilation and set the moral terms of community, such narratives set differences aside. They thus estrange the nation's origins, which, to begin with, are not national at all. The call to mourn the dead is an oblique acknowledgment that the nation is founded on what it cannot comprehend, much less incorporate. But it is also a means for disavowing this fact. Put differently, the substitution of the "sacrificial dead" for the intractable complications of history and technology is a way of remembering to forget the essential strangeness of national origins. One kind of alien presence, imagined as innocent and beneficial, comes to stand in the place of another that, while not exactly malevolent, produces effects that are contradictory, unpredictable, at times destructive, and at others emancipatory. What comes to be regarded as a guarantor of goodness and legitimacy is exchanged for that which works in the world as a principle of equivocation and a force of ambivalence.[6]

Nationalism, or the conjuring of the nation by way of substitution and estrangement, is the topic of this book. To that double process of appropriating and replacing what is foreign while keeping its foreignness in view I give the name *translation*. Nationalism understood as translation revises (in the strong sense of that word) origins for the sake of projecting a new basis of filiation. At the same time, it keeps in reserve something of the alien quality of origins, investing it with a power to explain the past and underwrite the coming of a future.

This book examines the beginnings of Filipino nationalism in the later nineteenth century until the eve of the revolution of 1896. It argues that early Filipino nationalism has its roots in the dual history of Spanish colonialism and Catholic conversion, and that it sought to account for its contradictory origins by means of translation. It sought, that is, to appropriate an aspect of the Catholic-colonial regime and invest it with a power it did not originally have. In this historical context, I focus on Castilian, the language of the colonizer, which captivated the thinking of Filipino nationalists.[7] The latter saw in Castilian a force of communication with which to address those on top of the colonial hierarchy, all the way to the metropole. Often to their surprise, they received all sorts of responses, though not always what they had hoped for. Castilian also allowed them to communicate among themselves, thereby enabling them to go beyond their linguistic and geographical differences. It gave them a medium with which to leave, even if only momentarily, their origins behind and identify with the coming of an alternative, pre- as well as postcolonial history.[8] Furthermore, when incorporated into vernacular literature, Castilian had a transformative effect, extending and amplifying the literature's communicative capacity and arguably laying the ground for the formation of a nationalist public sphere. The "Castilianization" of the vernacular—that is, the estrangement of the latter through its assimilation of the former—would characterize vernacular theater, the earliest form of mass entertainment in the colony, and would provide a point of convergence between elite and mass interests in the power they sensed was at work in Castilian.

Such developments were borne by a pervasive nationalist fantasy:

that of harnessing Castilian into a lingua franca with which to dispel the oppressive parochialism and social inequalities in the colony. Castilian, or more precisely the communicative power associated with it, would, or so nationalists thought, promote the assimilation of the colony's disparate peoples as full citizens of Spain, and when that project failed, as citizens of a new and independent Filipino nation. In this way did Castilian function as a technic for overcoming what nationalists could not fully account for: the ineradicable contingency of their differences and the contradictions of colonial society. In short, the foreignness of Castilian, the fact that it was a second language, enhanced Castilian's telecommunicative reach. Discovering a recurring foreignness within their "own" language and society, mass audiences and actors in vernacular plays, nationalist elites in exile, and, later on, revolutionary fighters in the colony sought in varying ways to appropriate it. Doing so meant tapping into previously inaccessible and secret sources of power that lay beyond the threshold of colonial society. Feeling the pressure of this power, nationalists saw in it the promise of nationhood, but also a recurring menace to its realization.

In what follows, I trace the genesis of this promise, the Filipino and Spanish responses to its call, and the progress and ramifications of its betrayal. What I hope comes forth in the chapters that follow is the jagged history of a specific instance of a much more general process: the emergence of a nation tied to the vicissitudes of translation practices rooted in colonization and Christian evangelization. This other legacy—the persistent need to translate, and the risks and opportunities it entailed—renders the nation's borders constantly open to the coming of something alien and other than itself. In the Philippine case, the experience of nationhood was—and arguably continues to be—inseparable from the hosting of a foreign presence to which one invariably finds oneself held hostage. The paradoxical nature of Filipino nationhood is perhaps characteristic of many other nations, especially those that were formerly colonized. But the exhilaration and the particular tragedy of its unfolding would come in time to belong to Filipinos alone, as would the names of the dead and their ghostly emanations.

FORGIVING
THE FOREIGN

"Above all," Philippine Commonwealth President Manuel L. Quezon declared in a 1937 speech to the Filipino people, "we owe to Spain . . . the foundations of our national unity."[1] Spanish conquest and the conversion of most of the native population to Catholicism transformed the archipelago from a collection of disparate and often warring communities into a "compact and solid nation, with its own history, its heroes, its martyrs, and its own flag, [with] its own personality, feeling a deep sense of worth and inspired by a vision of its great destiny." For this reason, Quezon claims, Filipinos ought to overlook the "mistakes" of their former colonial master. Instead, they should "raise in every heart . . . a monument of undying gratitude to the memory of Spain side by side with that which we should erect in honor of the American people." Speaking thirty-nine years after the collapse of Spanish rule and the onset of United States colonial occupation, Quezon (who had himself fought briefly in the revolution of 1896) stressed Filipino indebtedness to Spain. The "religion and education" the latter provided "had not only enabled us to assimilate another civilization such as brought about by the United States of America, but also prevented the basic and distinctive elements of our personality from being carried away by strange currents, thus bringing us to the triumph of our aspiration to be an independent nation."[2]

So immense is the debt owed to Spain that it cancels out whatever Spaniards might owe to Filipinos. Spain's "mistakes," Quezon points out, were "merely crimes of the times and not of Spain." By this logic, colonial oppression must be written off like a bad debt, impossible to collect, much less account for. In the face of these circumstances, Filipinos should forgive their former colonial master even and especially if the latter had not asked to be pardoned. Thus Filipinos on the threshold of receiving a grant of independence from one colonial power, the United States, inherit a double obligation to an earlier one. They must not only be grateful, they must also be forgiving. One requires the other. Forgiveness is conjoined with the call to "raise in every Filipino heart . . . a monument of undying gratitude" to the former master. Continually recollecting a debt they can never fully repay as well as forgiving one who has never asked for pardon, Filipinos remain forever bound to the legacy of the former master just as they anticipate doing the same for their current occupier. We might ask: what is the nature of this legacy?

Colonialism lies at the origins of nationhood, Quezon suggests. In this he is not alone, as some of the most significant works in the historiography of Filipino nationalism testify to this same claim, though with important qualifications and varying emphasis.[3] It was the Spanish legacy to transform disparate peoples into a nation capable of "assimilating" yet another civilization. Issuing from an alien presence, nationhood in this view is the condition of being endowed with the power to incorporate that which lies outside the nation, and to do so without any loss. Absorbing the influences of an other, the nation retains its integrity. The "basic and distinct elements of our personality," as Quezon puts it, do not change. They cannot be "carried away by strange currents." In his view, the nation absorbs outside forces without itself becoming different. It gives in without giving up what it essentially is. This magical capacity to remain immune to that which comes from the elsewhere, to harbor and domesticate the foreign, including the foreignness of its own origins, while remaining unaltered: such is Spain's grant to the Philippines. Continuing indefinitely into the future, this colonial gift leads to "independence," which thereby calls for the forgiveness of those who have not even asked for it.

It is not surprising that Quezon by 1937 had come to hold what would seem like a deeply conservative view of nationhood as a gift from above that holds its recipients in eternal debt to its source. As president of the American-sanctioned commonwealth—a transitional regime meant to prepare Filipinos for political independence—Quezon, along with the great majority of the Filipino elite who filled the ranks of the colonial legislature and bureaucracy, stood as the direct beneficiary of the U.S. occupation. American power was used not only to crush the incipient Philippine Republic of 1899 and the fierce Filipino resistance that lasted through part of the first decade of U.S. rule. It was also crucial to preserving and expanding elite privileges through the colonial legislature, the judicial system, free trade policies, and the military, which repelled local revolts and other challenges from within. Even as they occasionally railed against American hegemony, Filipino elites thrived under its protection. Heirs to the administrative machinery and political-economic infrastructure that emerged during the later period of Spanish rule and was subsequently overhauled under the Americans, Filipino elites like Quezon no doubt sought to legitimize their place by evoking the fatedness of their historical role as the very embodiment of nationalist sentiment. One way of doing so was to claim for the nation-state a kind of natural descent from its colonial forebears. As an example of what Benedict Anderson has called "official nationalism," Quezon's speech is perhaps just another anxious attempt to explain away the bastard origins of the nation while securing his position as its legitimate leader.[4]

Perhaps.

What is curious about Quezon's speech is its triumphal tone. It is as if the monumentalization of Filipino gratitude to Spain and to the United States indicates not an admission of defeat but a victory of sorts: that of preserving the "basic and distinctive elements of our personality," keeping these from "being carried away by strange currents." Using the foreign, Filipinos are able to withstand its full force. Here, there is a kind of inoculation at work, one with a history that dates back to the beginnings of Spanish rule in the second half of the sixteenth century. Resorting to local languages to convert the native populace to Christianity, working through local elites to collect tribute and enforce colonial edicts, relying upon native and Chinese labor to build ships, roads, and churches while deploying native armies to repel other European powers and repress local uprisings, the Spanish regime like all other colonial orders, required what it sought to subdue. It confronted and challenged forth what was alien to itself, seeking to transform it into a standing reserve. Hence conquest required the natives' conversion, not only to Christianity, but into a stock of labor, materials, and signs that could be readily called upon to augment and expand colonialism's reach. From translation to taxation, from military incursions to residential resettlement, from religious conversion to the exile and execution of "subversives," Spanish colonial power was sustained by the material and symbolic resources at times willingly, but more often coercively extracted from those it subjugated and subjectified.[5]

As a witness to this history, Quezon seems to be saying that something survived and persisted in the face of Spanish (and later, American) exactions and demands. Not all was "carried away by strange currents." On the one hand, the nation is the result of a kind of inheritance. It is constituted by the legacy of colonial incursions and institutions. On the other hand, the nation is also a site of survival, a living on that comes from taking the foreign in and remaking it into an element of oneself. Thus is the nation indebted to colonialism. Thanks to its exposure to the foreign, it has developed a powerful immunity to further alien assaults.

There is then another way of understanding Quezon's assertion of Filipinos' dual obligation to forgive while remembering Spain. It is tempting to regard the call to forgiveness as a recipe for officially administered amnesia and it undoubtedly was meant to have this effect. But to pardon those who have not asked for it is also to display magnanimity. Alongside "undying gratitude," there is a kind of unyielding generosity. The servant appropriates from the master something that the latter had not intended to give: the power to absorb that which is foreign while inoculating itself from its deracinating effects. The servant acknowledges this unintended gift. He thus shows that he is capable of something the master is not: that of recognizing his debts. Spain for its part is unable to reckon what it owes to the Philippines. It remains ignorant of its obligations. Filipinos respond by overlooking the Spanish inability to owe up to its "mistakes" and "crimes." By this act of forgiveness, Filipinos thereby reinforce their difference from the former master. They set themselves apart by recognizing what Spain cannot see in addition to granting the former master what it does not even think to ask for. Filipinos thereby reciprocate the unintended gift of Spain, this time augmented by a constant remembering. Headed toward the "triumph of our aspiration to be an independent nation," Filipinos acknowledge the ineluctably foreign origins of the nation, converting this foreignness from a sign of shame into a signal of impending sovereignty. Put differently, they regard colonialism as that which brings with it the promise of the foreign. This promise is felt as the coming of a power with which to absorb and domesticate the otherness that lies at the foundation of the nation.

This book inquires into the promise of the foreign—the wishfulness it induced, the betrayals it sowed, the vengeance it called forth—at the origins of Filipino nationalism during the latter half of the nineteenth century. How was nationalism infused with that which it desired, yet at times sought to disown, and whose arrival was always deferred? How did it emerge through the mediation of what was as irreducibly alien as it was undeniably intimate? And what of this mediation? Is it possible to think of the foreign in its various manifestations—for example, as language, money, "subversives," rumors, secret oaths, and ghosts, which all figure in the chapters that follow—as the medium for translating and transmitting those "strange currents" that at once enabled and menaced the coherence of nationalist thought? If the foreign can be regarded as a medium for forging nationalism, could we not regard it then as a kind of technology? Could we not think of the foreign languages, dress, ideas, and machineries that increasingly penetrated and permeated colonial society throughout the nineteenth century as infrastructures with which to extend one's reach while simultaneously bringing distant others up close? Expanding while contracting the world, transporting and communicating the inside outside and vice versa, exporting goods and people while importing capital, books, newspapers, political movements, secret societies, and ideologies, technological developments in the later period of Spanish rule brought the promise of the colony's transformation. They circulated the expectation of society becoming other than what it had been, becoming, that is, modern in its proximity to events in the metropole and the rest of the "civilized" world. In this way, the complex of technological developments, we might say, embodied the promise of the foreign, or more precisely, of the becoming foreign associated with the experience of modernity.[6]

To understand the link between foreignness and modernity, it is necessary to sketch some of the salient features of the Philippines' long nineteenth century.[7] By the 1820s, a number of important areas in the colony had undergone fundamental changes, moving from a subsistence economy to one geared toward the cultivation of cash crops for export to world markets. It is worth underlining that the Spanish colonial state did little to spur these developments. Rather, it sought to contain the effects of foreign commerce and the circulation of foreign capital through protectionist measures and regressive taxation, while censoring new ideas and sentiments that entered the colony from outside.

From 1565 to 1815 (or from the Battle of Lepanto to Waterloo, as the historian Benito Legarda reminds us),[8] the galleon trade served as the sole link between the colony and the rest of the Spanish empire. While it prevailed, Manila served mainly as a transshipment point for Asian goods made or gathered outside the colony in exchange for New World silver half a world away. Erratic and vulnerable to seasonal changes and piracy, the highly speculative trade was limited to Spanish residents while dependent on native shipbuilders and sailors as well as on Chinese traders. It mired the colonial state in constant fiscal insolvency, making it dependent on silver subsidies from New Spain. The Philippine colony thus remained an economic backwater, with neither precious metals, big plantations, nor manufacturing industries to attract large-scale Spanish settlements. Bourbon reforms from the 1760s sought to turn the colony's fortunes around by encouraging direct trade between the colony and Spain (thereby bypassing the Americas) and mandating the cultivation of tobacco as a cash crop in certain parts of the largest island, Luzon. The state-run tobacco monopoly was as close as the Philippines came to a system of forced deliveries characteristic of other Southeast Asian colonies. Prone to corruption, smuggling, and the intermittent eruption of local revolts, the tobacco monopoly was never profitable. Abolished in 1882, it showed once again the Spanish inability to reap benefits from the colony's agricultural resources. Nonetheless, the tobacco monopoly, unlike the galleon trade, had the effect of inaugurating an era of economic transformation by making conceivable crop production for export rather than for domestic use.

Spanish attempts at controlling the rate and modulating the tempo of change within the Philippine colony consistently failed due in large part to political turmoil in the Peninsula. Throughout the nineteenth century, Spain was immersed in ongoing civil wars pitting liberals against conservatives. In the wake of Napoléon's invasion and the loss of its American empire, the Spanish metropole's ability to direct the course of events in its Philippine colony was considerably circumscribed. The Carlist wars and the revolution of 1868 further intensified the pace of political instability in Spain, as conservative promonarchists vied for power with liberal republicans. Given the rapid changes of regimes at home, colonial officials appointed by the government in Madrid came and went with increasing frequency in the Philippines. Unsure of the length of their tenure, such officials often turned their positions into opportunities for amassing wealth. Given the rampant bureaucratic predisposition toward rent seeking, corruption became common at all levels of the state. Contradictory Spanish policies aggravated the conditions in the colony. For example, the government sought to liberalize trade by opening the colony's ports to foreign, mostly British and American, merchants. At the same time, they sought to pursue protectionist measures, limiting the flow of goods from other countries and slapping steep tariffs on them. Such measures, not surprisingly, were invitations for bribery and smuggling, further enriching those in the position to benefit from imposing, then circumventing, the law. In the same vein, Spanish policies for encouraging the growth of crops for export failed to benefit Spaniards themselves, for they had neither the capital, nor the interest, nor the knowledge to operate large-scale plantations. Always small in number (less than 1 percent of the colony's population by 1898), the Spanish community tended to reside within Manila's walls—medieval-like fortifications referred to as *Intramuros*, literally "within walls." They were dissuaded by the government from venturing into the countryside for fear of mixing with the native populace and giving rise to a restive mestizo population that might, as in the case of the Americas, come to challenge colonial rule. Most were thus consigned, if not content, to live off government salaries or subsidies, and in the case of the clergy, from tributes rendered by parishioners, rents collected from their estates, and funds from the Crown.[9]

In the absence of Spanish investments, foreign merchants stepped in. As early as the later eighteenth century, British and North American traders had been making regular stops in Manila en route to China. By the early nineteenth century, they had established flourishing merchant houses in the colony. Run by enterprising men, often with experience and connections to European and American trading houses in Canton, they set about advancing credit to local farmers who then promised to grow and sell them certain crops at a set price delivered according to a set schedule. Such crops as abaca, sugar, coffee, and tobacco proved highly profitable. Working through networks of Chinese wholesalers and retailers with long-standing ties to the countryside—in many cases having intermarried with local women—British and American merchants provided the inducements and rewards for surplus production that the Spaniards could not. They also made available new technologies for the processing of raw materials and in 1892 furnished the capital for building the colony's first railroad system that linked Manila to central and northern Luzon, leading to the increase in the production of crops and migration of labor.[10] Foreign merchant houses also took in deposits and paid out interest, thereby providing the colony with modern banking services. Along with Chinese traders who were also local sources of credit for those who could not access Manila's banks, foreign merchant houses allowed for the accumulation and circulation of capital within the colony. Where Spaniards at the end of the Galleon trade settled for using the state apparatus to collect rents and extract labor and natural resources without providing necessary capital investments, foreigners kept the colony financially afloat and economically productive. They encouraged the cultivation of cash crops, moving the colony decisively toward an export economy and linking its fortunes to the booms and busts of the world capitalist economy. Such was the influence of foreign merchants and capital that one Spanish observer in 1879 was led to write that "from the commercial view, the Philippines is an Anglo-Chinese colony with a Spanish flag."[11]

By the middle of the nineteenth century, the social consequences of the economic revolution became evident in the rise of a colonial bourgeoisie composed of *indios*, Chinese and Spanish mestizos, and a smaller number of creoles. Within a generation, they were sending their sons and daughters to secondary schools and universities in Manila and by the 1880s to Europe. They acquired cosmopolitan tastes in dress, furniture, food, and entertainment while absorbing liberal ideas from abroad. As the British consul remarked in 1858, "A very marked change has taken place in the dress and general exterior appearance of the inhabitants of the large pueblos . . . In the interior of the houses the same change is also observable in the furniture and other arrangements, and the more evident wish to add the ornamental to the more necessary articles of household uses."[12] Translating money into status symbols and consumable objects, this colonial middle class "gave proof of their intelligence and aspirations by . . . buying pianos, carriages, objects imported from the United States and Europe which came their way, owing to foreign trade."[13] Becoming middle-class was thus associated with things foreign, beginning with merchants and the capital with which they communicated and through which the movements of goods and people were instigated. Money as both an instrument and outcome of foreign trade enabled the bourgeoisie to gather foreign objects within domestic settings even as the very nature of the domestic itself began to appear strange and novel. Thanks to their connection to British, American, and Chinese merchants and their accumulation of money with which to call forth things at a great distance, the middle class found a way of bypassing what they considered the main obstacles to progress: the Spanish colonial state and its chief supports, the Spanish friar orders.

Where the colony's political economy was concerned then, daily life was increasingly coming under the sway of forces foreign to the Spanish regime. The colonial state sought to contain this other other, but did so through the most regressive means. It extracted tributes and forced labor from the masses while exempting the *principalia* or local elite. However, the latter were made responsible for collecting tributes and were held criminally liable for making up the inevitable shortfalls, creating widespread discontent among both local elites and those below them. Additionally, the state leveled the most onerous taxes on and restricted the movements of one of the most productive elements in the colony: the Chinese. It curtailed political participation among non-Spaniards, refusing in 1837 to restore the short-lived privilege of Filipinos to be represented in the Spanish parliament. More significantly, the state empowered the Spanish friars to oversee nearly every aspect of colonial politics and education, making the clerical orders the most powerful agents of colonialism in the Philippines.[14]

Subjected to liberal and nationalist attacks in Europe since the Enlightenment, the friar orders had most of their properties taken away from them in Spain during the nineteenth century, just as they had lost their holdings and influence in nearly all of Latin America after the wars of independence. The Philippine colony was the only place where friars still retained considerable power. Throughout the nineteenth century, while their influence waned everywhere else, it grew in the colony as the state found itself dependent on the clergy's knowledge of local languages and social practices among the populace. Because of their far longer tenure in the archipelago and their success in converting the vast majority of the natives to Catholicism, the friars proved indispensable for maintaining Spanish hegemony. Acting as bulwarks against the threats of foreign influences and ideas, friars came to regard themselves as patriotic Spaniards charged with preserving what was left of the empire. They were thus deeply hostile to liberalism, which they blamed for their retreat in Europe and elsewhere. It was also unsurprising that they came to regard the free flow of goods, money, and ideas as harbingers of moral ruin and social collapse. In response to the influx of things foreign, the religious orders with the support of the state presided over the censorship of books and newspapers while casting suspicion on and encouraging the repression of various calls for reform. With the important exception of the Jesuits, who had been expelled from the colony in 1768 and allowed back in 1859, the regular clergy restricted what could be taught in schools, including and most significantly the Castilian language (of which more will be said in the following chapters).[15] Where an emergent middle class saw in things foreign the promise of modernity— of the colony, for example, becoming other and better than what it had been—Spanish friars and their official allies could sense only the workings of a power they could barely contain. For the latter, the foreign could only be a source of instability and the taproot of uncertainty.

The Filipino intellectual T. H. Pardo de Tavera, who was among the first generation of nationalists in the later nineteenth century, retraces the path of this conflict. Writing in 1912, he observes that by the nineteenth century,

> freedom of trade was bound to bring capital and active people from outside the archipelago. Capital would be of use to develop production and, naturally, consumption and exportation. Persons who came freely brought new ideas, new methods, new intellectual needs, without the support of privileges which served for exploitation, so that such men had to influence favorably the general progress of Filipinos . . . Wealthy citizens would come to Manila, make purchases, become acquainted with the great merchants who entertained them in their quality [sic] as customers, whose trade they needed; they visited the Governor General, who would receive them according to the position that their money gave; they came to know the Justices of the Supreme Court, the provincials of the religious orders; they brushed up as a result of their contact, with the people of the capital, and on returning to the pueblo they took in their hearts and minds the germ of what was subsequently called subversive ideas and later filibusterismo. . . .
>
> Already the "brutes loaded with gold" dared to discuss with their curate, complain against the [Spanish] alcalde, defend their houses against misconduct of the lieutenant or sargeant of the constabulary. Such people were starting to emancipate themselves as a consequence of this economic independence. Their money permitted them effectively to defend questions involving money first, then those of a moral nature. They were actually becoming insolent, according to the [Spanish] dominators [sic]. In reality, they were beginning to defend their rights.[16]

For the foreign merchants and the Filipino colonial bourgeoisie, the circulation of money spurred movement in and out of the pueblos as well as outside the archipelago. In Pardo de Tavera's idealized account of national progress, "freedom of trade" allowed freedom of travel. And with travel came opportunities to bring distances up close, geographic as well as social. For money enabled one to reach those at the top of the hierarchy—the governor general, the Supreme Court justices, the provincials of the religious orders. It allowed one not only to speak directly to the state but to speak back to local representatives and get a response. Money was thus endowed with the power of a telecommunicative medium, allowing its possessor to address those from afar and solicit their recognition.

Money also allowed its holders to speak with one another regardless of their social origins or position. British and American merchants, Filipino farmers, Chinese traders, Spanish officials, and the clergy could address one another by means of a medium common to all because exclusive to no one. Money had the ability to subsume differences while itself remaining unchanged. Herein lay another dimension of its telecommunicative power: it could serve as the measure of value and medium of exchange—of goods, labor and interests, for example—and so functioned as a medium of communication arguably analogous to a lingua franca in colonial society.[17] However, insofar as money had a foreign origin, its movement and effects could not be fully controlled by the colonial state. Emerging outside of colonial society, it nonetheless animated its movements and articulated its disparate parts with one another and with the world outside. It allowed its holders to travel up and down the colonial hierarchy while it seemed to surpass that hierarchy's limits. It created material wealth but in so doing undermined the basis of colonial power. Its very familiarity could thus have defamiliarizing outcomes. In a word, money came across as an uncanny force within nineteenth-century colonial society. Those who, like Pardo de Tavera, came in close association with its workings and advocated its increased circulation through commerce, assumed that free trade with foreigners was the condition for freedom as such. It was not surprising that they would come under suspicion and in time be labeled as *filibusteros* or subversives at odds with the interests of the state and church (about which more will be said in the following chapters). As the "insolent" agent of modernity's promise, they seemed to the Spanish friars and officials to be out of place and to speak out of turn, recognizable as those who refused the usual modes of recognition. As filibusteros, they became categorical anomalies: the aliens from within rather than from outside, subject to surveillance, persecution, exile, and, on occasion, execution. The economic historian Benito Legarda remarks, "The rise of the native intelligentsia and Spain's repressive political policies were bound to culminate in an outburst of no mean proportions,"[18] including, of course, the anticolonial revolution of 1896.

It is the uncertain path leading up to this disproportionate outburst brought on by the simultaneous allure and danger of the foreign that I seek to trace in the chapters that follow. Unlike the numerous and in many cases fine works on the history of Philippine nationalism, this book does not offer a chronological account of this history. Rather, I have chosen to tack back and forth among different moments, texts, and figures to bring forth the uneven and contingent articulations of the *possibility* of nationalist emergence. I begin with the nationalist fascination with and hesitations about Castilian as a kind of telecommunicative technology in the late 1880s to the early 1890s, focusing in particular on the newspaper *La solidaridad* and, in reverse chronological order, the two novels of José Rizal, *El filibusterismo* (1891) and *Noli me tangere* (1887). Tracing the interplay of translation and revenge, secrecy and foreignness, and terror and authorship, I seek to foreground the hazards of pursuing the promise of a lingua franca.

I then loop back to the first half of the nineteenth century, examining the popular investment in the foreignness of Castilian as seen in the *comedia*, the most widespread genre of vernacular theater, and look closely at the most important example of this period, the Tagalog epic poem *Florante at Laura*, by Francisco Balthazar, more popularly known as Balagtas. As I try to demonstrate, the expropriation of untranslated Castilian words in these plays evidences an investment in the foreign that ran across linguistic, class, and geographical lines among Christianized lowland communities. Such plays amounted to acts of popular translation that reiterated missionary practices even as they revised them. In this way did vernacular theater furnish the grounds for a kind of protonationalist public sphere. This estrangement, this making uncanny of the vernacular in and through Castilian, arguably opened up the possibility for deploying *both* languages in the anticolonial revolution of 1896, a topic I leap forward to in the last chapters of this book.

In lieu of detailing the vicissitudes of the fighting against Spain, however, I focus on the crisis of address that obtained on the eve of the revolution, a crisis foreshadowed by the popular expropriation of Castilian in vernacular theater. What made the revolution revolutionary, I argue, was precisely the insistent ways it posed the questions "Who speaks?" and "Who is spoken to?" to those in the colony, to which no sufficient answer could be given, especially by colonial authorities. For the Spaniards, this crisis of address was felt most acutely upon the discovery of what they took to be nationalist conspiracies hatched in secret societies. Assailed by rumors and other traces of these conspiracies, colonizers and colonized were gripped by the specter of secrecy, of hidden forces at work pointing to other sources of power. And from such secret sources there issued what appeared to be a novel language positing an unsettling relationship between freedom and death.

The somewhat idiosyncratic architecture of this book, its zigging and zagging across temporal and textual realms, is meant to illuminate less the linear trajectory of nationalist thought as its many fits and starts, its uneasy cohabitation with colonialism, as well as its originary cosmopolitanism, oriented as it was to something other and far more variegated than the limits of colonial conventions.[19] In doing so, I hope to get at the stuttering vitality of early nationalism as it tendentiously mistranslated colonial idioms in search of alternative modes and loci of address. For Filipino nationalism, at least in its inception, was not merely fated to repeat the logics and logistics of colonial rule, contrary to what some postcolonial scholarship on nationalism has claimed about the nation form. Neither did it begin with the outright rejection of Spanish colonialism, as contemporary nationalists think. Rather, as we shall see, its origins lie with the discovery of an alien and alienating capacity to transmit messages across linguistic and social borders, reaching audiences and publics yet to be defined and consolidated by the authority of the state and the authorship of postrevolutionary (and counterrevolutionary) nationalist leaders.

To understand the initial experience of nationalism as the power of transmission, it is necessary to see it from the perspective of a history of translation. The first generation of nationalists, known in Philippine historiography as *ilustrados*, or enlightened, were particularly captivated by the possibilities of the Castilian language for furnishing a lingua franca that would reach across linguistically diverse regions of the archipelago. It would also draw together rulers and ruled, integrating the colony as a full-fledged province of Spain. The spread of Castilian promised, so the ilustrados thought, to make Filipinos equal to Spaniards as citizens of a common *patria*. They thus saw in Castilian an agency analogous to money. It would allow them to communicate at a distance, traversing differences in language, social rank, and territorial boundaries. It would translate the local into the national, which would simultaneously resonate with the languages of the larger modern world. At the same time, Castilian would also be brought into close association with local languages, as in the case of vernacular plays, augmenting the local languages' expressive capacities and expanding their reach to audiences whose social identities had yet to be determined. In so doing, such plays would set a horizon of address distinct from that of Christian discourse, making conceivable a public sphere at variance with that formed by evangelization and thereby available for more secular appeals.

As the potential lingua franca of nationalist thought, Castilian was idealized by nationalists as the medium of translation, a second language with which to articulate one's first. It was thus invested with the capacity to recast particular interests in ways that could address the metropole and whoever else in the colony cared to listen. And at a certain moment when it failed to win recognition for nationalist demands, Castilian, as I will try to show, would be reworked as an element in the oaths of secret societies and would come to terrorize its original speakers on the eve of the revolution. In the history of Filipino nationalism, then, Castilian presented an array of possibilities. To seize upon these possibilities was to recognize and respond to the promise of the foreign. It is these acts of recognizing, responding, and thereby assuming the responsibility for what comes before and beyond oneself that comprise what I take to be the practice of translation.

The importance of Castilian thus relates directly to the matter of translation. In the colonial context we are examining, translation begins with coming into contact with the foreign—with that which precedes and survives one's arrival, which does not properly belong to one, and which has origins beyond one's own language—and its subsequent reformulation into an element of oneself. It is about the discovery not of an identity, but of an alien presence residing within colonial society. How does this alien presence appear? What shapes does it take, what sounds does it make? How does it invite appropriation? How does it frustrate attempts at domestication, and to what effect? That is, how does it call out for translation, even and especially when it is left untranslated? Who hears its call and what becomes of those who are called? To consider these questions is to see how the beginnings of nationalism, at least in the Philippine context (but no doubt elsewhere), was enmeshed in a linguistic politics that anticipated and accompanied an economic revolution. The latter, as we have seen, let loose things foreign within the colony: merchants, money, goods, ideas, and so on; the former, as we shall see, put forth the irreducible foreignness of what would come to be regarded as "common" to the history of the nation. This letting loose and putting forth of the alien constitutive of nationalism involved ways of doing and making do, rhetorical practices, mechanical instruments, and repetitive gestures that could be summed up as the technics of translation.

Such technics underwrote nationalism's attempts to claim the power of the foreign in its various incarnations while seeking to inoculate itself from its indeterminate effects. As a technical ensemble, translation is not simply a means for substituting the language and meanings of one for another. It is also the letting loose and putting forth of the foreign, tasks made possible only by way of repeatable acts of promising and believing in the possibility of communicating with others into the future. Felt as the recurring transmission of a response to the call of the foreign, translation practices keep the foreign in circulation, hence saving it for those who come later. With translation then, there is a sense of futurity harbored and kept in reserve, of the radical otherness of language surviving and producing effects beyond the moment of its articulation. Joining response to responsibility, translation safeguards the promise of the foreign. It thereby gives rise to the possibility of historical thought as the opening to that which is new and therefore always yet to come.[20]

With this opening, however, there comes as well the risk of mistranslation: not simply miscommunication, but the sheer lack of connection that threatens the terrifying dissolution of communicative possibilities. The promise of translation brings with it the risk of betrayal even before and certainly beyond the circulation of messages, and prior to the constitution of social identities. One can fail to translate and reach the other. Or reaching the other, one faces the danger of blurting out what is taken to be nonsense instead of meaning. One is thus left unrecognized as the bearer of messages and the author of one's speech. Misrecognized, one appears foreign oneself, carried away by "strange currents."

In the Philippine colonial context (and perhaps elsewhere), there was always the danger that one would be contaminated rather than immunized from one's exposure to the foreign, confounded rather than empowered by the technics of translation. Such would be the fate of the first generation of nationalists. Regarded as subversives by virtue of their association with the foreign, they were harassed, ridiculed, persecuted, and in some cases killed by the Spanish regime. Taking in the foreign, they were mistaken as aliens within. In time, they would come to offer a different response: the call not for assimilation as citizens of Spain, but for separation and independence. They would reconsider their debts and plot their revenge. Hence did the prospect of modernity also consign them to a future of violent, terror-filled struggle for recognition. The risk of misrecognition inherent in translation threatened to ignite a commerce in vengeance. Such was the other side of the promise of the foreign. It would come to define in many cases the relationship between the nationalist figures and the colonial authorities they sought to address, culminating in an "outburst of no mean proportions." Given revenge, forgiveness would have to wait.

TRANSLATION
AND
TELECOMMUNICATION
Castilian as a Lingua Franca

The Fantasy of Communication

In the spring of 1889, the editors of the Filipino nationalist newspaper, *La solidaridad*, then based in Barcelona, wrote in celebration of the tenth anniversary of the inauguration of a telegraph cable system in the Philippine colony. Running between Manila and Hong Kong, and from there to Europe, the system furnished an "electric language" (*lenguaje electrico*) with which to transmit "patriotic thoughts" directly to the motherland, Spain. Thanks to telegraphy, the Philippines was put in contact with the world in new ways.

This "brave instrument" (*valioso instrumento*) engaged the interest of the editors involved in a campaign for reforms that sought to extend the rights of Spanish citizenship to all those living in the colony. Telegraphy made it seem possible to speak directly and intimately with the metropole and beyond. Its promise of rapid communications at great distances meant bypassing the mediation of the colony's more "retrograde elements" and "enemies of progress," an allusion to the Spanish clerical orders and their bureaucratic allies. Hence, it did not seem to matter that the first transmission, reprinted by the editors, was a profession of fealty and devotion to the Crown sent by the governor general on behalf of the colony's subjects. It seemed less important that modern technology was used to convey a traditional message of feudal subservience. The editors were drawn instead to the sheer fact of this "sublime discovery" capable of speedy transmissions: a "language of lightning" (*lenguaje del rayo*) that triggered fantasies of immediate communication. Sidestepping the content of the message, they celebrated the capacity of a technology to overcome existing barriers to speech.[1]

The existence of such barriers in large part accounts for the foreign location of *La solidaridad*. Colonial censorship, fed by the suspicion and hostility of the Spanish friar orders toward any attempt at challenging

their authority, along with the threats of imprisonment, exile, and execution made it dangerous to ask for reforms in the colony. Hounded by
colonial authorities, many of those in the first generation of nationalists
were forced to leave the Philippines for Spain and other parts of Europe
where a more liberal political climate allowed them to speak out.[2]

It is important to underline at the outset the ethno-linguistic heterogeneity of this first generation of nationalists. Though they were all
young men of mostly middle-class backgrounds with university education in Manila and Europe, they came from the various linguistic regions of the archipelago and differed, at least in the eyes of colonial law,
in their ethnic makeup. Most spoke the local vernaculars such as Tagalog, Ilocano, Kapampangan, Ilongo, and so forth as their first language
and counted among themselves mestizos (both Spanish and Chinese),
indios or "natives," criollos (Spaniards born in the Philippines distinguished from the more privileged *peninsulares*, or Spaniards born in
Spain). Collectively they came to be known as *ilustrados*, enlightened. In
Europe during the 1880s and early 1890s they were joined in their
campaign for reforms by Spanish liberals and Freemasons, at least one
Austrian intellectual, and an older generation of Filipino exiles in En-
gland and Hong Kong who had suffered earlier in the hands of colonial
authorities. Known in Philippine historiography as the Propaganda
Movement, their activities were based in Barcelona and later in Madrid,
with ties to Manila and surrounding towns. Ilustrados themselves traveled widely to study at universities in Paris, Berlin, and London, and it
was not uncommon for them to be multilingual. Their efforts, largely
liberal in character and inspired no doubt by their understanding of the
Spanish revolutionary legacy, focused on seeking the assimilation of the
Philippine colony as a province of Spain, restoring Filipino representation in the Spanish parliament, encouraging greater commercial activities, and securing equal treatment of the colony's population regardless of race before the law. That is, Filipino nationalists at this time
wanted to be recognized not just as "Filipinos," for this merely meant in
the late nineteenth century one who was not quite indio or Chinese, yet
not quite Spaniard. They also wanted to be seen as Spanish patriots, at
home in Spain as much as they were in the Philippines.

Nationalism in the Philippines thus began as a movement among
groups uncertain about their identity and anxious about their place in
colonial society. Beneficiaries of the increasing commercialization of
agriculture and the penetration of European trade starting in the later

eighteenth century,[3] they sought not a separate nation—at least not yet—but a claim on the future and a place on the social map. Their initial appeal was not for the abolition of colonial rule but for its reformation in ways that would expand the limits of citizenship and political representation. The first generation of nationalists thus initially sought not separation but recognition from the motherland. This wish brought with it the imperative to communicate in a language that could be heard and understood by those in authority. Such a language was Castilian.

Traversing ethno-linguistic differences, Castilian served as the lingua franca of the ilustrados. Learned haltingly and unevenly first from their parents or private tutors and later on, for those who could afford it, at clerically controlled universities in Manila, Castilian allowed this small group of nationalists to speak with one another.[4] Equally important, Castilian provided them with the medium for communicating with others both within and outside of colonial society. Thus could they address Spanish officials in Spain as well as in the Philippines; and Europeans and later on Americans who knew the language. With the exception of a very small group of criollos for whom Castilian was presumably a first language, most nationalists found in Castilian a second language common to each because native to no one.[5] At the same time, they found in Castilian the means with which to translate their interests in terms that were audible and readable within and beyond colonial society. The foreignness of Castilian, the fact that it did not belong to them, was precisely what made it indispensable as a lingua franca for seeking recognition.

There is a sense then that Filipino nationalism did not originate with the discovery of an indigenous identity by the colonized and his or her subsequent assertion of an essential difference from the colonizer. Rather, its genesis lies in the transmission of messages across social and linguistic borders among all sorts of people whose identities and identifications were far from settled. Further, such transmissions had foreign origins and destinations, crossing provinces and continents, emanating from distant cities and strange locales. These transmissions were in Castilian for the most part, a language long heard in the colony but, because of the colonial practice of dissuading natives from learning it, largely misunderstood and barely spoken by the vast majority of those living in the archipelago. Castilian was in this sense a foreign language to most; and among ilustrados, it was a second language with which to represent the interests of the majority of the colonized. Thus we can think of Filipino nationalism as a practice of translation, here understood first as the coming into contact with the foreign and subsequently its reformulation into an element of oneself. From this perspective, nationalism, as I hope to show, entails at least in its formative moments neither the rejection nor the recapitulation of colonialism. Rather, it is about the discovery of an alien aspect residing within colonial society and its translation into a basis for a future history.

The Promise of Castilian

The sense of exhilarating possibilities opened up by contact with the foreign comes across in the *La solidaridad* article on the telegraphy cable system. Reaching outside the Philippines, it was a system that surpassed the communicative limits of colonial society. The "language of electricity" cut across linguistic differences to the extent that it belonged to no particular group or country. It could send messages to the world because all languages could be translated into its codes. It was thus exterior to all other languages, and this is what gave telegraphic technology the quality of a new kind of lingua franca.[6]

The nationalist editors identified neither with the inventors of the telegraph nor, as we saw, with the contents of its transmission, but with its peculiar power to cross linguistic and geographical boundaries. Such crossings were crucial to their project. We can see this heightened fascination with communication in their reliance on the Castilian language. *La solidaridad* was not the first Filipino nationalist newspaper although it proved to be the most influential publication of the movement. An earlier nationalist paper was *Diariong Tagalog*, founded in 1882 (fittingly enough, the same year as the appearance of Renan's essay on nationalism) by Marcelo H. del Pilar, who would later become the editor of *La solidaridad*. Based in Malolos, a city north of Manila, it was a bilingual publication, featuring articles in the Tagalog vernacular and in Castilian. Though it did not last long, *Diariong Tagalog* was the first in a long line of bilingual nationalist newspapers that would appear in the Philippines from the late nineteenth to the first half of the twentieth century.[7]

Throughout the history of nationalist publications, then, print Castilian always had a significant place. While vernacular languages such as Tagalog or Cebuano were used in specific regions to express political sentiments, the Spanish language invariably accompanied these expressions, allowing them to circulate beyond their regional confines. We can think of Castilian as a second language for translating the primary languages of the archipelago. It relayed sentiments and wishes not only across linguistic regions; for those who could use it, it had the power to convey messages up and down the colonial hierarchy, linking those on top with those below. In this capacity, Castilian played a function analogous to that of the telegraph, transmitting messages within and outside the colony.

Given the power of Castilian to expand the possibilities for contact and communication, it comes as no surprise that nationalist ilustrados should become invested in its use. Hence, in the pages of *La solidaridad* we read of the persistent demand among nationalists for the teaching of Castilian to all inhabitants of the colony. Colonial policy from the late sixteenth through the end of the nineteenth century had installed Castilian as the official language of the state. The Crown had repeatedly mandated the education of natives in this language. However, as with many other aspects of colonial policy, such injunctions were honored more in their breach than in their observance. In 1863, as part of a series of reforms of the colony's educational system, the Escuela Normal de Maestros, or Teacher's School, was established and supervised by the more liberal Jesuits to enable Filipino teachers to learn and teach the Spanish language. However, such a school met with scorn and "bitter opposition" from the friar orders, especially the parish priests who no doubt saw the prospect of Castilian-speaking Filipino teachers as a threat to their influence.[8] Given the weakness of the colonial government and the vigorous resistance of the friar orders to spreading Castilian, only about 1 percent of the population had any fluency in the language at the end of more than three centuries of Spanish rule.[9]

There were other reasons for the limited spread of Castilian. The Philippine colony was located at the furthest edges of the Spanish Empire. Even with the opening of the Suez Canal in 1869, travel to the Philippines from Spain was still a matter of several months. Possessing neither the gold nor silver of the New World colonies, the Philippines had few attractions for Spanish settlers. Fearful of repeating the large-scale miscegenation between Spaniards, Indians, and Africans in the New World, the Crown had established restrictive residency laws discouraging Spanish settlement outside of the walls of Manila. As a result, no sizeable population of Spanish-speaking criollos ever emerged, and there persisted a paucity of teachers, Spaniard as well as Filipino, to teach Castilian to the wider population.[10]

Ilustrado nationalists argued that such limitations could be remedied. Enforcing existing laws, the government, if it chose to, could devote resources to building schools and providing for the more systematic instruction of Castilian. Yet, the state seemed not only incapable but unwilling to carry out these measures. It seemed then to be violating its own laws. Such conditions came about, as ilustrados saw it, largely because of the workings of the Spanish friars. They had long blocked the teaching of Castilian to the masses in the interest of guarding their own authority. Their steadfast opposition to the widespread teaching of Castilian kept the colony from progressing. Cast as figures opposed to modernity, the Spanish clergy became the most significant target of ilustrado enmity. In their inordinate influence over the state and other local practices, the friars were seen to stand in the way of "enlightenment," imagined to consist of extended contact and sustained exchanges with the rest of the "civilized" world. Thanks to the friars, colonial subjects were deprived of a common language with which to address one another and reach those at the top of the colonial hierarchy.[11]

How did the Spanish clergy assume such considerable influence in the colony? To answer this question, one needs to keep in mind the immense significance of Catholic conversion in the conquest and colonization of the Philippines. Spanish missionaries were the most important agents for the spread of colonial rule. Colonial officials came and went, owing their positions to the patronage of politicians and the volatile conditions of the home government. They often amassed fortunes during their brief tenure and with rare exceptions remained relatively isolated from the non-Spanish populace. By contrast, the Spanish clergy were stationed in local parishes all over the colony. They retained a corporate identity that superseded the governments of both the colony and the mother country. Indeed, they claimed to be answerable only to their religious superiors and beyond that to a God who transcended all other worldly arrangements. This access to an authority beyond colonial hierarchy proved essential in conserving their identity as indispensable agents of Spanish rule.

Through the clergy, the Crown validated its claims of benevolent conquest. Colonization was legitimized as the extension of the work of evangelization. Acting as the patron of the Catholic Church, a role it had zealously assumed since the Counter-Reformation, the Crown shared in the task of communicating the Word of God to unknowing natives. While the state relied on the church to consolidate its hold on the islands, the church in turn depended on the state in carrying out its task of conversion. Missionaries drew on the material and monetary support of the state, relying upon colonial courts to secure its land holdings especially in the later nineteenth century, on military forces to put down local uprisings and groups of bandits, and on the institution of forced labor for the building of churches and convents.

However, the success of the Spanish missionaries in converting the majority of lowland natives to Catholicism rested less on coercion—it could not, given the small number of Spanish military forces in the islands—than on translation.[12] As I have elsewhere discussed at length, evangelization relied on the task of translation. God's Word was delivered to the natives in their own tongue. Beginning the latter sixteenth century, Spanish missionaries following the practice in the New World, systematically codified native languages. They replaced the local script (*baybayin*) with Roman letters, used Latin categories to reconstruct native grammars, and provided Castilian definitions in constructing dictionaries of the vernaculars. Catholic teachings were then translated and taught in the local languages. At the same time, the missionary policy insisted on retaining key terms in their original Latin and Castilian forms. Such words as *Dios, Espíritu Santo, Virgen,* and the names of saints, along with the language of the mass and the sacraments, remained in their untranslated forms in Latin and Castilian so as not to be confused, or so the missionaries thought, with pre-Christian deities and animistic beliefs. From the missionary point of view, translation, the exchange of one language for another, was predicated on a notion of untranslatability that marked the limits of exchange and prohibited further substitution.

Through the translation of God's Word, natives came to see in Spanish missionaries a foreign presence speaking their "own" language. As I have demonstrated elsewhere, this appearance—as sudden as it was unmotivated from the natives' point of view—of the foreign in the familiar and its reverse, the familiar in the foreign—roused native interests and anxieties.[13] For what they apprehended in the friar was the force of communication—the power to establish contact across borders and speak in ways otherwise unanticipated and unheard of and to do so in a language other than their own. Conversion was thus a matter of responding to this startling because novel emergence of alien messages from alien speakers from within one's own speech. It was to identify oneself with this uncanny occurrence and to submit to its attractions, which included access to an unseen yet omnipresent source of all power.

Conversion translated the vernacular into another language, converting it into a medium for reaching beyond one's own world. But the intermediary for addressing what lay beyond was the Spanish missionary. He stood at the crossroads of languages, for he spoke not only the vernacular but also Castilian and Latin. And because of his insistence on retaining untranslated words within the local versions of the Word, he evinced the limits of translation, the points at which words became wholly absorbed and entirely subservient to their referents. The imperatives of evangelization meant that translation would be at the service of a higher power. Unlike the telegraph cable (or print and telephone for that matter), which opened up to a potentially limitless series of translations and transmissions, evangelization encapsulated all languages and messages within a single, ruling Word, Jesus Christ, the incarnate speech of the Father.

Through the missionaries, converts could hope to hear the Word of the Father resonating within their own words. Put differently, Catholic conversion in this colonial context was predicated on the transmission of a hierarchy of languages. Submitting to the Word of the Father, one came to realize that one's first language was subordinate to a second, that a foreign because transcendent presence ruled over one's thoughts, and that such thoughts came through a chain of mediations: roman letters, Castilian words, and Latin grammatical categories superimposed on the vernaculars.

We can think of the missionary then as a medium for the communication of a hierarchy of communications that was thought to frame all social relations. Through him, native societies were reordered as recipients of a gift they had not expected in the form of a novel message to which they felt compelled to respond. What made the message compelling was precisely its form. The missionary's power lay in his ability to predicate languages, that is, to conjoin them into a speech that issued from above and was meant to be heard by those below at some predestined time. The power of predication therefore also came with the capacity for prediction, that is, the positing of events as the utterance of a divine promise destined to be fulfilled in the future. To experience language hierarchically unfolding, as for example in prayer or in the sacraments, is to come to believe in the fatality of speech. All messages inevitably reach their destinations, if not now, then in the future. Moreover, they will all be answered, if not in one way, then in another. The attractions of conversion thus included the assurance that one always had the right address.

In tracing the linguistic basis of missionary agency, one can begin to understand how it is they became so crucial in legitimating colonial rule and consolidating its hegemony. The rhetoric of conversion and the practice of translation allowed for the naturalization, as it were, of hierarchy, linguistic as well as social. They made colonization seem both inevitable and desirable. At the same time, one can also appreciate the depth of nationalist fascination with the friars and their obsessive concern with the Spanish fathers' influence over the motherland. As "sons" of the motherland, the ilustrados wanted to speak in a language recognizable to colonial authorities. To do so meant assuming the position of the friar, that is, of becoming an agent of translation who could speak up and down the colonial hierarchy, making audible the interests of those at the bottom to those on top. It also implied the ability to speak past colonial divisions: to address the present from the position of the future and to speak from the perspective of what was yet to arrive. With these historical matters in mind, we can return to the nationalist demand for the teaching of Castilian.

The Risks of Misrecognition

Remarking on the royal decrees providing for the teaching of Castilian to the natives, a writer for *La solidaridad* deplores the failure of authorities to enact these laws. All the more unfortunate, since "the people wish to express their concerns without the intervention of intermediary elements (*elementos intermediarios*). Moreover, in the Philippines, the ability to speak and write in Castilian constitutes a distinction. There, it is embarrassing not to possess it and in whatever gathering it is considered unattractive and up to a point shameful for one to be in a position of being unable to switch to the official language."[14] To speak Castilian is to be able to address others without having to resort to the help of "intermediary elements"—the Spanish friars. Unlike in the Dutch East Indies, for example, where Melayu existed as a common language between colonizer and colonized and would in time become the basis for the national language, Indonesian, in the Philippines, colonial officials almost never learned the local languages, just as most natives were unable to speak Castilian.[15] Both relied on the missionary to translate and therein, as we saw, lay the basis of missionary influence. Educational reforms that would spread Castilian would eliminate this "shameful" situation. "Direct intercourse between rulers and ruled" would be possible, as the writer would go on to say, as both would come to dwell in a common linguistic milieu.

However, as the writer notes, Spanish friars have refused to give up their position. Instead of recognizing the desire of natives to learn Castilian, friars have come to suspect their motives. Those who advocate the teaching of the Spanish language are treated as potential "enemies of the country . . . a *filibustero*, a heretic and depraved (*perverso*)" (11). Not only do Spanish fathers stand in the way of direct contact between the people and those who rule them. Worse, they misrecognize colonial subjects who speak Castilian as subversives and criminals. While nationalists associate the learning of Castilian with progress and modernity, the Spanish friars see it as a challenge to their authority and a veritable theft of their privileges. Indeed, the word for "subversive," *filibustero*, also refers to a pirate, hence to a thief.

Blocked from disseminating Castilian, nationalists also become suspect. Rather than accept the position laid out for them as natives and subjects, they insist on speaking as if they were other and thus foreign to colonial society.[16] Responding in Castilian, nationalists claim they have been misrecognized. It is not they who are criminals, but the friars who accuse them. Over and over again, writers for *La solidaridad* refer to friars as "unpatriotic Spaniards," hence the real filibusteros. In an article typical in tone and content, one writer asks:

> In fact who is the friar? Somebody egoistic, avaricious, greedy . . . vengeful. . . . They have been assassins, poisoners, liars, agitators of public peace . . . They have . . . stirred the fire of the most violent passions, aroused in every way the ideas of rebellion against the nation . . . converted the people thus into parricides . . . [They] enjoy the sight of fields strewn with cadavers and sing of their prowess to the accompaniment of the sad lamentations of the helpless mother, the afflicted wife, and the unfortunate orphan. Look at the true picture of those great men . . . those hypocrites, executioners of mankind, monopolizers of our riches, vampires of our humble society.[17]

Undoubtedly influenced by Spanish liberal anticlericalism, the nationalist imaginary regards the crimes of the friars to progress along the path of covetousness, followed by murder and ultimately parricide. From their perspective, the friars are subversives who stand in the way of a happier union between the colonial state and its subjects. Yet, neither the state nor the church recognizes this fact. Authorities refuse to listen, or more precisely, they mishear, mistaking the ilustrado desire for Castilian as his or her rejection of Spain. The delirious enumeration of clerical criminality in the passage above reflects something of a hysterical response to repeated miscommunications. Such alarm is understandable, given the grave consequences of being misheard in the way of imprisonment and executions.[18]

What is clear is that having a common language does not guarantee mutual understanding, but precisely the reverse. Castilian in this instance is a shared language between colonizer and colonized. Yet the result is not the closer union that nationalists had hoped for but mutual misrecognition. Each imagines the other to be saying more than they had intended. Acting upon each other's misconceptions, they come to exchange positions in one another's minds. Questions about language lead to suspicions, conflict, and violence. Rather than reconcile the self with the other, Castilian has the effect of estranging both precisely by confusing each with the other.

Historically, as we had seen, it was the Spanish friars who had monopolized the ability of the self to speak in the language of the other, controlling the terms of translation by invoking a divinely sanctioned linguistic hierarchy. Conversion occurred to the extent that natives could read into missionary discourse the possibility of being recognized by a third term that resided beyond both the missionary and the native.[19] But by the late nineteenth century, this situation had been almost reversed. Nationalists addressed Spaniards in the Spaniards' own language. The friars did not see in Castilian-speaking subjects a mirror reflection of themselves. For after all, given the racial logic of colonialism, how could the native or mestizo be the equivalent of the European? Rather, friars tended to see nationalists as filibusteros guilty of stealing what rightfully belongs to them and compromising their position as the privileged media of colonial communication. In their eyes, nationalists were speaking out of turn. Their Castilian had no authority because it was uttered outside of the hierarchy. From the friars' perspective, nationalist attempts to translate their interests into a second language only placed them outside of the linguistic order of colonial society. Thus were nationalists rendered foreign. Speaking Castilian, they appeared to be other than mere natives and therefore suspect in the eyes of Spanish fathers.

Speaking Castilian produced strange and disconcerting effects. For nationalists, Castilian was supposed to be the route to modernity. Progress came, so they thought, in gaining access to the means with which to communicate directly with authorities and with others in the world. It followed that the Spanish language was a means of leaving behind all that was "backward" and "superstitious," that is, all that came under the influence of the friars. To learn Castilian was to exit the existing order of oppression and enter into a new, more "civilized" world of equal representation. Castilian in this sense was a key that allowed one to move within and outside of colonial hierarchy.

Nonetheless, such movements came with certain risks. Speaking Castilian, one faced the danger of being misrecognized. We saw this possibility in the vexed relationship between nationalists and colonial authorities in the Philippines. The dangers of misrecognition, however, also carried over into Spain. Seeking to escape persecution, nationalists often fled abroad. Most gravitated to Barcelona and Madrid, which became centers of nationalist agitation from the 1880s to the mid-1890s. In these cities, Filipinos found themselves reaching a sympathetic audience among Spanish liberals and other Europeans. Their writings were given space in Spanish liberal newspapers. Filipino artists such as Juan Luna and Felix Resurrection Hidalgo won a string of prizes in Madrid and Paris painting in the academic style of the period, which one might think of as speaking a kind of Castilian. And in the pages of *La solidaridad*, one reads of political banquets where nationalists addressed Spanish audiences and were greeted with approval and applause.

Castilian seemed to promise a way out of colonial hierarchy and a way into metropolitan society. However, in other nationalist accounts we also see how this promise fails to materialize. Nationalists find themselves betrayed by Castilian in both senses of the word. Out of this betrayal, other responses arise, including phantasms of revenge and revolution. We now turn to these successes and failures of translation and recognition and the responses they incur.

The Ambiguities of Assimilation

Reading once again the newspaper *La solidaridad*, we get a sense of the attractions that Castilian and Spain held for Filipino nationalists. An instructive example is the speech delivered by Graciano Lopez-Jaena, one of the paper's editors, during a political banquet in Barcelona in

1889.[20] He begins with a declaration of his own foreignness. He announces to the Spanish audience that he is "of little worth, accompanied by an obscure name, totally unknown and foreign to you, with a face showing a country different from your generous land, a race distinct from yours, a language different than yours, whose accent betrays me" (28). That is, he comes before an audience and tells them in their language that "I am not you." Hence, not only am "I" a foreigner, but one who is in some respects lower than "you." Lopez-Jaena calls attention to the difference of his appearance, aligning it with his accented Castilian, which "betrays me." Yet, he continues, even if "I am a nobody" (*si nada soy*), "I am encouraged by the patriotic interest that my speech might awaken in everyone. . . . Be indulgent toward me." The audience responds with a murmur of approval, "good, very good" (*bien, muy bien*).

Here, the native addresses the other in the latter's language. He appears as someone acutely conscious of his difference from those he addresses. "I" am not "you," he seems to be saying, yet "I" (*yo*) announce this in your language. The audience hears and responds with approval. In this way, the native not only maps the gap between himself and the other; more important, he succeeds in crossing it. Traversing racial and linguistic differences, his "I" is able to float free from its origins and appear before a different audience. When the audience responds with a murmur of approval, it identifies not with the speaker but with his ability to be otherwise. The audience comes to recognize the native's ability to translate: that is, to transmit his "I" across a cultural divide. The native defers to his audience—"I am nobody"—and that deference, heard in the language of the audience, meets with approval. Recognized in his ability to get across, to keep his audience in mind, and to know his place in relation to theirs, the native can continue to speak, now with the confidence of being able to connect.

The contents of Lopez-Jaena's speech are themselves unremarkable and predictable. It contains the usual call for reforms—economic, political, and educational—that would lead to the improvement of the colony. It extols the riches of the archipelago while lamenting the state's inability to make better use of them. And it invariably sets upon the friar orders as those responsible for resisting changes in the colony. Finally, Lopez-Jaena calls on Spain to rid the colony of friars and devote attention to the development of commercial opportunities in the Philippines and to answering the needs of its inhabitants.

What is worth noting is the reception he gets. As was the common practice in newspapers of the era, the printed version of his speech is punctuated by the sound of applause ranging from "mild and approving" to "prolonged and thunderous," particularly when Lopez-Jaena lauds Spanish war efforts in repulsing German attempts at seizing its Pacific island possessions. By the end of the speech, the audience explodes with "frenzied, prolonged applause, bravos, enthusiastic and noisy ovations, congratulations and embraces given to the orator" (46).

In the course of his speech, Lopez-Jaena goes through a remarkable transformation. He starts out an obscure foreigner, but by the latter half of his speech, he begins to refer to himself as a Spaniard. In criticizing the ineptitude of the colonial state and denouncing the ill effects of the friars, he says, "There are efforts to hide the truth. But I, a Spanish patriot above all, for I love Spain, I must raise the veil . . . that covers the obstacles that prevent the Philippines from forging ahead" (44). From being a mere native, a "nobody," "I" am now a Spaniard like "you." This transformation is both recognized and produced by the audience's response. Using a language not his own, Lopez-Jaena is heard. Castilian in this case allows for what appears to be a successful transmission of messages, of which there are at least two: the contents of the speech, and the mobility and transferability of the "I" and "you" into a "we" (*nosotros*). We can understand the frenzied applause at the end of the speech as a way of registering this event. That a foreigner appears, proclaims his difference from and deference to his hosts in their own language, thereby crossing those gaps opened up by his presence; that an audience forms around his appearance, seeing in him one who bears a message and recognizes his ability to become other than what he had originally claimed to be: this is the dream of assimilation. It is the materialization of the fantasy of arriving at a common language that has the power to take one beyond hierarchy. Although it begins with an acknowledgment of inequality, Castilian as a lingua franca allows one to set hierarchy aside. To become a "patriot" is thus inseparable from being recognized by others as one who is a carrier of messages and is therefore a medium of communication. It is to embody the power of translation.

What happens, though, when there is no applause, or when the applause is replaced by something else? What becomes of the movement from a native "I" to a Spanish "I" when the sources of recognition are unknown or uncertain? Outside of the banquet, such questions arose to confront nationalists in the streets of the metropole. We can see this, for example, in the travel writings of Antonio Luna.

La solidaridad regularly featured the travel accounts of Luna, who would later become one of the most feared generals of the Philippine revolutionary army in the war against Spain and would subsequently become enshrined as part of the pantheon of national heroes by the republic. As a student in Paris, he visited the Exposition of 1889 and under the pseudonym "Taga-ilog" (which literally means "from the river" and is a pun on the word "Tagalog") wrote of his impressions. He was fascinated by the exhibits from other European colonial possessions but felt acutely disappointed that the Philippine exhibit was poorly done. In one article, he praises the exhibits from the French colonies. He is particularly envious of the displays from Tonkin, which show the regime's attempts at assimilating the natives through the teaching of French. Such brings to mind Spanish refusal to spread its language in the Philippines. By comparison to those in the French colonies, "We Filipinos [*nosotros filipinos*] are in a fetal and fatal condition." In the very next paragraph, however, Luna writes, "The path is shown to us [by the French] . . . But we, Spaniards [*nosotros españoles*] do not want to follow this path. . . . It behooves this race of ours—this race of famous ancestors, giants and heroes—to think of greater things. Our Filipinos already know the most intricate declensions of classic Latin; never mind if they do not understand a word of Castilian." And then in the next paragraph: "We who had the fortune of receiving in those beautiful regions (of the Philippines) the first kiss of life. . . . learned Castilian . . . without understanding it. Later in that town, isolated from all cultures, we saw among 14,000 inhabitants a teacher without a degree, a priest who alone knew Castilian, a town with one deplorable school without equipment for teaching and without students."[21]

There are at least three references invoked by the pronoun *we* (*nosotros*) in the passages above: *nosotros filipinos, nosotros españoles*, and a *nosotros* that is left unspecified as it sees (*vimos*) the conditions in the colony. What triggers this switch from one referent to another is the embarrassment and disappointment Luna feels in seeing the Philippine exhibit. Its crudeness and inadequacy become suddenly apparent when compared with that of the French. Comparison leads him to think of the latter as somehow superior in that it reveals what is lacking in the former. In this sense, we might think of "French" as that which encapsulates "Spanish." Through the perceived modernity of the French, the Spanish comes across as woefully unmodern. The invocation of "French" seems here to have the effect of joining the colonizer to the colonized in the

Philippines implied by the rapid changes of registers in Luna's "we." "We Filipinos" can also, in the next instance, become "we Spaniards" precisely because another term, the French, appears as a point of reference.

Here, a different kind of assimilation is at work, one that contrasts with the banquet scene. The audience in Lopez-Jaena's case responded to his speech and took note of his capacity to distinguish, then suture, differences. In Luna's case, the slide from "Filipino" to "Spaniard" and back is provoked by embarrassment, not applause. He sees the Philippine exhibit and imagines others seeing it, then comparing it to the French, as he does. He thus becomes aware of another "we," an unmarked and anonymous presence that wanders into the exhibits and sees him looking. He is of course also part of that anonymous "we," whom we could think of as the crowd.

A crowd by definition is something that exists outside of oneself. To become part of a crowd is to feel oneself as other. As James T. Siegel writes, "The crowd . . . is a source of self-estrangement within society. One becomes like it and unlike oneself and one does so precisely by responding to it. Becoming alien to oneself and replying . . . are one movement."[22] As part of a crowd of onlookers, Luna's sense of foreignness is intensified. He finds himself split not only between "Filipino" and "Spaniard," but also between one who sees and one who is seen. Castilian addressed to Spaniards allowed Lopez-Jaena to reconceive hierarchy and set it aside, even if only momentarily. In Luna's case, however, Castilian spoken even to oneself amid a crowd produces only a redoubling of his alienation. Assimilation occurs without recognition. He finds himself to be where he is not: in Paris, as part of an anonymous crowd, not quite Filipino nor Spaniard. He thus fails to gain recognition, as he shuttles between identifications, unable to consolidate either one.

One can translate, be understood by the other, yet find oneself unrecognized. Luna's dilemma in Paris becomes even more pronounced on the streets of Madrid. In one essay, he reports the following exchange with a Spanish woman:

> "But how well you speak Spanish."
> "Castilian, you mean, madam."
> "Yes, señor. I am surprised that you speak it as much as I do (*lo posea tanto como yo*)."
> "It is our official language and that is why we know it."
> "But, dear God! Spanish is spoken in your country?"

"Yes, madam."

"Ahhh!!!"

And in that long "Ahhh," suspicious and expressive, would be wrapped all the opinions formed by that Madrid woman. . . .

Perhaps we are thought to be little less than savages or Igorots; perhaps they ignore the fact that we can communicate in the same language, that we are also Spaniards, that we should have the same privileges since we have the same duties.[23]

In speaking Castilian, Luna is greeted with astonishment, then an "ahhhh!!!" He reads into that response a series of possibilities, all of which rest on the suspicion that what he has said has been misplaced. Rather than arrive at its intended address, his message—that yes, "I," too, am a Spaniard; that "I" am not a savage—has been lost. The self that speaks Castilian cannot get across. The native finds himself stranded in that "ahhh!!!" which is neither his first nor second language, but simply a sign for all that has been left unsaid. On the streets, he discovers that "possessing" the Spanish language, as the woman put it, renders one into an oddity, to which the only appropriate response is suspicion. Her suspicion in turn, triggers his, as he finds himself assimilated into what he thinks is her image of him: a "savage." Castilian as a lingua franca in this context draws him to anticipate misrecognition. That is, he is forced to assume the place of the other from where he appears as one who is relentlessly foreign. Rather than embody the power of translation, Luna finds himself the target of insults. In another essay on his impressions of Madrid, he writes:

My very pronounced Malay figure which had called extraordinary attention in Barcelona, excited the curiosity of the children of Madrid in the most glaring manner. There is the young girl [chula], the young woman, or the fashionably dressed [modistas] who turn their heads two or three times to look at me and say in a voice loud enough to be heard: "Jesus! How ugly [¡Que horroroso!] He's Chinese. He's an Igorot." For them, Chinese, Igorots or Filipinos are all the same. Small and big boys . . . not content with this proceed to yell out like savages: Chino! Chiiinitoo! Igorot! In the theaters, in the parks, in gatherings everywhere, there was the same second look at me, the mocking smile . . . the half-stupid stare. Often, in thinking about these spontaneous manifestations, I asked myself if I were in Morocco, in the dangerous borders of the Riff, and I come to doubt that I lived in the capital of a European nation.[24]

Subject to racial insults, Luna begins to doubt again. He wonders if he is in Morocco rather than Madrid—whether he is in a civilized society or among those it considers less so. Indeed, he starts to regard his body as if it were not his own, forced to see it as it is seen by others. He thus experiences it as excessively visible, the object of second looks, its difference too pronounced. His mere appearance comes across as a provocation, almost an affront to those who see him, and thus an invitation to respond. They do so not by hearing him speak or even by asking about his identity but by supplying him with others. Called an assortment of names except his own, Luna finds himself assimilated into the category of the "foreign." Yet, this foreignness is not that of the crowd. A crowd forms around his appearance, but it is one that sets itself against him. In Paris, he could at least disappear into the crowd and find a place in its anonymity. In Madrid, he is set upon by it.

Being targeted by the crowd—being taken in by being taken apart—drives Luna to speak, but this time to a separate audience. He ends his essay on Madrid with the following warning: "Filipinos who are in the Philippines: do not be carried away by the siren song, the immense flights of fantasy, because the disenchantment will be terrible. We are told so much about her (that is, Spain) . . . we think so much of her beauty . . . that when the image melts before the heat of realism, the disappointment is fatal" (686). Assaulted by suspicions and insults in Castilian, Luna talks back. However, his message is directed no longer at Spaniards but to an audience that is absent from the streets of Madrid: Filipinos in the Philippines. It is as if the crowd enables him to find another address. Walking in Madrid, he cannot even recognize Spain, thinking that he might as well be in "Morocco," or at least the Morocco that exists in Spanish minds. The image of Spain, so mystified in the colony, turns out to "melt" upon contact with reality. The crowd's speech has the effect of dissipating the colonial aura. It returns Luna back to the very conditions he had sought to escape: those of being a foreigner under suspicion. Like Lopez-Jaena in the banquet, he, too, transmits messages he did not originally intend. However, rather than win recognition as one who embodies the power of translation, Luna finds himself made to embody an excess of messages beyond his control.

It is not surprising that amid these scenes of rampant misrecognition, he stops referring to himself as a Spaniard. He turns instead to an absent audience, the "Filipinos in the Philippines," thereby imagining an alternative destination for his words. He thus separates Castilian from Spain, appropriating the other's language not in order to return it to him, but to set him aside. In doing so, Luna assumes the position that had been imputed to him by colonial authorities. He becomes, that is, a filibustero who in speaking Castilian chooses not to return it to its source. He thus begins to traffic in stolen goods. In addressing "Filipinos in the Philippines" from Spain in the Spanish language, he establishes for himself and others in his position a different route for the transmission of messages, one that takes on a new kind of immediacy in circumventing the mediation of colonial authority. By shifting the locus of his address, Luna converts his foreignness into a constitutive element of his message.

But what of the response? Was there any way of knowing in advance what would be heard in the colony? What would get through the colonial censors, and in getting through elicit a reply? And by whom, given the plural nature of colonial society? What forms would such responses take, especially since the smuggled message would be in a second, foreign language? What would nationalism look and sound like once its multinational linkages were localized and its communicative energies redirected back home? To address these questions, I turn in the following chapter to the novel titled, appropriately enough, *El filibusterismo*, by the most renowned Filipino nationalist, José Rizal.

2 THE PHANTASM OF REVENGE
On Rizal's Fili

*The question of the self: "who am I?" not
in the sense of "who am I" but who is this "I"
that can say "who"? What is the "I" and what
becomes of responsibility once the identity of
the "I" trembles in secret?*

JACQUES DERRIDA

The Strangeness of Rizal

In nearly all of the towns in the Philippines today, one finds monuments to the country's national hero, José Rizal (1861–96). Most of these are smaller variations of the main monument located in Manila. Erected in 1912 during the U.S. colonial regime, it contains the hero's remains and stands close to the site where he was executed by the Spaniards in 1896 for the crime of fomenting the revolution.

What is worth noting about the monument is its foreignness. It was built by the Swiss sculptor Richard Kissling, whose design was chosen in an international competition sponsored by a committee of Filipino nationalists that included Rizal's older brother.[1] Shipped in pieces from Europe and assembled in the Philippines, the monument depicts Rizal in a winter coat holding a copy of one his two novels, both of which were written in Castilian. The monument has since become the focus of official commemorations of Rizal's death as well as the gathering point for various civic and religious groups dedicated to preserving his memory.

Yet the figure of Rizal in this and other monuments remains odd.[2] Attired in nineteenth-century European clothing suitable for winter climates unimaginable in the tropics, he cradles one of his two novels written in a language that less than 1 percent of the population could read, much less write in.[3] Even during his lifetime, Rizal was regarded as unusual, if not out of place in the Philippines. Colonial authorities suspected him of being a German spy because of his fluency in German and

FIGURE I

Rizal monument, Luneta Park, Manila

his praise for German schooling. Common folk who had heard of him or seen him perform medical treatments (for he was a doctor) regarded him as a miracle worker, while others saw him, especially after his death, as a Filipino Christ.[4] The Katipunan, the revolutionary organization, took him as their guiding spirit, using his name as their secret password, even though Rizal himself had disavowed their movement. It was as if his appearance and name provoked everyone in the colony to see in him a range of references that he did not originally intend. He had what seemed like a remarkable ability to cross geographical borders (by virtue of his frequent travels in and out of the colony) and linguistic differences. (Aside from Tagalog, his mother tongue, he spoke and wrote Castilian fluently and was adept enough in German, French, English, and Italian to translate works in these languages into Castilian and Tagalog. He also knew Greek and Latin and dabbled in Japanese and Arabic.) In this sense, we could think of him as a figure of translation. Linking disparate linguistic regions and social groups inside and outside the archipelago, Rizal's image was deemed capable of transmitting messages from outside to those inside the colony and vice versa. The image of Rizal—its reference to external origins and foreign languages—lends it the character of a lingua franca. As with Castilian, which was the language common to ilustrado (literally, "enlightened") nationalists who spoke a variety of local languages, Rizal's image seemed capable of crossing linguistic boundaries, circulating up and down the social hierarchy. In the Philippine colony, then, both Castilian and Rizal's image appeared capable of becoming common to all because native to no one.

Put differently, Rizal's monuments bear the trace of the foreign origins of the nation: that original aspect of nationalism which owes its genesis to something outside the national. That foreignness, however, has been by and large domesticated. Rizal's monumentalization seems to be saying that he now belongs to "us"; that "we"—Filipinos, not Spaniards—claim him as our own. "We" heard his message, which was meant only for "us," and we responded by rendering to him the recognition denied by Spanish authorities. His memory is now "our" property.

One then can think of Rizal's monuments as a means of acknowledging his foreignness while simultaneously setting it aside. As with all national monuments, that of Rizal's marks his death, bringing those of us who recognize him into a relation with his absence. Yet his death, which is another dimension of his foreignness, no longer need exercise any pressure on the nation's self-conception. If Rizal's strangeness is still palpable in the Philippines today, there is a generalized sense that it has nonetheless been contained, buried, as it were, in the popular assumption that he is the "father" of the nation and, as one of his biographers put it, the "first Filipino."[5]

In a similar vein, it is rare today for Filipinos to read his novels in their original form. These have long been translated into English and other local vernaculars. In 1956, as part of the so-called Rizal Bill, Congress, over the objections of the Catholic Church, required the reading of the novels in English (which is the medium of instruction in schools) among college students, which further dampened interest in the originals.[6] And in recent years, film, operatic and comic book versions of the novels have tended to displace the originals themselves altogether. The monumentalization of his novels has effected the flattening out of their heterogenous language and the stereotyping by Filipino readers of the novels' characters as stand-ins for the various political positions opposed or held by its author. In the same vein, the literary nature of his books has been summarily typed as "realist" and "derivative" of Spanish and French models, while their nature as social documents for the late nineteenth century or as quasi-biblical sources of nationalist wisdom is emphasized by most scholars. As if to reiterate Renan's dictum, the nation remembers Rizal in order to forget him, burying his intractable strangeness.

As with Rizal's image, his novels also have foreign origins. The *Noli* and the *Fili*, as they are popularly referred to, were written while Rizal traveled and studied through Europe. The first novel was composed mostly in Paris and published in Berlin in 1887; the second was begun in London, continued in Biarritz, Paris, and Brussels, and finally published in Ghent in 1891. While monetary considerations forced Rizal to find the cheapest publisher, there is nonetheless the sense here of nationalist writings emanating from the unlikeliest places beyond the colony similar to that of the primary nationalist newspaper, *La solidaridad* (published in Barcelona and Madrid from 1889 to 1895). Both novels were declared subversive by Spanish authorities, their transport and possession criminalized. Rizal and his friends had to arrange for their clandestine delivery to the Philippines. They were smuggled in, usually from Hong Kong, and bribes were routinely paid to customs officials to allow for their entry.[7]

The conditions under which the novels were composed and circulated further underline their strangeness. They were written outside colonial society, addressed to an audience absent from the author's immediate milieu. Their clandestine circulation required the corruption of officials, while their possession, declared a crime, could result in imprisonment. Their author was himself exiled in the southern Philippines for four years and eventually executed. Thus were the alien origins of the Noli and the Fili conjoined to the putative criminality of their effects. Indeed, it is this connection between foreignness and criminality that is thematized most persistently in the second novel.[8]

To inquire about this link, I will reverse my treatment of the novels, turning first to the second, El filibusterismo, before going back to the first, Noli me tangere, in chapter 3. In doing so, I regard the second as a revision of and therefore a screen through which to read the first. In any case, both novels, as we shall see, are about the living finding themselves blocked from responding to the messages of the dead, and the catastrophic consequences of such blockage.

The Figure of the Filibustero

Along with a few other nationalists, Rizal early on entertained the possibility of Philippine separation from Spain as an alternative to the political assimilation favored by most of the other ilustrados. As early as 1888, he was complaining in several letters that Spain was simply "unwilling to listen."[9] Within months of finishing his second novel in 1891, he left Europe for Hong Kong, then went on to the Philippines, convinced that the struggle should be waged there. He would follow the train of his words, returning as it were to the scene of the crime.

We might ask: what was the manner of this return and the nature of the crime? We get a sense of both in Rizal's dedication of the Fili: "To the Memory of the priests Don Maríano Gomez, Don José Burgos, and Don Jacinto Zamora," it begins, referring to the three Filipino secular priests who were falsely implicated in a local uprising in 1872 and unjustly executed by Spanish authorities.[10] Having earlier criticized the Spanish friars' monopoly over the colony's wealthiest parishes in the 1860s, these three secular priests had also challenged Spanish assumptions about the inferiority of natives and mestizos and the inability of non-Spanish secular priests to run their own parishes. They were thus regarded by ilustrado nationalists as their precursors. Representing protonationalist instances of resistance to friar rule, which was regarded as the most repressive aspect of colonial rule, the fate of Fathers Gomez,

Burgos, and Zamora also signified assimilationist aspirations gone wrong.

In the novel's dedication, Rizal recalls their deaths by commemorating their innocence. He "in no way acknowledges [their] guilt"; instead he holds Spain "culpable for your deaths." "Let these pages serve as a belated wreath upon your unknown graves; and may all who . . . attack your memory find their hands soiled with your blood!"[11] Like a gravestone, the book's dedication marks the death of Filipino fathers. Their execution had made a lasting impression on Rizal when he was a young student in Manila. Later on, he wrote to friends that had it not been for Gomez, Burgos, and Zamora, he would have been a Jesuit.[12] In their deaths, Rizal hears a message and is compelled to respond. Mourning their deaths not only leads him to mark their "unknown graves," it also spurs him to utter a threat: that those who attack your memory will be soiled in your blood. They, too, should be made to suffer your fate. The deaths of the Filipino priests instill in Rizal a desire for vindication. The dedication of the *Fili* thus brings together mourning and revenge as two parts of the same reply that he directs to the fathers: those who are dead as well those who are guilty. Writing thus becomes a practice of gathering and giving back what one has received. In the *Fili*, returning a message means remembering what was said and responding in kind.

But again we might ask: who determines the nature of the message and decides the forms of its return? There is, of course, the author Rizal. Yet in the *Fili*, the author is shadowed by another agent who returns the call of death: the figure of the *filibustero*. In the book's epigraph—what we might think of as its other dedication—Rizal quotes his Austrian friend and nationalist sympathizer Ferdinand Blumentritt, who writes: "It is easy to suppose that a filibustero has bewitched [*hechizado*] in secret the league of friars and reactionaries, so that unconsciously following his inspirations, they favor and foment that politics which has only one end: to extend the ideas of *filibusterismo* all over the country and convince every last Filipino that there exists no other salvation outside of that of the separation from the Motherland." In Spanish dictionaries, one of the definitions of *filibustero* is that of a pirate, hence a thief. But as one who, we might say in English, "filibusters," she or he is also one who interrupts parliamentary proceedings, smuggling his or her own discourse into those of others. In either case, we can think of the filibustero as an intruder, breaking and entering into where she or he does not properly belong, doing so by surprise and often in disguise. Small wonder then that by the late nineteenth century, *filibustero* was also glossed as "subversive," in the sense of a disruptive presence, a figure who, by word or deed, suddenly and surreptitiously steals upon the social order.[13] Thus were nationalists referred to by Spanish authorities as filibusteros. Their wish to speak and disseminate Castilian as a route to economic and social reform challenged the friar-sanctioned practice of dissuading natives from learning the language. As we saw in chapter 1, the friars from the beginnings of colonization in the sixteenth century had administered God's Word in the many local vernaculars. They also translated native languages into Castilian for the benefit of the colonial state and their clerical orders. Thus did the friars long enjoy the role of privileged mediators between the metropole and the colony. For Filipino nationalists to seek to spread Castilian to the populace would in effect undercut the mediating authority of the Spanish fathers. In their desire to communicate in Castilian, ilustrado nationalists were asking to be recognized as other than what colonial authorities regarded them to be: the equal of Spaniards. Instead, Spanish authorities, prodded by the friars, saw nationalists to be speaking out of place. Speaking in a language that did not belong to them, they appeared alien to and disruptive of the colonial order.

The political implications that grow out of linguistic disruptions takes on a particular inflection in Rizal's citation of Blumentritt. The filibustero here is put forth as a kind of sorcerer, a malevolent medium. Later on, Rizal in his preface will refer to the filibustero as a "phantom" (*fantasma*) who roams about, haunting the populace. Its presence is thus a secret, so that one may be in contact with a filibustero without being aware of it. The power of the filibustero lies in his or her ability to make you think what she or he wants you to without your knowledge. Possessed by the thoughts of an other you cannot even recognize, you begin to act in ways you did not intend. Thus does the malevolence of the filibustero consist of separating you from your own thoughts. In a colonial context, such a separation can bring you to cut yourself off from the mother country, that is, to mistake separation from Spain for independence.

While the filibustero is thought to subvert one's control over one's thoughts and that of the mother country over her sons and daughters, it also insinuates its way to the top of the colonial hierarchy, inserting itself where it does not belong and causing authority to act in ways that go against its interests. The filibustero then is a kind of foreign presence who exercises an alienating effect on all those it comes in contact with. Being out of place, it can travel all over the place, promoting the misrecognition of motives and words. For this reason, we can think of the filibustero's foreignness as the force of a transmission that troubles social hierarchy. The filibustero possesses the power of translation—the capacity to cross boundaries and put diverse groups in contact with one another—but translation in the service of something outside of colonial society.

What is the "outside" that the filibustero works for? Independence, perhaps? Rizal himself remained uncertain. Until the end of his life, he never explicitly favored a final break with Spain, even though he considered political assimilation to be doomed. We can think of the *Fili* as the site within which he rehearsed this ambivalence that haunted nationalist sentiments. The novel is a record of hesitations and anxieties raised by the failure of assimilation giving rise to the specters of separation. The figure of the filibustero was its medium for tracking and trafficking in the emergence, spread and containment of such anxieties. This fundamentally unsettling nature of the filibustero as both medium and message infects, as it were, both author and his characters. I try to trace the spread of this infection below.

Misappropriating Castilian

Nearly all commentaries on *El filibusterismo* rank it as an "inferior" because less polished work when compared to Rizal's first novel. The second lacks, for these commentators, the narrative coherence and biting humor of its predecessor, putting in their place polemical pronouncements and sarcastic laughter.[14] In most writings about nationalism and Rizal, the *Fili* is quickly passed over, its complications put to the side.

Such complications begin with the absence of a single narrative line. Instead, the novel is loosely woven around two plots, from which several others emerge. One concerns the attempts, ultimately foiled, of an association of university students to establish a self-supporting academy for the teaching of Castilian in Manila autonomous from friar control. The other plot deals with the story of Simoun, a mysterious jeweler of unknown origins who, having ingratiated himself with the governor general, friars, and local officials, uses his wealth to spread corruption in the colony in the hope of intensifying general misery and hastening a popular uprising. An important twist to this story is this: Simoun is actually Crisostomo Ibarra, the protagonist of the first novel, who was thought to be dead. Persecuted in the earlier novel for his reformist ideals and his love for María Clara, the illegitimate daughter of the Spanish friar Damaso and a devout native woman who had been unable to conceive with her feckless native husband, Ibarra flees the country. In the *Fili*, he returns years later disguised as Simoun the wealthy merchant, intent on rescuing María Clara from her seclusion in the convent and orchestrating a revolt to wreak revenge on all those he deems responsible for ruining his future.

Both plots end in failure. The students' petition for a Spanish academy is denied. They are subsequently blamed for the mysterious appearance of posters deemed "subversive" at the university. Many are rounded up and imprisoned, and though they are all eventually released, they also retreat into an embittered cynicism. At least one of them, Basilio, is drawn to Simoun's plot. However, Simoun's plans also unravel. He discovers that María Clara has died, and his plans for instigating an uprising are discovered by colonial authorities. He flees to the rural retreat of Padre Florentino, an older Filipino secular priest from the generation of Gomez, Burgos, and Zamora. In the end, nothing is resolved. Simoun dies of his wounds and disappointment and Rizal, speaking through Padre Florentino, launches on what by then was a familiar polemic about the necessity of education, virtuous intentions, and sacrifice in confronting oppression and injustice. The novel is remarkably inconclusive. Its plots do not add up to a political program—in fact, such a program is studiously avoided. Rather, disillusionment takes on almost baroque proportions. What remains in the end is the author's voice speaking through Padre Florentino, asking the "youth" to come forth and sacrifice themselves for the nation. And after hurling them to the ocean, he addresses the jewels of Simoun, which Simoun used for corrupting officials and buying weapons for his uprising, commending them to the care of "Nature" for use in more noble purposes in the future.

What interests me are the ways this open-endedness and negativity produce a space for the emergence of an authorial voice addressing an absent audience. In between the twisting and twining of these plots, Rizal constructs a series of scenes around particular characters. Many of these have only the most tenuous connections to the narratives. Instead, they bear out another kind of emplotment. In these scenes, Rizal obsessively details the recurrence and effects of the foreign detached from its origins in hierarchy. What emerges in these foreign encounters is a certain politics, colored by anticipation, shame, and resentment, that envisions a response through translation. It is my contention that the receipt of the foreign, its recognition and its return, marks the domestication of nationalism as specifically "Filipino." Additionally, the failure of recognition and the deferral of the return are built into such a politics, one whose translation requires a voice whose appearance seems new. Such would be the voice of the author.

Where and how do we come to see the emergence of the foreign? How does it call for as much as it evades translation and domestication? And what are the consequences of such an event for understanding the linguistic basis of nationalism?

One place to see the emergence of the foreign and its domestication is in the classroom. Rizal writes at length about education in his political essays. For Rizal, education is the key to reformulating social relations. It places youth in the position of receiving and realizing a future. Education thus converts the future whose futurity cannot be known into a set of promises pledged to youth. But what blocks this promise from being realized, as we saw, are the friars who controlled the educational institutions in the colony. To understand how this blockage is produced, we can turn to a chapter in the novel titled "La clase de fisica" ("The Class in Physics") (98–108).[15] Rizal describes the conditions at the colony's Dominican university: "No one went to class in order to learn but only to avoid getting marked absent. The class is reduced to reciting lessons from memory, reading the book and once in a while, answering one or other trivial, abstract, profound, cunning, enigmatic questions. True, there was no shortage of little sermons (*sermonitas*)—they were always the same—about humility, submission, respect for the religious" (89). In class, one's main concern was to avoid being marked absent. Yet one's presence amounted to little, since it entailed the mechanical recitation of texts and the occasional answer to questions as trivial as they were abstract. Education was a matter of hearing what one has already heard before, such as the sermonitas on submission and humility, just as it required the repetition of formulaic answers to predictable demands. Nothing truly new was allowed to emerge, and in this sense the classroom was an extension of the church. Hence, for example, the scientific instruments in the physics laboratory were never used by the students and were taken out only on rare occasions to impress important visitors, "like the Holy Sacrament to the prostrated faithful: look at me but do not touch" (90). In a similar vein, to memorize and repeat the words of a textbook is to turn oneself into a vessel for the passage of the words of authority. One is expected not to make these words one's own, but rather to submit to their force and bear them back to their source as the friar stood by and measured one's fidelity. Schooling led not to a future but to the perpetuation of familiar forms of servility. It was meant to maintain students in their stupidity.

Yet what made the classroom different from the church was that students were required to recite individually. They could not receive a grade and pass the course, Rizal writes, until they had been recognized (*ser conocido*) and called upon by the professor. By recognizing the student, it is as if the professor sees in him a capacity to speak up. At the same time, that capacity constitutes a potential for disruption. In speaking up, the student might also talk back; in repeating the textbook, he might make a mistake and thus utter something uncalled for and unexpected. Such possibilities make the classroom a volatile arena for the reiteration of authority, a place for the potential exposure of authority's limits.

In the physics class, Rizal describes the professor, Padre Millón, as one who "was not of the common run." He knew his physics, but the demands of colonial education required that he assume his role in the ritual of the classroom. Having called the roll, he begins calling on students to recite the day's lesson "word for word." Rizal describes their response: "The phonographs (*los fonografos*) played, some well, others bad; others stuttered and were prompted. He who recited without a mistake earned a good mark while he who committed more than three mistakes a bad one" (92). Used as a medium of instruction, Castilian here has a curious role. In speaking like "phonographs," students mechanically reproduce the lesson. They respond in a language that is wholly exterior to them. Castilian thus comes across as a means not of self-expression but of self-evacuation. One who recites Castilian phonographically demonstrates, among other things, that this language has no place in one's mind. One speaks it without knowing what one is saying, so that it seems to be merely passing through one's body. Drained of intelligibility and detached from intentionality, Castilian thus becomes truly foreign to the students. In speaking it, they become mediums for the reproduction of its foreignness.

One's capacity to reproduce Castilian earns one a mark. One's presence is noted down and one is left alone by the friar as he moves on to call another student. The student's grade signifies his submission to the demand for repetition. However, repetition not only signifies his acknowledgment of the professor's authority, it also conveys his distance from the professor's language, for speaking Castilian in this context requires its separation from the rest of one's thoughts. That is, it entails the recognition of the foreign as foreign, as that which belongs to someone else and over which one does not have a proper claim. In speaking up to authority, one acknowledges the sheer passage of the latter's language through oneself. One thus confronts Castilian as the inappropriable: the materialization of an alien presence that periodically assails one and which one periodically is required to fend off. When called to recite, one speaks Castilian in order to put it out of mind, in the hope of sending it back to where it came from.

However, these recitations are never smooth. Both students and professors find themselves in the midst of other signs that can at times interrupt the circulation of the language of authority. Rizal's interest lies precisely in recording the static against which these signals take place. Amid the tedium of recitations, the friar-professor scans the faces of his students looking to catch someone unprepared, "wanting to startle him" (*quiso asustarle*). He spies on a "fat boy with a sleepy face and hair stiff and hard like the bristles of a brush, yawning almost to the point of dislocating his jaw, stretching himself, extending his arms as if he were on his bed." The professor zeroes in on the unsuspecting student:

> "*Oy*! you [*tu*], sleepyhead, *aba*! What! And lazy, too! Maybe [*seguro*] you don't know the lesson, *ja*?!" Padre Millón not only addressed all the students informally [*tuteaba*] like a good friar, but also spoke to them in the language of the marketplace [*lengua de tienda*]. . . . The interpellation, instead of offending the class, amused them and many laughed: this was something that happened routinely. Nevertheless, the sleepyhead did not laugh; he rose up with a jump, rubbed his eyes, and like a steam engine gyrating a phonograph, began to recite. (92)

The boredom of one student triggers the interest of the professor. The latter sees in the former an opportunity to break the monotony of the class. It works. He surprises the student, much to the delight and laughter of his classmates. What is worth noting here is the mode of the friar's speech. He not only speaks down to the students, addressing them individually as *tu* rather than with the more respectful *usted*. More significant, he speaks to the class in lengua de tienda, the language of the marketplace, or what has also been referred to as *español de la cocina*, kitchen Spanish.[16] Consisting of an unstable mix of Castilian and Tagalog, it is a language spoken to and at the lower end of the social hierarchy. In addressing his students in this language, the friar momentarily disrupts the ritual of recitation and turns the classroom into another place closer to that of the market than the church.

Hearing this linguistic disruption, one that was a matter of daily routine, the other students laugh. In their laughter, they find themselves occupying a different position. No longer are they anxious and expectant targets. Rather, they become spectators to a comical encounter. Thus are they momentarily released from the grip of Castilian. Instead, they come to share as audiences in another language that belongs neither to them nor to the friar: the lengua de tienda.

Their identification with one another, however, finds its locus in the body of the fat boy. Interrupted from his reverie, he bursts out in a convulsive repetition of the lessons like a "steam engine gyrating a phonograph." Startled, he takes shelter in repeating what he does not understand. As if wielding an amulet, he repeats the lesson hoping to protect himself from further intrusions. But rather than fend off authority, his response sets him up for another ambush. " '*Para, para, para!*' the professor interrupted. 'Jesus! what a rattle!' " The professor then proceeds to ask the student a question about the day's lesson on the nature of mirrors that is not mentioned in the textbook. Uncomprehending, the student tries once again to recite the text. And again he finds himself interrupted by the friar, "inserting *cosas* [what] and *abas* at every moment," while mocking his appearance. Rather than receive a mark for his submission, the student is marked as the object of derision in the common language of the market and the laughter of the other students.

Throughout this exchange the professor's authority comes less from speaking Castilian as from interrupting its flow. He dominates the production of surprise, thereby controlling not only the circulation of Castilian but also its possible deviations. Herein lies the importance of "market Spanish." Through lengua de tienda, he alerts students to the fact that he is able to hear in Castilian the outbreak of another form of speech. He knows what they are aware of but cannot say: that Castilian can be spoken in ways that evade linguistic authority. He thus communicates the miscommunication intrinsic to colonial sociality and thereby shows himself capable of anticipating the semantic crisis built into the economy of colonial communication.

The students in their laughter also come to recognize their professor's authority. However, it is not in this instance an authority that derives from the language of God or the state, but one that comes from the ability to overhear and transmit the intermittent and interruptive language from below. They see in their professor one who can draw from other sources the means with which to get across in ways that evade the language of the textbook. Mixing linguistic registers, he appears to mimic the speech of those at the periphery of the linguistic hierarchy. Thanks to the friar, Castilian appears to give way, becoming another language that makes possible a momentary joining of his interests with those of his students.

That joining of interests, however, is as evanescent as it is transitory. More significant, it relies on the targeting of an other who can barely speak and cannot laugh. Such is the fate of the fat boy who is finally reduced to saying, in response to a long-winded question that ends with, "What do you say?": "I? Nothing!" (*Yo? Nada!*). When he does speak in a Castilian other than that of the textbook, it is to say that the "I" who speaks is one who has "nothing" to say and so by implication is no one at all. The boy speaks Castilian and finds himself unrecognizable even to himself. Compelled to answer in a foreign language, he finds himself converted into one who is utterly foreign. The professor and his students are thoroughly complicit in the interruption of Castilian by sharing a language from below. But the result is not the end of hierarchy, only its reconfiguration at the expense of a designated alien. Interrupting the possibility of interruptions, the friar and his students are led to discover and domesticate the foreign residing in their midst, which includes both the Castilian of the lesson and the embodiment of its failure to be correctly returned in the fat boy.

Rizal, however, raises a third possibility. Rather than repeat the language of authority or disrupt its demand in order to reformulate hierarchy, one can say "no" to both. In such a case, conflict would replace subservience. Rather than scapegoating, there would be confrontation; in place of laughter, revenge. This third possibility is played out when Padre Millón calls on another student, the felicitously named Placido Penitente (95–99). Placido is caught by the friar trying to prompt another student who was being grilled. Seeing the native student's embarrassment (*verguenza*, which means shame but also refers to the private parts of an individual), the professor relishes the thought of further humiliating him. He attacks Placido with a barrage of tendentious questions meant to confuse him, to the usual amusement of others. Indiscriminately mixing registers, the priest punctuates his questions with Latinisms and lengua de tienda, repeatedly punning on Placido's name and forcing him to stutter and commit several errors while reciting. Throughout, the student finds himself the recipient of the professor's assaults and the laughter of the class.

However, something unexpected happens. Turning to his record book to grade the student, the friar discovers that Placido had been marked absent for the day. He had come in late just after his name had been called on the roll. Officially, he was not there. Yet, not only was he being given a grade; he is also told by the friar that he has fifteen absences and is one short of failing the class. Placido takes exception, for he knows that he has been absent only three times and tells the friar so in impeccable Castilian. The priest replies once again in Spanish pidgin, "Jusito, jusito, señolia! . . . si te descuidas un mas, sulung! Apuera de la fuerta!" ("Enough, enough, *señorito* [little master] . . . any more discussions and you're out of here, out of the door!"),[17] only this time spoken with a Chinese accent that gives a sharper edge to his mockery of the student's protestations. He tells him that he multiplies each absence by five to make up for all the times he does not call the roll. Hearing this, Placido is outraged. He is doubly misrecognized, taken as a mere indio incapable of speaking Castilian even when he does, and as a fool incapable of telling the difference between his absence and presence. At this point, Placido's embarrassment is converted into anger. Cutting off the friar at midsentence, he says,

> "Enough, father, enough! Your Reverence can mark me for mistakes as much as he wants, but he does not have the right to insult me. Your Reverence can stay with the class, but I cannot stand it any longer."

> And without taking leave, he left.

> The class was shocked [*aterrada*]. Similar acts of indignity were almost never seen. Who would have thought that Placido Penitente . . . ? The professor, surprised, bit his lips and watched him leave, moving his head with a menacing motion. With a trembling voice, he then began a sermon on the usual themes, though with much more forcefulness . . . about the increasing arrogance, the innate ingratitude, the

vanity, the excessive pride that the demon of darkness had infused in the youth, the little education, the lack of courtesy, etc., etc., etc. (98)

Rizal imagines a moment when the indio speaks up not in order to confirm authority in its place but to reject it altogether. Placido tells the Spanish father "enough!" in the latter's language. Addressing the friar as "Your Reverence" (V. R.), he discovers in Castilian a place from which to separate his interests from those on top. Castilian allows him to fashion an "I" that can say "I can't stand it anymore," an "I" that can get across to and, more important, surpass hierarchy. Through Castilian, the "I" appears as one who, in saying "no" to the father, can begin to imagine taking the latter's place. In Castilian, Placido interrupts the friar, until then the master of interruption, thereby ceasing to reproduce the friar's interests. Instead, he converts Castilian into his own language, seeming to possess and contain its alien force.

The sudden appearance of this mastery shocks (aterrar) the rest of the students. They hear Placido and understand what he says, yet they can no longer recognize him. "Who would have thought that Placido Penitente . . . ?" It is as if the students sense in Placido a communicative force that, in responding directly to authority, overtakes its demands. He thus comes across as someone other than who he was supposed to be. Refusing the father, he also separates himself from the rest of the class. He manages to return the surprises of the friar with a surprise of his own: he leaves. But in leaving, he takes on the risk of failure and shows that risk to be an element of his speech.

Where the other students speak Castilian in order to put it out of mind, Placido turns Castilian into a language for staking his own. In this way, he becomes a new kind of figure, one who is "rarely seen." Like the ilustrado nationalists, Placido's newness appears strange to those who see it. The friar can respond only with stunned silence, then with a mechanical sermon, the usual harangue whose tediousness Rizal signals with "etc., etc., etc." The friar finds himself in the place of the fat student, retreating behind the repetition of words that everyone has already heard. Both he and the rest of the students find themselves faced with a different kind of foreignness, one that is not available to the usual modes of domestication. While it speaks in the language of authority, it exceeds hierarchy as if it were addressing another location.

What is this other location? How else might one come to discover it? What sort of recognition flows out of this other locus of address? In the case of Placido Penitente, the discovery of this address begins with a sense of embarrassment that is converted into anger through the misappropriation of Castilian, both on the friar's and on his part. But what of those who cannot speak Castilian, or at least cannot do so in the ways that might skirt around or go beyond hierarchy? How are they to be recognized? And by whom?

To address these questions, I want to turn to one of the chapters in the *Fili* concerning the story of Julí, a young native woman whose entire family had suffered in the hands of the colonial authorities (227–35). Her father, Cabesang Tales, is a farmer whose lands are unjustly taken away by the friars and their native lackeys. He is subsequently kidnapped by local bandits, forcing Julí to place herself in the domestic service of an older, wealthy woman in town in order to pay his ransom. Her fiancé is the student Basilio, who is arrested by Spanish authorities on charges of putting up subversive posters at the university. She is compelled to seek the aid of the parish priest, Padre Camorra, popularly known in town as *si cabayo*, or "the horse," for his "frolicsome" ways with women. Julí is terrified at the prospect of having to submit to his advances even as she is desperate to seek his intercession to free Basilio from jail. She is thus overwhelmed by guilt. She would be guilty of giving up her honor should she submit to the friar and guilty if she does not, since it would mean abandoning any hope of helping Basilio. Either she sacrifice her beloved to keep her virtue, or sacrifice her virtue to save her beloved.

Her predicament is articulated through a series of dreams, "now mournful, now bloody." In these dreams,

> complaints and laments would pierce her ears. She imagined hearing shots, seeing her father, her father who had done so much for her . . . hunted like an animal because she had hesitated to save him. And her father's figure was transformed and she recognized Basilio, dying and looking at her reproachfully . . . blood issuing forth from his mouth and she would hear Basilio say to her: "Save me! Save me! You alone can save me!" Then a burst of laughter would resound, she would turn her eyes and would see her father looking at her with eyes full of reproach. And Julí would awaken and sit up on her mat, would draw her hand over her forehead and pull back her hair; cold sweat, like the sweat of death, would dampen her. (232–33)

In her dreams, Julí is assailed by voices and stares from her father and her fiancé, each meshing into the other. In their absence, their dream images occupy Julí's mind, insisting to be heard and attended to. She has no control over their return and cannot find the means to meet their demands. Here, guilt is associated with the sense of being filled with voices and images from beyond one's waking life. Such presences convey a single message: "Save me!" Unable to keep from hearing it, Julí is nonetheless unable to reply. Guilt arises from this failure to stop listening and the inability to fashion an answer. Instead, one is burdened with a sense of obligations unmet and losses unmourned. In Julí's case, this failure to return what has been given to her keeps returning, lodging itself inside, like an alien presence she cannot get rid of. She is held hostage to the recurring presence of absent fathers. She does not have a language with which to address these figures, to welcome them and send them on their way. Instead, she is burdened by a responsibility she cannot respond to. In this way, she finds herself in a position far more desperate than the students in the physics class. At least the students had the possibility of mimicking the language of authority in order to evade its full force, or to misappropriate it for themselves and thereby confront it directly. Julí's only alternative—consorting with the Spanish father—is really no alternative at all, since it amounts to incurring further guilt. It is as if to undo one crime, she must commit another.

What might have saved her from this spiraling guilt would have been the intervention of a third term coming between her and her ghostly fathers. It would have been a figure who might have spoken on her behalf, fending off the fathers' demands and effectively absolving her of her debts. Without this third term, debts can only pile up, pushing one to do what one shouldn't, triggering more guilt, and so on around the circle. In Julí's story, the only resolution turns out to be death. Entering the priest's quarters, she is "filled with terror . . . she saw death before her" (235). Before the priest could advance on her, she plunges to her death out of the convent's window. Unable to domesticate the spectral presences of her fathers and unable to speak past the expectant friar, Julí is driven to her death. Hearing of her death, the people of the town can do no more than murmur their dismay, "dar[ing] not to mention names." They, too, it would seem, are unable to respond adequately to her death. For this reason, they become complicit in her demise and infected with her guilt.

In hearing the story of Julí, everyone seems implicated. Her guilt may have been absolved by her death, but it is nonetheless passed on to those who hear of her fate. Rizal in retelling this tale takes on her guilt and distributes it to his readers. Just as Julí was overcome by the insistence of a message she could not return, so we the readers are placed by Rizal amid a loss we cannot account for. In the midst of this guilt, there are at least two possibilities. One might, as in Julí's case, feel blocked and be driven to suicide, symbolic or otherwise. But one might also take a different route, which Rizal had laid out in the dedicatory section of his novel: repaying debts by way of revenge. By doing so, one would constitute oneself as an agent of recognition: as one who receives and registers messages of distress by virtue of one's proximity to another address: that of death. It is this route of revenge that others take that I now want to take up in the following section.[18]

The Gift of Vengeance

As we saw in the dedication of the *Fili*, the question of revenge is linked to the imperative to mourn the dead. The author styles himself as the agent of this double duty. In writing, he pays tribute to the memory of dead fathers and sends a message to those he deems responsible for putting them to death. He faces two ways. In doing so, he also finds himself speaking from two places. As an author, he stands outside of his text, marking the threshold of its fictional reach. But he is also a voice that, in addressing his readers and characters, exists inside the text. His identity as the singular author from whom the novel originates is contingent on the dispersal of his presence and the dissemination of his voice throughout other voices and figures in the book.

We might think of Rizal then as a double agent: his role as an author is a function of his shifting positions in the stories he tells. We can see this doubleness refracted in the language of the novel itself. Though written in Castilian, the *Fili* is remarkably heteroglossic, full of regional slang, idiomatic expressions, Latinisms, bits of untranslated French, German, and Tagalog, and broken up by the occasional appearance of lengua de tienda and Chinese-inflected Spanish. Just as the author's position is split and unstable, so are the languages he finds himself using. Mixing identities and linguistic registers, Rizal as "Rizal" is a figure in the historical emplotment of Filipino nationalism as much as he is a figure whose presence haunts the *Fili*. He is an author as much as a fictional character: not one or the other but both/and. He thus remains eccentric to any particular identity and at a remove from any one position. His historical specificity lies precisely in his unspecifiability.

In his doubleness, it is tempting to see Rizal approximating the situation of the filibustero, for in the novel, the filibustero is a figure of corruption as well as critique. It stands astride the tasks of mourning and revenge, translating the demands of one into the force of the other. Yet, as we shall see, the figure of the filibustero is precisely what Rizal must conjure up in order to renounce. In that renunciation, he clarifies his status as the author of this text, a status far from settled in the unsettled conditions of the late nineteenth century.

In the novel, the figure of the filibustero looms most ominously in the character of the jeweler Simoun. Central to Simoun's identity is his mysterious appearance. He speaks with a "strange accent, a mixture of English and South American . . . dressed in English fashion . . . his long hair, completely white in contrast to the black beard . . . which indicated a mestizo origin." Always he wore "a pair of enormous blue-tinted glasses that completely covered his eyes and part of his cheeks, giving him the appearance of a blind man or one with a defective vision" (5–6). Wherever he appears in the colony, people take notice. His unknown origins are the regular subject of gossip and speculation. Alternately referred to as a "Yankee" because of the time he spent traveling in North America, as an "American mulatto," an "Anglo-Indian," or a "mestizo," the mysteriousness of Simoun's origins is compounded by his "strange [Castilian] accent" and his ability to speak Tagalog and English. And because of his reputed access to both the friar orders and to the governor general, he acquires such nicknames as the "brown cardinal" and the "black eminence" (44). While Simoun is thought to originate outside of the colonial order, he is nonetheless able to traverse the various levels of colonial society and move up and down the linguistic hierarchy.

What enables him to circulate within colonial society are his powerful connections, cultivated by his wealth. Money allows him to cross geographical and social distances without having to be absorbed by any locality or social group. In this sense, money augments his mysteriousness, drawing others to further speculate on what lies beneath his appearance. Such speculations suggest that the figure of Simoun is seen as something more than what he appears to be. He compels others to read him as a sign of and for something else—secret arrangements, unaccountable events, unexpected possibilities, hidden conspiracies—which escape detection.[19]

Simoun's mysteriousness, however, is a disguise. Early on in the novel, while walking through a cemetery the student Basilio sees Simoun without his glasses and, much to his surprise, realizes that he is in fact Crisostomo Ibarra, the ilustrado protagonist of Rizal's first novel. Ibarra as Simoun has come back to exact vengeance from the colonial authorities he holds responsible for destroying his life. Thanks to the machinations of the friars in particular, Ibarra's father was thrown in prison, where he eventually dies. His body is then dumped in the river by local grave diggers, never to be found. Ibarra's fiancé and the focus of his future happiness, María Clara, is taken away from him and sequestered in a convent. And his name is ruined by association with a revolt he did not even know of. Hounded as a filibustero for seeking to introduce educational reforms, he barely manages to escape from the colonial police, who think they have shot and killed him as he goes down a river with the aid of a native boatman, Elias.

As Simoun, Ibarra returns. Long thought to be dead, he comes back to life, but now as a disguised presence. Whereas Ibarra had in the past sought to use Castilian as a way of securing for himself a place in a reformed order, now as Simoun he seeks to use money to blast that order apart. He explains himself to the stunned Basilio:

> "Yes, I am he who [was here] thirteen years ago . . . Victim of a vicious system, I have wandered throughout the world, working night and day in order to amass a fortune and carry out my plan. Today I have returned in order to destroy this system, precipitate its corruption, hurl it into the abyss . . . even if I have to spill torrents of tears and blood . . .
>
> "Summoned by the vices of those who govern, I have returned to these islands and under the cloak of a merchant, I have traversed the towns. With my gold I have opened the way . . . and since corruption sets in gradually, I have incited greed, I have favored it, the injustices and abuses have multiplied; I have fomented crime, and acts of cruelty in order to accustom people to the prospect of death . . . I have instigated ambitions to impoverish the treasury; and this being insufficient to lead to a popular uprising, I have wounded the people in their most sensitive fibers . . ." (46–47)

Revealing his secret to Basilio, Ibarra implies that underneath his disguise he has not changed. The "I" that announces its return in order to mourn its losses is the same "I" that has wandered the world and now brings with it a plot of revenge. "Simoun" is a fiction, a ruse that allows Ibarra to circulate in the colony. As such, it is a second, malleable identity within which to conceal an unchanging one. The strangeness of

Simoun is thus recognizable to Basilio and the reader as that which refers to Ibarra, carrying out the latter's plans, acting on his behalf, serving to collect what is owed to him. Here, disguise seems to conceal one's identity only in order to consolidate one's claims on the world and one's certainty about oneself.

Money plays a crucial role in Simoun's plans. Through money, he— or they, that is, Ibarra and his double, Simoun—is able to incite greed and spread corruption. Simoun is thus not really a merchant, since his interests lie not in the conversion of money to capital and the accumulation of surplus value. Rather, he seeks to harness money into an instrument of his will. It is as if at the end of each transaction, he expects not to receive more money but rather to produce more misery. Contrary to Marx's capitalist who sweats money from every pore, Rizal's fake merchant exudes money in order to sow crime and incite popular uprisings. Like disguise, money is an object whose foreignness is here readily transparent and whose disruptive effects are meant to be calculable and knowable in advance, at least from the point of view of Ibarra. Money and disguise encapsulate a set of prior wishes and are made to serve the self-same identity. Behind "Simoun" there stands Ibarra; behind money, Ibarra's plan. Thus can Ibarra imagine himself the author of his plot, the one who holds its secret and determines its unfolding.

Thinking of himself at the origin of his appearances and his plot, Ibarra, speaking through Simoun, depicts his return as a response to a summons issued by "the vices of those who govern." Arriving at the scene of the crime, he sees that neither the victim nor the perpetrator can be helped. Both are so corrupt and so weakened that only through more corruption can they be saved. What might seem like a paradoxical notion takes on a certain force when Simoun declares to Basilio, "I am the Judge come to punish a system by availing myself of its own crimes" (49). Ibarra as Simoun thus sets himself up as a third term that intervenes and adjudicates matters between colonizer and colonized. He speaks beyond the law and thereby becomes a law unto himself. As judge, he regards himself as the locus of all address and the source of recognition. Such is possible insofar as he is also the author of a plot whose elements take him as their privileged referent. As judge and author, Ibarra-Simoun surpasses and subordinates all others in colonial society.

Revenge here entails a particular kind of fantasy. It gives rise to a particular scenario about one's place in relation to others. The self idealizes itself as one who was once misrecognized and made to suffer for it but now returns in control of its appearances. It thus imagines itself as one capable of distinguishing and disentangling itself from the misperceptions of others. Hence, though one may look and sound foreign, underneath one is in control of one's identity. In effect taking vengeance is simultaneous with putting the foreign in its "proper" place: outside of oneself, a mere disguise and thus an instrument with which to carry out one's will.

We see this fantasy at work in Simoun's emphatic dismissal of assimilationist politics. Addressing Basilio in proper Castilian, he mocks the students' efforts to encourage the learning of the language. For Simoun, such a project is doomed. The friars and the government will never allow it; the people will never take to it since it is a foreign language incapable of expressing their native sentiments. At most, Castilian will become the language of a privileged few, thereby aggravating one's separation from the people. Indeed, the students' advocacy of Castilian amounts to the betrayal of their mother tongue (47–48), while their wish for Hispanization is like the desire of "the slave who asks only for a little rag with which to wrap his chains so these would make less noise and not bruise the skin" (53). Instead of "slavish thoughts," he urges them to think "independently," which means that "neither in rights, nor customs, nor language should the Spaniard be considered here as being in his own home or thought of by people as a fellow citizen, but always as an invader, a foreigner, and sooner or later, you will be free" (49).

For Simoun, freedom lies not in identifying with the colonizer, even as equals, but in separating oneself from him. One needs to forget about Castilian and remember only that Spain is a foreign presence that belongs elsewhere. In this way, one need no longer look toward Spain for reforms. Rather, one can in one's own language constitute oneself as an agent of change and recognition.

We can think of revenge then as a relationship of reciprocity whereby one returns what one has received wrongfully back to where one imagines it came from.[20] To take vengeance is to communicate something about Castilian: that it came as a result of an invasion; that it does not belong here; and that it should therefore be returned to its original owners. Only then can "we" regain our proper place at "home." This separatist logic assumes that the domestication of the self occurs simultaneously with the containment of the foreign, its relocation as that which is external and distinct from oneself. One who speaks Castilian wrenched free from its origins in Spain no longer need feel burdened by the stirrings of that which it cannot possess. The economy of revenge allows one to think of assuming the place of the other as the privileged agency of translation and recognition. Rid of this foreignness, "I" can be free from the need to seek the other's recognition even as "I" continue to speak in its language. In this way, revenge entertains scenarios of authorship as the basis of authority, exclusion as the basis of freedom. Dissolving one kind of hierarchy, it promotes the desire for another to take its place.

In Simoun's scenario, revenge is associated with a violent uprising coming as the culmination of widespread misery and indiscriminate deaths. Basilio, for example, will eventually come to join his plot when he learns of Juli's death. Vengeance takes a violent form because it entails responding to a prior violence. It is as if one who takes vengeance speaks in the place of the dead, as the dead's representative. And given the semiotic logic of revenge, to represent the dead is a matter of not only speaking in its place, but speaking as if one came from the dead. This intimacy with the dead is of course the position of Simoun, who speaks for Ibarra come back to life, and of Ibarra, who, like Rizal, speaks for his dead father. Thus can one see revenge as a form of mourning, a way of commemorating the dead in that they are given a proper place in the world just as the foreign is returned back to where it came from. Violence imaged as the flow of blood links the two, serving as a kind of lingua franca that enables one to commemorate the absence of the dead while absenting the foreigner from one's midst. In this way does the phantasm of revenge seek to domesticate nationalism as that which now refers back "here," to the "Filipinos" in the Philippines, where the genealogies of the living can be traced to the unmourned dead rather than something that translates and transmits Filipino demands for reform to the rest of the world.

In the *Fili*, however, revenge ultimately fails to deliver on its promise. All of Simoun's plans unravel. He is betrayed by Basilio, who cannot reconcile himself to the use of violence. But even before Basilio, Simoun is detained by Rizal himself. Alone in his room on the eve of the uprising, Simoun's reveries about the revolt he has planned are "suddenly interrupted":

A voice was asking in the interior of his conscience if he, Simoun, were not also part of the garbage of the cursed city, perhaps its most malignant ferment. And like the dead who are to rise at the sound of

the oracular trumpet, a thousand bloody phantoms, desperate shadows of murdered men, violated women, fathers wrenched from their
families . . . now arose to echo the mysterious question. For the first
time in his criminal career since starting in Havana . . . something
rebelled inside of him and protested against his actions. Simoun
closed his eyes . . . he refused to look into his conscience and became
afraid . . .

   "No, I cannot turn back," he exclaimed, wiping away the sweat
from his forehead. "The work has gone far and its success will justify
me . . . If I had behaved like you, I would have succumbed. . . . Fire
and steel to the cancer, chastisement to vice, and if the instrument be
bad then destroy it afterward! . . . The end justifies the means . . ."

   And with his brain swirling he went to bed and tried to go to sleep.
(145–47)

Revenge holds out the promise of domesticating the alien in both its
forms: as the dead whose ghostly returns intrude on the living, and as
the colonizer whose language assails one into shame, guilt, and submission. But what domesticates revenge? If vengeance is the exchange of
violence for violence, does it not, like guilt, risk spiraling out of control?
Can the language of blood call into existence a response other than more
of the same? If not, can revenge do any more than increase the frequency of ghostly returns? Rather than lead to the domestication of
nationalism, revenge in this case would keep the foreign in circulation,
forcing one to dwell amid its incessant returns.

   Perhaps seeing this possibility, Rizal intervenes. He addresses Simoun by way of the latter's conscience. Breaking and entering into his
thoughts along with a chorus of ghostly voices, this interior voice mimics the sound of God at the Last Judgment. One might say that the author
appears in disguise. His voice emanates from within his character's
head yet confronts him like the sound of voices from the edge of the
grave. Speaking from a posthumous perspective, the author situates
himself as a foreigner residing within his characters. He periodically
interrupts their speech to confront them as a fearsome presence orig-
inating beyond the colonial order yet understandable only within its
linguistic confines. Thus is the author's voice like that of a second language. Its sudden emergence from within one's own language compels
one to reframe one's thoughts. Simoun is asked by this second voice:
aren't you also guilty? It forces him to reformulate his thoughts in

response to this demand. The second holds the first accountable and so contains the latter's speech in both senses of the term. Under the cover of a fictional voice, the author subordinates all other fictional voices, enframing all other plots. The foreign returns in its most intimate yet most impersonal form.

In seeking revenge, Simoun disguised as a foreigner sought to exceed and thereby take the place of the law. But Rizal as the second voice seeks to surpass revenge and put it back in its place, as a criminal act answerable to a higher law. Simoun tries to talk back to the author, seeking to separate himself from his characterization. Refusing Rizal's intervention, he imagines himself at the origin of hierarchy, not subject to it: a source of terror, not its recipient. But he falters, his "brain swirling." His plans already doomed, he finds himself in the grip of authorship's interruptive arrival.

Authorship and the Politics of Naming

What did it mean to be an author in Rizal's time? Given the paucity of scholarship on the sociology of authorship in nineteenth-century Philippine colonial society, we must speculate. We might start with the question of Rizal's name. According to his own accounting, this was a name that did not originally belong to him, nor did it come down from his father. His father's name was Francisco Mercado and his mother's Teodora Alonso. "Rizal" was added, he claims, by a provincial governor, "a friend of the family," as a second surname in order to distinguish them from the other Mercados in the country to whom they bore no relation.[21] It is difficult to ascertain the veracity of this story. Before the Decree of 1849, which required colonial subjects to take on permanent surnames, a person's name was not meant to signify their family of origin. Upon baptism, converts were given a first and at times a second name derived from that of a saint but did not assume the surname of their parents. Surnames were not routinely passed down from parent to child, even among mestizos or wealthier indios, through the eighteenth and early nineteenth century. This changed in 1849 when Governor General Narciso Clavería issued a decree ordering that colonial subjects acquire permanent surnames (*apellidos*), whether Spanish or native, from a catalog of names (compiled by parish priests) in the interest of rationalizing colonial administration and tribute collection. These surnames were to be passed down to succeeding generations. With the aid of parish priests, the decree was successfully enforced within a few years, though older naming practices did not entirely disappear.[22] Rizal's claim that his surname was not inherited from either of his parents was thus not unusual, given the transitional nature of naming practices at the time of his birth. It should also come as no surprise that the family of Rizal referred to themselves in the father's surname, Mercado, while the mother used her father's name, Alonso, following the Claveria decree of 1849. Whatever the truth in Rizal's story, the fact remains that the surname *Rizal* originated as a supplementary formation, something that came from outside the family rather than being handed down through the father's or mother's line.

It was not until 1872, the year of the Cavite revolt that resulted in the execution of the three Filipino secular priests, Gomez, Burgos, and Zamora, that the name *Rizal* took on a new significance. In a letter to his Austrian friend, Blumentritt, Rizal recalls how his older brother, Paciano, enrolled him at the Jesuit-run secondary school Ateneo de Manila under this second name. Paciano had been associated with one of the martyred priests, José Burgos, and out of a desire to protect the younger José he had him enrolled in another name. "My family never paid much attention [to our second surname]," Rizal wrote more than a decade later, "but now I had to use it, thus giving me the appearance of an illegitimate child!"[23] Rizal sees in the history of his name the convergence of a set of contingencies—the act of a colonial official, the effects of a state decree, the shadowy but no less tragic events of 1872, the predicament of his older brother—all of which give him the appearance of something other than who he was supposed to be. His surname functions not as a way of linking him to his father and family, as post-1849 naming practices would have it, but precisely as a way of obscuring such a link. *Rizal* offered José a disguise. The second name concealed the first and thus allowed him to pass through the suspicious gaze of colonial and clerical authority.

The secondary name, however, comes to take on a primary importance out of proportion to its intended function. José as "Rizal" soon distinguished himself in poetry-writing contests, impressing his professors with his facility with Castilian and other foreign languages. In Europe, he signed his name to a series of political essays critical of the colonial order and challenging Spanish historical accounts of precolonial Philippine societies. Though he occasionally used pseudonyms, everyone, ilustrados and Spanish authorities alike, knew exactly who these names referred to. And his two novels bear not only this name but also the phrase "Es propiedad del Autor," the property of the author. Indeed, by 1891, the year he finished the *Fili*, this second name had become so well known that, as he wrote to a friend, "All my family now carry the name Rizal instead of Mercado because the name Rizal means persecution! Good! I too want to join them and be worthy of this family name." His mother had previously been harassed and arrested by the colonial police because, among other things, "she did not identify herself as Realonda de Rizal but simply as Teodora Alonso! But she has always called herself Teodora Alonso!"[24]

His name thus came to signal a certain notoriety, and his family, having been compelled to take it on, were subjected to persecution. Originally meant to conceal his identity, his second name became that through which he was widely known. For this reason, what was meant to save him from suffering now became the means with which to harm and ruin others. As his foremost biographer, Leon María Guerrero, wrote, "He must have felt utterly alone, surrounded though he was by his family, for he alone must bear the responsibility for their ruin; because of him they had been driven from their homes in his name."[25] Racked by guilt, Rizal returned to the Philippines. His return was a response to the distress caused by his name, one that he had used to authorize a series of texts.

Authorship in this instance brings to Rizal recognition that leads to ruination. He feels himself responsible for his family's fate. The "illegitimate child" now assumes the focal point of the family's identity, at least from the point of view of colonial authorities. His name takes on a patronymic significance, as that through which his family comes to have a public identity and is made into a target of colonial pressure. His name reverses the family genealogy. It is now through the youngest son that the family comes to be known. In taking responsibility, Rizal stands as the author of this reversal, one whose effects are linked to criminal acts of subverting authority and reversing hierarchy.

The colonial state thus invested the name *Rizal* with a certain communicative power, seeing in it the medium through which passed challenges to its authority. They recognized in his name far more than Rizal himself had ever intended. In his trial, colonial prosecutors claimed that his name had been used as a "rallying cry" by the Katipunan revolutionary organization to enlist the support of Filipinos and indios, of the wealthy and the poor alike.[26] Indeed, what Guerrero refers to as the "magical power" of Rizal's name was used by the members of the Kati-punan as a secret password (382). The name *Rizal* in this sense worked like a second language, crossing the line between the upper and lower levels of colonial hierarchy while bringing the disparate groups in each level in touch with one another. It was a watchword through which one came into contact with something new and unexpected.

During his trial, Rizal repeatedly objected to the state's accusations and lamented the rampant misappropriation of his name. "I gave no permission for the use of my name," he wrote in response to the charges that it has served to instigate the revolution, "and the wrong done to me is beyond description."[27] It was as if Rizal found himself confused with Simoun as the author of a separatist conspiracy, caught within a phan-tasm of revenge he had sought to control. He condemns the revolution as a "ridiculous and barbarous uprising, plotted behind my back . . . I abominate the crimes for which it is responsible and I will have no part to do with it."[28] Unlike the ruination of his family, he could not be held responsible for the catastrophe he thought was about to befall the col-ony. "How am I to blame for the use of my name by others when I neither knew of it nor could stop it?"[29] Against the misreadings of his name by those above and those below, Rizal claimed innocence. "I am not guilty either of organizing a revolutionary society, or taking part in such societies, or of participating in the rebellion."[30]

In claiming innocence, Rizal disavows responsibility for the uses to which his name had been put outside the domestic circle of his family. The colonial state sought to attribute the upheavals of 1896 to a singular author. Rizal for his part could not or refused to recognize these events as anything but "barbaric" and "criminal." Revolution appeared as the fail-ure to sublimate revenge. For him, it involved the emergence of a kind of speech from below that was not properly traceable to his thoughts and which eluded his ability to translate. For as we had seen in the *Fili*, authorship was about the rehearsal and subsequent containment of shame, guilt, and revenge. In his God-like interventions within his char-acters' speech, he had sought to transform such affects of identification into a discourse of responsibility constituted by "education," "virtue," and "sacrifice." Nationalist authorship, "properly conceived," was a mat-ter of identifying with and domesticating the force of translation, thereby displacing the hegemony of the Spanish friar. As the various scenes of the *Fili* show, the corruption of authority is imagined by Rizal to give rise to an interruptive voice that seeks to re-form relations of inequality. Translation in this context brings with it the desire for hierarchy, not its elimination. Insofar as nationalist authorship concerns the designation of the foreign as an ominous but potentially domesticatable element of oneself, as that which one can recognize and so control, it mirrors the logic of Christian conversion in its colonizing context. In both, there exists the wish for communicative transparency: that all messages, whether intended or not, have the same address, and that figures such as the missionary or the author serve as indispensable relays for their transmission.

However, Rizal's life, especially his trial, reveals something of the unexpected and unaccountable consequences of this wish for authorship. Just as evangelization resulted in conversions and translations beyond the reach and outside the expectations of Spanish missionaries —resulting, for example in the emergence of "folk Catholicism," or figures such as the "filibustero," or even "Rizal"—so nationalist authorship sparked readings that it could not anticipate, much less control. For rather than lead to the domestication of desires and languages out of place, nationalist authorship tended in fact to spur them into uncharted and at times revolutionary directions.

In all cases, Castilian played a key role, keeping a sense of the foreign —that is, that which escaped assimilation either into the colonial or the national—in circulation, available for all kinds of use and misuse. The history of conversion made Castilian over into a medium for transmitting a fantasy about direct communication and unlimited transmissions across sociogeographical divides. Like Castilian, the name *Rizal* by the late nineteenth century retained and kept in circulation the sense of the foreign that even he himself could not recognize and account for at the point when the Spanish language (and all it implied about the power of transmission and translation) was denied to the rest of the colony's subjects. Proclaiming in the trial that "I am innocent" meant that "I" did not intend to commit a crime that nevertheless bears his signature. His innocence then implies his guilt, the culpability he incurred in ignoring the effects that a second, foreign name would have on those who felt its force.

3   THE CALL OF DEATH
On Rizal's Noli

The Contingencies of Authorship

We have seen how misrecognition bred phantasms of revenge in the travel writings of Antonio Luna and in the novel *El filibusterismo* by José Rizal. Speaking Castilian and seeking to assimilate as Spanish citizens, Filipino nationalists were instead regarded as foreigners and thieves by crowds in Spain and colonial authorities in the Philippines. Taking on that foreignness, they threatened to return it to its source. Rizal saw that such exchanges might well lead to uncontrollable violence. Usurping the law, nationalist vengeance threatened to replace the terror of colonial rule with its own. Rizal thus called for the sublimation of vengeance into sacrifice at the end of his book.

Such a solution required the mediation of an author. Assuming the voice of God, the author insists on replacing terror and corruption with education and virtue. Authorship's authority consisted of its ability to transmit a language and speak in a voice that surpassed colonial hierarchy. In this way, Filipino nationalists and Spanish friars shared something in common. Both believed in and appealed to an authority that lay outside of colonial society yet determined its limits. Nationalist authorship emerges as a voice that bases its authority on its ability to reach a higher power. Infinitely exterior and inherently inexhaustible, such a power is conceived, as we saw in the *Fili*, as an interruptive presence that breaks into the circle of vengeance and thereby claims to be the destination of all messages. By drawing on this power, the author could challenge friar domination over speech and translation. At the same time, by presuming to take on the language of God, Rizal could demand that the desire for revenge be transformed into an ethos of sacrifice.

However, authorship had other effects. Rather than establish a new sacrificial order that would domesticate the desire for revenge, nationalist authorship led to other possibilities. For example, we saw how the publication of the *Fili* set off a train of thoughts among those who read or heard of it, both Spaniard and Filipino. Relaying bits and pieces of the book, plots were fabricated and charges and accusations were made, leading to events beyond the author's knowledge or control. Authorship in this case found itself unable to negotiate the divide opened up between what was said and what others heard and understood. In the space of that gap, all sorts of misappropriation took place. For the Spaniards, the name *Rizal*, for example, came to be associated with filibusterismo, with the specter of vengeance rather than with its containment and conversion. For the Katipunan separatist organization, *Rizal* became a watchword of the revolution used as a password to gain entry into secret meetings. It was as if the movement to separate the Philippine colony from Spain were triggered in part by the possibility of separating an author's work from its original intentions, letting the work drift into other contexts and other meanings. We can imagine how such a work, disseminated clandestinely among an anonymous readership and relayed by word of mouth to those unable to read Castilian, generated a current of expectation that led into different directions, including the revolutionary uprising of 1896. Perhaps this is why Rizal could only disavow Spanish charges of fomenting the revolution. He could not recognize himself as the author of such a movement even if he had rehearsed both its occurrence and failure in his writings.

Nationalist authorship thus not only raised the possibility of Filipino ilustrados speaking in the place of the Spanish friars directly to and on behalf of higher authorities, worldly and otherwise, it also opened a line of transmission to those lower in the social hierarchy. It found itself addressing the crowd, or more precisely, depicting the conditions under which such a crowd could be stirred, their interests organized and directed; but also showing how such attempts could fail and the ongoing consequences of that failure. Such might be the story of the revolution, or at least one version of it. To get a sense of the complications entailed in addressing the crowd, I want to turn to Rizal's first novel, *Noli me tangere*.[1] Looking at the first novel from the perspective of the second novel will allow us, I hope, to think of Rizal in relation to the practice of translation characteristic of colonial rule. The *Fili* as the sequel to the *Noli* chronologically comes later, yet the belatedness of the second enables it to serve as the horizon against which to discern and assess the movement of the first. In this way, neither has any clear priority. Each is integral to the other; they echo each other's plots and haunt one another's characters. Such an approach gives us a chance to see how questions of recognition, revenge, and sacrifice in the second novel are shadowed by the anxieties about paternity, the attractions of anonymity, and the recurring circulation of rumors and gossip in the first within the context of the colonial linguistic hierarchy.

Nationalism and Technology

While he dedicated his second novel to victimized fathers, Rizal offers his first to *mi Patria*, the motherland. Like the *Fili*, the *Noli*, as it is commonly known, was composed during Rizal's travels and studies in Europe. But unlike the *Fili*'s more separatist sentiments, the *Noli* clings, however ambivalently, to earlier assimilationist aspirations, whereby much of nationalist energy was directed toward securing political representation, educational changes, and economic reforms. All of these efforts, the ilustrado nationalists hoped, would culminate in the recognition of Filipinos as equals of Spaniards and lead to the Philippine integration to Spain as one of its provinces. In this context, the reference to mi Patria is not entirely clear. It denotes the colony, *Filipinas*, but also refers to the metropole, *España*, rhetorically acknowledged as *madre*. Mi Patria is not at this point easily locatable in the world. Its geographical uncertainty makes it seem as though Rizal were conjuring an image rather than positing a settled and clearly demarcated entity.

Indeed, it is a "beloved image" (*querida imagen*) that Rizal addresses when he speaks of mi Patria: "And while many times in the midst of modern civilizations I have wanted to evoke you, now to accompany me with your memories, now to compare you with other countries, so often has your beloved image appeared to me as if [suffering] from a social cancer." The image of mi Patria simultaneously evokes love and disease, further highlighting its unsettled nature. It is when Rizal compares "my nation" with those of others that he sees its affliction. Mi Patria literally suffers by and from comparison. Set against others, it appears plagued by malignant cells multiplying within its body and the ulceration, which is to say corruption of its tissues. He further adds, "As I am your son, I too suffer from your defects and weaknesses." The beloved nation, as a carrier of a fatal disease, infects the author himself. He inherits this suffering and the weakness it brings, sharing with the motherland a body divided against and so foreign to itself.

What is worth noting is how Rizal comes about such a vivid picture of the nation as the host of a series of intractable contradictions. Through what he will later in the novel call "the devil of comparisons" (*el demonio de las comparaciones*), he sees what had previously remained invisible to him: that the beloved image is also host to a deadly presence hidden away from view.[2] As we have seen, the *Fili* associated such a presence with the specter of the *filibustero*. In the *Noli*, however, the sources and carriers of this cancerous growth are not easily identifiable. What interests Rizal, in fact, is the process by which one arrives at such identification. We get a sense of this when he writes in the rest of the dedication:

> Desiring your health which is also ours, and searching for the best cure, I will do with you what the ancients did with their sick: they exposed them on the steps of the temples so that each person who came by to invoke the Divinity might propose a remedy. And to this end, I will try to faithfully reproduce your condition without much contemplation [*sin contemplaciones*]; I will lift part of the veil that hides the evil, sacrificing all to truth, even my own self-respect [*amor propio*], since as your son, I too suffer from your defects and weaknesses.

A doctor himself, Rizal was prone to using metaphors of disease to describe the conditions that had befallen the motherland, a practice common enough in his time. As a doctor, one might have expected him to prescribe a cure. Instead, he asks others to do so. His task as an author is to "expose" the cancer's spread by "faithfully reproducing" the nation's state. And he does so *sin contemplaciones*, "without much ado," as one of his English translators puts it,[3] but which we might gloss as "without much contemplation or thought," as if he were in a state of distraction. Although he compares the novel to an ancient ritual of exposing the sick on the steps of the temple, he seems uninterested in presiding over its performance. Lifting the veil that covers the "evil" underneath, Rizal is concerned with revealing what has been concealed for others to see. He wants, that is, to reproduce faithfully the traces of this sickness he himself carries within and to make it available for public viewing, "without contemplation." How do we understand this odd juxtaposition of a pathos-laden gesture of revelation on one hand with a kind of noncontemplative, nondramatic, yet faithful reproduction of what is unveiled on the other?

Reproduction without contemplation comes across mechanically, even automatically, as if abstracted from human agency. In the case of the novel, the exposure of the nation is tied to a particular set of technological conditions: the mechanical reproduction of printed words on the page and its circulation through clandestine means. Let me suggest that we can clarify such mechanically reproduced images taken "sin contemplaciones"—at a glance, without much ado, and in a state of distraction—by referring to another technic for mechanical reproduction distinct from but anticipated by print: photography. The printed word and the photographed image bear the traces of one's original intentions and map the trajectory of one's thought and vision. Yet, as with all traces, once made public by way of mechanical reproduction, they drift away from their origins, assuming a life related to but also distinct from them. Thus do they become available for all sorts of appropriations.

Ilustrados were familiar with and avid users of photography. Though they did not write about photography as did other European intellectuals, they posed for studio portraits, informal group shots, and historical tableaux that were used as models by such nationalist painters as Juan Luna. Rizal himself carried photograph albums of his family and friends when he traveled, and while exiled in Dapitan considered photographing the indigenous populations there. His own portraits were featured on his books and were prominently displayed in the meeting places of the Katipunan.[4] As we saw earlier, his statues in the Philippines are based on a studio photograph taken in Madrid before his return to the colony. Photography, like print technology, not only allowed ilustrados to view the world up close and compare it to the colony, it also furnished the means for projecting ilustrado thinking and appearances beyond the local confines of colonial society. As with telegraphy, photography and print were regarded to have a certain telecommunicative capacity.

When Rizal writes that the purpose of his novel is to "unmask the hypocrisy" of colonial authorities, "unveiling what lay hidden behind the deceptive . . . words of our government" and laying out "facts which . . . are true and real: I have the proofs,"[5] we can think of the "proofs" he speaks of as analogous to photographs that reveal and reproduce faithfully what is otherwise inaccessible to our eyes. Photographs duplicate what they depict. They are in this sense doubles of what they convey. Their appearance suggests that each thing or person photographed is accompanied by an image that is at the same time fundamentally distinct from it. Hence, what we see in a photograph is always a likeness that is never fully identifiable with and assimilable to its referent. The faithful representation of the image of mi Patria, at once beloved and diseased, is intimately available only in and through its public exposure by way of print technology. Print technology, by allowing for the mechanical reproduction of the appearance of what was once hidden, makes visible to the mind's eye what had remained obscured or dimly perceived. In this sense print, while certainly distinct from photography, is analogous to the workings of the latter.[6] Both suggest surfaces infiltrated by hidden depths, presences haunted by secret histories, and visible forms sustained by invisible forces.

My point is that Rizal's interest not only in writing but also, just as significant, in publishing the *Noli* can be regarded as part of the wider ilustrado fascination with technologies of communication capable of translating and transmitting words and images across boundaries and at great distances. As we have seen, the power of such technologies is twofold: they bring one in touch with the foreign, with what is unknown and yet to come, and they reproduce and disseminate such experiences again and again far beyond the point of their initial occurrence. Hence, while ilustrados like Rizal never explicitly wrote about the matter of technology as such—whether photography, print, or telephony—we can sense the intensity of their investment and the alacrity of their response to its workings in their attempts to articulate images of and sentimental attachments to the nation. Such is evident, as we have seen, in their intense interest in Castilian. Nationalism is thus always engaged in the question of technology, including the technics of translation, exploring its promise and possibility in the world.[7]

Originally, Rizal had wanted to write the *Noli* in French but decided finally on Castilian so as to reach, as he wrote to a friend, "my countrymen . . . and wake from its slumber the spirit of my fatherland."[8] Print Castilian would reach those who should listen but so far had been inattentive. Like the propaganda newspaper *La solidaridad*, the novel was part of the nationalist attempt to speak to authority in ways that would bypass the mediation of the Spanish friars. The novel was meant by Rizal to convey images of colonial society as accurately as possible. With its numerous vignettes and characters that go against the grain of colonial stereotypes, we could think of the novel as an album of snapshots as well as a recording machine for gathering and assembling such pictures. The novel's effect is to leave indelible images whose meanings and referents, like those of any photograph, evade the closure of any one viewing and reading so that they continue to generate interest among future readers and viewers.[9] As we shall see, the *Noli*'s ability to faithfully reproduce scenes from colonial society hinged on the ways such scenes also brought with them a sense of something more, of something hidden or repressed whose sources could neither be fully disclosed nor determined. Revealing the nation meant showing its doubleness, the way it was divided within and against itself. In short, Rizal's interests led him to depict the Patria as a set of idealized images fatally accompanied by their mysterious other bringing in their train intimations of illegitimacy and death.

In what follows, I try to demonstrate how the characters in the *Noli* are besieged by their secret others. The others eventually reveal the origins of the main protagonists to be illegitimate and criminal. Once repressed, origins return as the ghostly traces of the past and form the basis of nationalist identity. The public exposure of the Patria through the lens of the novel results not in the cure for its cancerous image but in its metastasis. We can think of the novel then as a kind of camera that not only brings the surfaces of the Patria into view, but, by way of comparison, also suggests something unsettling beneath such surfaces. As such, the novel is a kind of technic for placing the author and readers at a remove from what they see while bringing them ever closer to its appearances and hidden aspects.

Images of the Patria, however, also include and implicate those at the lower levels of hierarchy. They appear most commonly in the form of a crowd. In the novel, they are often depicted as those who are exposed to Castilian without quite understanding it. Yet they find themselves intermittently drawn to and curious about its speakers. Elsewhere, I have tried to show something of the history of this mass fascination with the foreignness of Castilian in connection with Christian conversion during the earlier period of Spanish rule.[10] In the *Noli*, Rizal periodically takes up the strands of their curiosity. It is as if he feels the pressure of their interests and is compelled to follow the different routes of their desires especially as these are expressed in the form of rumors and gossip. In this way, the *Noli* differs from the propaganda writings in *La solidaridad*. The newspaper, based in Barcelona and then Madrid, was concerned primarily with establishing lines of contact among ilustrados and their European sympathizers in the hope of being heard by officials in the metropole. Though he shared in the aims of this project, in writing the *Noli* Rizal was also intensely interested in hearing what those below had to say, or at least in imagining what they might if given a chance to be heard. There is then a persistent fantasy about the crowd as a site of apprehending other possibilities, recognizing other figures, and registering as well as responding to other messages. In recording the crowd's presence, Rizal sought to accommodate and account for an expressive force that emerges from its midst.

The Illegitimacy of Origins

Where the *Fili* begins with plots of revenge and ends with the call for sacrifice, the *Noli* brings our attention to the weakness of authority, parental as well as colonial. For Rizal, each contributes to the corruption of the other, thereby blocking sons and daughters from realizing their aspirations. Spanish friars wield inordinate influence over mothers and fathers, to the point of monopolizing the education and future disposition of their children. Mothers and fathers in turn submit readily to the friars' demands and so neglect their children's interests. Colonial officials from the highest to the lowest levels stand by helpless and unwilling to regulate these relationships and thus end up complicit with them. The weakness of authority, therefore, means not that they lack force—for if anything they are excessively forceful—but that they are bereft of legitimacy.

The novel's main plot, from which several other subplots spring, involves the romance between Crisostomo Ibarra and María Clara. He is an ilustrado youth just back in the colony after spending several years studying in Europe. Full of liberal ideas, he wants to establish a school that would teach Castilian and introduce new ideas to the students of his hometown, San Diego. María Clara is Ibarra's childhood sweetheart, daughter of a wealthy merchant, Capitan Tiago, and his wife Pia Alba, also from a well-off family. Nowhere in the novel does Rizal indicate the precise racial makeup of María Clara's parents. They are most likely indio, but the reader is led to believe that at least one of them must be a Spanish mestizo (Tiago, who speaks good Castilian? Alba, whose father was a wealthy merchant?), because of María Clara's light skin and semi-European features. While there are some resemblances between her features and those of her mother, traces of her father's are nearly absent from her face.

María Clara's beauty is widely celebrated. Those who see her are invariably taken by her stunning features. Her hair appears "almost golden" in color, "her nose of correct profile, neither sharp nor flat, her mouth small and perfect with two beautiful dimples on her cheeks. Her skin had the fine texture of an onion layer, the whiteness of cotton according to her most enthusiastic relatives" (32). She is "everyone's idol" (33), including that of the Spanish fathers. During the town's procession, she comes across as someone who "manifested her love with that virginal grace to whom nothing came but pure thoughts. . . . Ecstatically contemplating the beauty of María Clara, some old women murmured while chewing their betel nut, 'She looks just like the Virgin!' " (151). In fact, this comparison with the mother of Christ comes up repeatedly, as when the author gushes forth about María Clara as "this divinized image of woman, the most beautiful idealization of the most ideal of creatures, this poetic creation of Christianity that unites in herself the two most beautiful states of woman, Virgin and Mother, [but] without her miseries, that we call María" (203).

María Clara stands out for being the image of the image of Mary. She resembles not divinity itself but its popular representation. Her appearance, in its remarkable proximity to the idealized notion of woman in Christianity, sets her apart and stirs the interest of everyone, up and down the social hierarchy. By making her unlike those around her, her beauty turns her into an alien figure who is at the same time universally recognizable. Like the lingua franca, her recognizability depends on her foreignness. Those who see her are drawn to her difference. She does not look like her parents nor, for that matter, does she resemble anyone else in the world. One might be tempted to infer that her mestiza features, if that is what her ethereal appearance can be called, signal the happy fusion of European and native qualities as much as they suggest the image of the re-embodiment of the divine in the human. In describing her appearance, Rizal engages in the dream work of assimilation, seeing in her a benevolent foreign presence available for domestication. In her perfection, she does not even know the miseries of Mary and thus seems exempt from the burden of colonialism's original sin.

It is this freedom from history, this originary innocence that constitutes her attraction, especially for men like Ibarra, the youthful Filipino, and Damaso and Salvi, the Spanish fathers. Each sees in her his object of desire. For this reason, each jealously guards against the other's possession of her. As with all romances, envy drives the action. Padre Damaso seeks to ruin Ibarra by first accusing his father, a Spanish mestizo beloved by the town, of sedition, conniving to have him locked up in jail till he dies, and, as a final abomination, desecrating his corpse by arranging to have it dug up and thrown into the river. Later on, he seeks to ruin the son in order to keep him from marrying María Clara by having him excommunicated after a violent encounter with the priest. For his part, Padre Salví, through the help of native mercenaries, orchestrates a rebellion implicating Ibarra as the leader. To cover up their crimes, Spanish fathers turn ilustrado sons into criminals.

Ibarra is imprisoned but escapes with the help of a mysterious indio boatman, Elias. One of the novel's subplots involves the friendship between the two, which begins after Ibarra saves Elias from being eaten by a crocodile during a picnic by the river. Elias reciprocates by saving Ibarra from being killed by a falling derrick during the groundbreaking ceremonies for his proposed school. Subsequently, the two have extended discussions on the fate of the colony and the measures that might be taken to change existing conditions. Initially, Elias seems more pessimistic of reform and hints at the possibility of separation, while Ibarra is more optimistic and cautious. By novel's end, the two have nearly reversed their positions.

While helping Ibarra escape in the wake of the failed uprising, Elias accidentally discovers Ibarra's genealogy. Sorting through Ibarra's papers, Elias learns that *Ibarra* is actually the shortened form of the Basque name *Eibarramendia*. Elias is stunned, for he realizes that in Ibarra he has found the object of his wanderings. Elias's secret mission is revealed just as Ibarra's "real" name is uncovered. Elias turns out to have been the grandson of a bright and educated indio whose future was ruined by Ibarra's great-grandfather, a cruel Spaniard. Falsely accused of arson, Elias's grandfather was tortured and killed, his grandmother driven to prostitution, his uncle-turned-bandit caught and mutilated by the colonial police, and his father forced to become a servant of his rich lover's family after they had stood in the way of their marriage. Elias and his sister, adopted by their mother's family, find out that his own father had been the servant he had treated with disdain. Shocked at this revelation, his sister commits suicide while Elias leaves the family and wanders about in search of revenge. A string of humiliations and crimes thus join Elias to Ibarra as each discovers the other's true identity. Ibarra is guilty by descent. In him, Elias finds what he had long searched for, a target for his vengeance. But unlike Simoun in the *Fili*, Elias checks his desire and instead converts it into sacrifice. In the end, he helps Ibarra escape to the point of giving up his own life.

Going by boat across the river, Ibarra stops to bid farewell to María

Clara, who had grown disconsolate over the prospect of losing her fiancé and being forced to marry someone else. At the moment of their parting on her balcony, she reveals to Ibarra the secret of her paternity and thus the reason for her difference. Coming across letters written by Padre Damaso years ago, she learns that he is in fact her "real" father. Her mother, who died from guilt shortly after her birth, had conceived her in an adulterous and, in the context of the paternal relationship between the clergyman and his flock, incestuous affair with Padre Damaso without the knowledge of her impotent husband, Capitan Tiago. When she found herself pregnant, María Clara's mother and real father had wished her dead, using drugs to try to abort the fetus and thus avoid any scandals. In exchange for keeping this knowledge secret, María Clara agrees to give up letters written to her by Ibarra while he was in Europe. Passages of these taken out of context were then used to convict Ibarra of being a filibustero.

Ibarra is at first stunned by this revelation and then overtaken with pity and admiration for what he sees as María Clara's sacrifice in the face of impossible demands (333–35). In sacrificing Ibarra, her love, she sacrifices her own future in order to protect the memory of one dead mother and the honor of two live fathers. Bidding farewell, Ibarra flees across the lake that hid his father's corpse with the help of Elias, the man whose own father was driven to death by Ibarra's paternal ancestors. Pursued by the police, Elias creates a diversion and dives off the boat. Ibarra succeeds in escaping while Elias is shot and killed. As we saw, in the *Fili* Ibarra returns as Simoun to wreak vengeance and rescue María Clara from her self-imposed exile in the nunnery. But he is too late.

Despite her sacrifices, María Clara was not without her own vengeful designs. With Ibarra's arrest, her two fathers, Capitan Tiago and Padre Damaso, arrange for her to marry Damaso's Spanish nephew. She refuses and insists on going to the nunnery. "The cloister or death" (343), she repeats, against the entreaties of Damaso. Shuttered within the convent's walls, she in fact suffers a kind of social death. She removes herself from circulation and, dropping out of view, keeps her secret intact. She resists the wishes of the fathers. But in doing so, she reinforces their hold. By clinging to the secret of her paternity, she becomes the agent for containing the spread of scandals that would have exposed the weakness of authority. Harboring the crimes of her parents and the priest, she covers up, as it were, their corruption and so takes on their guilt. Just as the beloved image of the Patria nursed within it a cancerous growth, so the beautiful image of María Clara hid the illegitimacy of her origins and the crimes committed for the sake of its concealment. She appeared to be the image of that impossible being, the Virgin Mother, but only to the extent that she was also the bastard child of a Spanish father and his native "daughter." And although she rebuffs the designs of her two fathers by entering the nunnery, she also chooses to protect their weakness. She takes her secret to her grave and thereby leaves paternal authority undisturbed.

In this sense, María Clara is a double agent, a figure whose appearance arouses the ilustrado hope for regenerating colonial society but whose secret identity forecloses the realization of such hope. She is one who suffers from an excess of domestication and therefore cannot be wrenched free from her parents to serve ilustrado male desires. It is for this reason that by novel's end, we are told that "nothing had been heard about [María Clara] again except that the sepulcher apparently guards her in its bosom." Nothing except rumors of a ghostly figure (*fantasma*) appearing on the convent's rooftops during raging thunderstorms, moaning in "a voice sweet and plaintive, full of hopelessness" (353) as if despairing of reaching God. Like the dead Elias and the fugitive (and eventually dead) Ibarra/Simoun, María Clara remains unmourned in the novel. Unmarked and uncommemorated in their deaths, such figures exist as phantom signs of the ilustrado failure to communicate and be heard by those on top.

The *Noli* excavates the hidden foundations of colonial kinship and discovers it to lie in deception and crimes ranging from murder to incest. But it also dramatizes the persistent failure of nationalism to redeem the colonial family and reform parental authority. Instead, nationalist figures suffer from untimely deaths in the novel, much like the author himself in real life. But as we have seen, Rizal's death came to be memorialized and his sacrifice acknowledged as a generative force in the emergence of the Filipino nation. Ibarra-Simoun, María Clara, and Elias, however, continue to die with each reading of the novel. Their deaths remain unchanged and continue to exert an unsettling pressure on the reader. They do not disappear from sight; rather, they are transformed into ghostly figures who return to haunt the Patria and in the process begin to demarcate its borders. In the *Noli*, the nation is imagined as the site of particular deaths and specific hauntings. The return of the dead, however, begins even before any of the main characters die. Throughout the novel, the appearance of death is often linked to the formation of the crowd. In what follows, we will see how the crowd's appearance becomes one of the conditions for recognizing another place for death outside of colonial hierarchy and friar domination.[11]

The Pleasures of Anonymity

As he wrote in the dedication, Rizal was concerned with exposing the illness that lay within the Patria, not with providing a cure. In fact, every attempt at a cure—sacrifice, educational reform, marriage, revenge, deception, social banditry, rebellion—turns out to aggravate the disease. Authority, in whatever form, fails, and so do resistances to it. What succeeds, however, is the recording of those failures. Rizal's authorship emerges from his ability to convey the illegitimacy of colonial authority and the inability of nationalists to replace it. The strength of that portrayal is seen in the fact that more than a century after its writing, the *Noli* continues to be read, and that each reading produces different effects. Scholars have referred to the novel as a "charter of nationalism" in that "it calls on the Filipino to recover his self-confidence."[12] That the recovery of "self-confidence" is the substance of the book is debatable. The fact however, remains: its *call* has never stopped. Reaching beyond the time of its writing, it has continued to circulate in a future it could never have anticipated.[13] This is perhaps what makes the *Noli* a literary work: its capacity to exceed the historical conditions of its production rather than simply mirror them. For this reason we might say that the *Noli* escapes the failure it describes. How so?

Rizal had confessed to sharing in the disease of the Patria. But he also repeatedly finds for himself another position from which to examine the progress of its contamination. As author, he is able to move and see in ways that his characters cannot. This sort of authorial mobility and omniscience was, of course, a convention that was becoming widespread in the late nineteenth century. Benedict Anderson has called attention to the conditions that allowed for such practices.[14] The spread of capitalist relations conjoined to technologies of mechanical reproduction had a corrosive effect on traditional notions of community based on face-to-face contact. There emerged a new experience of time that was characteristically "empty" and "homogenous," capable of encompassing heterogeneous experiences within a common temporal horizon. Clock and calendar rather than apocalyptic prophecy and seasonal rhythms measured the duration of lives to produce an effect of secular simultaneity—what Anderson refers to as the sense of a "meanwhile"—associated with modernity. At the same time, the standardization of languages by way of print and their wider dissemination by way of the marketplace made available lingua francas that allowed for communication on a new basis: across local differences and sociocultural particularities, but within the boundaries of new linguistic usages.

Under such conditions, community emerges amid anonymity. The novel, like the newspaper, becomes a site for conjuring the sense of belonging to a place without ever actually meeting, much less knowing the identity of all but a small number of its inhabitants. One reads a newspaper or a novel and one senses that it refers to a world one knows, that one could easily find oneself in the streets and houses it describes and the stories it tells. In this case, one feels called by those one does not and could not see; but just as important, one feels able to return these calls in the same language. It is as if anonymity, the fact of mutual estrangement, is a condition for community. Such is conceivable in view of the availability of a lingua franca, a language that, as we saw, becomes common to all by virtue of belonging to no one in particular. It is in this sense a second language that allows for communication across social and geographical distances. Placing one in touch with unseen and/or unknown others, a lingua franca becomes a medium of telecommunication. To speak in the lingua franca is to have access to this mediumship and thus to stand in relation to those absent from one's midst.

As we learned earlier, nationalists saw in Castilian the possibility of developing a lingua franca that would put them directly in touch with those on top of the colonial hierarchy while its spread to the rest of the colony's population would allow those below to be heard. Rizal's own interest in exposing what lay underneath appearances was intertwined with evoking the conditions under which a line of communication could be established with those below the social hierarchy. But they did not speak Castilian and had only the most fragmentary and intermittent comprehension of the language. What might be an alternative language with which to communicate with them? One possibility was Tagalog, because Rizal from Laguna was himself a native speaker of that language. But Tagalog was located at the bottom of the linguistic hierarchy. It did not carry sufficient authority to surpass Castilian and certainly would not be understood by colonial officials except through the mediation of religious authorities.[15]

The question of arriving at a lingua franca that could bridge social differences while being powerful enough to overcome the constraints of linguistic hierarchy is one that Rizal addresses indirectly. We can approach it initially by way of a detour. Here, I want momentarily to return to the question of telecommunicative technology.

Let us look back for a moment to the image of María Clara. We first see her in the novel through Rizal's eyes, or more precisely through a pair of imaginary opera glasses that he brings out. Following Ibarra up to his room where he sits in deep contemplation about the fate of his dead father, Rizal directs the reader's attention to the scene of the dinner party that the youth had just left, visible from the window of his room.

> If the young man had been less preoccupied and more curious, he would have wanted to see with the aid of a pair of opera glasses what had been happening in that atmosphere of light; he would have admired one of those fantastic visions, one of those magical apparitions that at times can be seen in the grand theaters of Europe in which to the muted melodies of an orchestra, there appears in the midst of a rain of light and a cascade of diamonds and gold, in an oriental decoration wrapped in vaporous gasses, a deity. . . . Ibarra would have seen a beautiful young woman . . . dressed in the picturesque costume of the women of the Philippines at the center of a semi-circle formed by all classes of people . . . there were Chinese, Spaniards, Filipinos, military, clergy, old, young, etc. (23)

Rizal sees what Ibarra cannot, because the author imagines peering through a pair of opera glasses. Through the glasses, the colony appears transformed, as if it were the stage for an elaborate performance. The world as a stage places both author and reader in the position of audiences separate from the characters in the book. We see what they cannot, and we do so through a prosthetic device used by the author for extending his, and our, vision. By framing colonial society as a scene, the glasses simultaneously distance us from it, yet bring us closer to the point of being able to see details that otherwise would remain unnoticed.

When María Clara appears, she is already an idealized image. The opera glasses magnify her ideality. In her, one sees an excess of possibilities. It is for this reason that she draws "all classes of people" (*toda clase de personas*) around her, inciting them to see in her something of what they want but till now could not express. Rizal sees this scene without himself being seen. He, too, is drawn to her image but, unlike those in the party, knows it to be an image that conceals an invisible and secret other. Though seduced, he keeps his distance, lingering, then moving on.

The author's situation is strikingly different from the other male characters who see María Clara. In one chapter, for example, the parish priest of San Diego, Padre Salví, wanders into the woods in search of a picnic to which he had been invited. He is surprised by the sound of women's voices and, hiding behind some trees, eavesdrops on their conversation. Peeking through the thickets, he sees María Clara along with some of her friends bathing, their hair loose, arms bare and the "wide folds of their bathing skirts outlining the gracious curves of their thighs" (125). The friar is struck "pallid and immobile" as he spies on María Clara's "white arms, the graceful neck ending in a suggestion of a bosom." Such sights "awakened in his impoverished being strange sensations that made him dream [sonar] new thoughts in his feverish brain" (126). The women disappear around a bend in the river, leaving the friar "like one drunk, unsteady and covered with sweat . . . with a dazed look . . . motionless and uncertain." When he finally recovers and finds his way back to the party, they notice his disheveled look and soiled cassock. "Did your Reverence suffer a fall?" somebody asks. "No!" he answers. "I lost my way" (126).

Here, Rizal gives us a picture of a colonial authority unable to check his desire. Salví gives in to his urges by listening to what was not meant for him and looking at what was meant to be kept out of sight. In a way, he does nothing that the author himself and his readers do not already do: overhearing and peering into spaces not meant for us, but to which we find ourselves drawn, seeing without being seen. The difference, however, is that Salví is caught looking by Rizal. The author takes obvious delight as much in the revelation of the women's bodies as in the exposure of Salví's reactions. The latter is described as "immobile" and "uncertain," "like one drunk" and thus without self-control. This loss of the father's self-control is occasioned by his illicit viewing of a woman young enough to be his daughter. He finds himself gripped by "strange sensations" and "dreams." That is, he finds himself beside himself, paralyzed and delirious. He is one who, as he later says, got lost and comes across as an embarrassing sight.

Nothing could contrast more with Rizal's position peering through a pair of opera glasses at the sight of María Clara. The author, like the friar, spies on a scene but remains in control of himself and what he sees. He never comes into view except to his readers, who find themselves invited to share his position. Through a narrative and technological device, the author avoids the fate of the friar. Instead he records the latter's delirium and embarrassment. Rizal sees the scene of women bathing through Salví's eyes, as if he were a kind of lens or another pair of glasses. Looking through the friar, the author also looks *at* him and in so doing stays out of view. He thereby overcomes the father's limitations and finds for himself another place from which to indulge *and* control his desire. Equally important, he draws readers to share his triumph. Rendered as a mobile and anonymous presence in the novel, the author becomes like the anonymous reader. Both share in the ability to overhear without being overheard, to see without being seen.

The Call of Death

But what of anonymous others who would not have been able to read Castilian, or any other language, for that matter? How might the author register their presence and seek to account for it? To answer this, we can turn to Rizal's description of the crowd. In another chapter, Rizal once again follows Ibarra as he rides a carriage through one of Manila's busier streets. Absent from the country for several years, the youth takes delight at the scene that unfolds from his carriage window.

> The animation that bubbled everywhere, so many coaches that came and went swiftly, the *carromatas*, the *calesas*, the Europeans, the Chinese, the natives, each with their own dress, the fruit vendors, the brokers, the shirtless porters, the food stalls, the lodging houses, restaurants, shops, even the carts drawn by the impassive and indifferent *carabaos*, which appeared to be entertaining philosophical thoughts while dragging their load, all, the noise, the movement, even the sun itself, a certain particular smell, the motley colors awakened in him a world of dormant memories. (41)

Ibarra is caught up in the rush of appearances outside his carriage window. The sight of Europeans is replaced by that of Chinese, who are then promptly substituted by natives and so forth. The only thing that identifies each type as such is their attire. Yet there is little sense here of one group deferring to another. The swiftness with which they displace one another from Ibarra's vantage point suggests the suspension of the protocols of recognition that is demanded by the colonial order. To

Ibarra, it seems that each group passes the other by without acknowledging its presence. Moreover, the law here does not seem visible, and its agents, if they are present at all, seem only to give way to the rush of images.[16] In this scene of nonrecognition, racial and class identities ascribed by the colonial regime seem to count for little. Instead, they give way to the indiscriminate substitution and equivalence of one entity with another: of fruit vendors with brokers, then half-naked porters, and so on. Ibarra is confronted with a series of images that has no beginning and no end, where all is "noise," "movement," and "odor." Anonymity takes on a sensuous quality as Ibarra's mind drifts and slides along the pathways opened up by the crowd. Unlike the crowd in Madrid, which singled out then verbally assaulted Luna, the crowd in Manila offers Ibarra the pleasure of losing himself in the sensation of indiscriminate mixing and substitution. For what is at stake in the loss of the self in the crowd is also the disappearance of authority and the flattening of hierarchy.

This experience of exhilarating loss through continuous movement is punctuated, however, by something else Ibarra sees. He passes by a group of convicts chained to one another working on the street. He is drawn to their "somber faces" and the way their eyes "glittered" in pain whenever they were whipped. This sight awakens a childhood memory of seeing a dead man, also a convict, lying on a wooden cart on the street. The corpse's eyes were half open while,

> two other [convicts] silently arranged a bamboo litter, without anger, without impatience, just as the native character is believed to be. "You today, we tomorrow," they might have been saying among themselves. People moved about without taking notice of them, in a hurry; women passed by, looked and continued on their way; the spectacle was common, and it had hardened their hearts. . . . Only he, a boy of eleven who had just arrived in the city, was moved; only he had nightmares the following night. (41–42)

To be in a crowd is to experience the momentary dissipation of both self and authority. In the streets, one seeks neither recognition nor deference from anyone else and so escapes the scrutiny of the law. What exists is a certain freedom from hierarchy, the freedom afforded by anonymity. In the midst of such freedom, Ibarra finds himself suddenly confronting the "somber faces" of convicts. Their appearance brings back what had been displaced by the crowd's movement. They stand apart from the crowd in that they bear signs of captivity and thus evince the workings, however distant and abstract, of authority. Their eyes "glitter" in response to the whip coming down on their backs. Looking at them, Ibarra begins to think of something else: the death that awaits each of these men. In their anticipation of death, the convicts share something in common. They seem to be in contact with each other because they are in proximity to something wholly alien to their lives: their own death. They sense their coming death and thus can hear its approach. Such a possibility is framed by Ibarra's childhood memory of seeing a dead convict. He imagines the silence of the other convicts around the corpse to amount to a kind of response to the dead: "You today, we tomorrow." Silence here is precisely a medium for transmitting a message from afar, so far that it reaches beyond life.

What Ibarra recalls is not only the sight of death but also the moment of its recognition. It is as if the corpse speaks and thereby instigates a silent exchange among the convicts. Ibarra finds himself a party to this scene. Seeing the convicts looking at the dead, he imagines them talking to one another and imagines himself being the recipient of that exchange. For this reason, Ibarra and the convicts find themselves set apart from the crowd. They see in the appearance of death the beginnings of mutual recognition, for when the convicts address one another their thoughts also reach a third party, Ibarra. Death forms the basis for a common language that passes through the corpse and connects the living around it. The corpse as transmitter of the language of death links the convicts to Ibarra amid the indifference of the crowd. This is what gives Ibarra nightmares and what gives the convicts pause: that the dead is not quite dead in that it continues to send messages from someplace else. The corpse exposed in public is alive with a communicative force that can reach past social divisions.

The convicts know what others around them do not. They submit to the inevitability of their deaths, bearing that knowledge in silence. It is the secret they harbor and which Ibarra, quite by accident, stumbles upon. The crowd delivers this secret knowledge to him without realizing it. The others move on without looking at the dead, indifferent to its presence. But Ibarra, moved, is the only one who has nightmares. That is, he internalizes the image of the dead and cannot but respond to its demand for recognition. Feeling the power of the dead—its ability to communicate across social lines and to bind oneself to others—Ibarra thus discovers another path to a different kind of authority outside of colonial society. It comes amid anonymity and leads past the Spanish friar and the state. Ibarra looks at the crowd and he sees death punctuating its ceaseless movements, conveyed by the silent communication among those who already know of their own fate. Through the corpse, the call of death establishes a connection, running a current that links him to those below as well as to his past. Lost in the crowd, Ibarra momentarily finds himself by finding in death an alternative locus of recognition.

Such moments of recognition and self-recovery have significant consequences. Passing the convicts, Ibarra's carriage is once again in the thick of traffic. He glances at the sights of the city but does so this time with a difference. He begins to compare what is visible with what is invisible. The new Escolta is unlike the old; the recently built Puente de España brings to mind early morning baths he used to take; the "animated conversations" he hears reminds him of a barrio in Madrid; and the sorry state of Manila's botanical gardens and the city's old walls makes him think of the gardens and cities of Europe (43). His viewing takes on a different syntax. "The devil of comparison," as Rizal refers to it, compels Ibarra to see in one place the traces of other times and places. He begins to see the city as a set of images abstractable from their physical location and therefore comparable to other similarly abstractable sights. In his mind's eye, "past" and "present," "Manila" and "Europe," are so many pictures that can be put side by side with each other. He thus sees what is present before him in terms of what is absent from his midst. The images of the city receive a new clarity precisely by appearing to summon the images of the Europe he had left behind. Looking out into the ocean, Ibarra says to himself, "Ah, on the other side of the sea, there is Europe!" where nations are "in constant agitation . . . happy in the midst of their catastrophes."

In Manila, Ibarra finds himself thinking of what is missing: earlier times and other places. The surfaces of the visible are so intensely permeated by the invisible that it is as if the latter makes possible the appearance of the former. Just as Ibarra sees in the face of the convicts the presence of death, so he senses in the city's views something that lies hidden elsewhere, at the other side of what is present. He is in a crowd yet is able to see past it. In the midst of their indifference, Ibarra takes note of differences, remarking on the line between life and death, and between this side of the ocean and that which lies beyond. Drawing differences, he then imagines himself traversing the gap between them.

Moving between temporal and spatial zones, he shows himself capable of bringing one site in communication with another.

At this point death looms up once again. Passing by Bagumbayan, the place for public executions (where Rizal himself would be shot), Ibarra's thoughts drift to the memory of a beloved "old priest" who had been executed there—undoubtedly an allusion to the martyred secular priest José Burgos, who, along with others, had challenged friar dominance over parishes in the 1860s. Reminded of this injustice, "he responded murmuring in a low voice: 'No, despite everything the Patria first, Filipinas first, daughter of Spain, first the Spanish nation! [la patria española].' " (43) The devil of comparisons leads Ibarra's thoughts back to death, that is, to the very point where what is invisible and past returns to haunt the present. Once again, death speaks through parts of the landscape, breaking through the indifference of the crowd. He responds not with thoughts of vengeance—at least not yet—but with a renewed sense of obligation to mother Spain and daughter Filipinas. Thus is the crowded street as much a site of freedom from hierarchy and the pressures of recognition as it is the place for encountering the compelling call of death to take up one's obligations.[17] Between these two possibilities, the figure of the youthful nationalist loses himself in the crowd only to find himself in contact with death.

However, as we saw earlier, the *Noli* is a novel about failure. The nationalist attempt to place the crowd in the ambience of death—to awaken it from its state of indifference and bring it to recognize its obligation to an authority beyond itself, to transform it, in short, into a people—does not succeed. Ibarra at first tries to set up a modern school that would teach Castilian and supersede the outdated lessons of the friars. At the same time, he had hoped to marry María Clara and start a family dedicated to improving the country. Finally, he sought to honor the memory of his dead father. Events conspire to block the realization of all these. He cannot mourn his dead father, whose corpse is missing in the river. He loses María Clara to the convent. His plans for a school trigger an attempt on his life and, through a series of complications, lead to his implication as the leader of a rebellion. Held captive by the colonial police, Ibarra, along with the rest of those suspected of participating in the uprising, is paraded down the streets of San Diego en route to prison. Branded a filibustero, he is exposed to the crowd that in Manila had not bothered to take notice of him. Like Luna on he streets of Madrid, Ibarra on the streets of his hometown becomes a target of derision. His distinctiveness from the crowd, once hidden, becomes revealed as a kind of crime. The public exposure of his putative criminality stirs the crowd. Yet they do not see in him their own fate the way that he had earlier seen his on the faces of the convicts. When they see him, they address him as if he were an alien presence:

> "That one is the one who is guilty!" shouted many voices. "That one is to blame . . ."
>
> "What have you done to my husband and my son?" Doray said crying. "Look at my poor son! You have deprived him of a father! . . ."
>
> "You are a coward!" screamed Andong's mother-in-law . . .
>
> "Damn you!" an old man said following him. "Damn all the gold amassed by your family to disturb our peace! Damn you! Damn you!"
>
> "They should hang you, you heretic!" shouted a relative of Albino, and no longer able to contain himself, he picked up a stone and threw it. This example was quickly followed, and over the unfortunate youth fell a rain of dust and stones.
>
> Ibarra suffered impassively, without anger, without complaint, the just vengeance of so many mournful hearts. This was his farewell, his adios, from his town where he had all his loves. . . .
>
> The tears, repressed for so long, burst forth from his eyes, he lowered his head and cried without having the consolation of being able to hide his grief, handcuffed as he was, and neither did he arouse compassion from anyone. Now he had no country [*patria*], no home, no love, no friends, no future! (316–17)

Blaming Ibarra for the loss and suffering of their loved ones, the crowd turns into a mob and carries out its desire for revenge. It hurls insults, then rocks, wishing his death as compensation for their pain. Here again we see a scene of recognition that leads to exclusion rather than assimilation similar to that experienced by Luna. The crowd in this case does the work of colonial authority. In targeting Ibarra, they become an extension of the Spanish friars who had wanted to see him dead. They hurl oaths and stones at him the way friars had laughed and insulted natives who tried to address them in Castilian. For this reason, the prospect of Ibarra's death remains disconnected from the lives of those who see him. As payment for their loss, his death would merely be his own, one that required neither mourning nor vengeance.

As if resigned to this fate, Ibarra assumes the pose of the convicts. He suffers in silence, taking on the "justified vengeance" of the crowd. His body registers the crowd's language just as the convicts' backs had been the recipients of authority's whips. However, he does not only serve as the passive destination of the crowd's message. At one point he also converts this message, translating it into a call for compassion. Unable to hold back any longer, he begins to cry, "without the consolation of being able to hide his grief." His tears form a kind of message. But this message reaches no one in the crowd, which consumed by its own anguish does not hear.

Nonetheless, the call is made, carried by Rizal, who then relays it to the reader. The author and reader both know that Ibarra has been wrongly accused and unjustly vilified. Knowing he is innocent, we share with Rizal the sense of Ibarra's loss. We are made to stand in relation to him in the same way that he stood in relation to the convicts and the way they in turn stood in relation to the corpse. Like the corpse, Ibarra becomes a transmitter of messages that have other, unknown origins. The author and reader for their part constitute a destination for messages outside of the crowd and thus beyond the limits of colonial authority. Rizal allows us to hear not only the crowd's speech but also its transformation by Ibarra into a new message. Herein lies the power of Ibarra's grief: it is a kind of second language that encapsulates the first, in this case, the crowd's speech. His grief takes on the qualities of a lingua franca that is capable of reaching beyond the particular place and time of its utterance. Surpassing the voice of the crowd, which in this instance acts as an extension or effect of the language of colonial authority, Ibarra's call carries over into the uncertain and contingent future of the novel's circulation. His loss may be unmarked in his own time and his suffering unlamented by the crowd, but not by the author. By the force of a writing enabled by the technologies of narrative exposure and print, he transmits it to anonymous readers. Thus the pathos of Ibarra's failure: he finds himself deprived of everything. Exiled within his own Patria, which as we saw is already divided within itself, he is rendered homeless within his own home. He becomes estranged, an enemy to his friends. His strangeness, damned in its own time, could thus be redeemed only in the future reading of the novel. And the author, standing between Ibarra's speech and its reception, sets the initial terms of that redemption. As with the author, so with the nationalist figure. His place is neither at home nor abroad, but always somewhere else: in a future that returns to haunt colonial society and its postcolonial successors.

If nationalism is, as Anderson's famous formulation has it, an imag-

ined community, in Rizal it is also a spectral one. It begins with technologies of telecommunication, the transmission of messages across
geographical and social distances, and includes the exposure of what
was once invisible into a set of reproducible images available for comparisons, the drawing near of visibilities from afar, and the mobility of
the authorial voice. Such conditions spring from and contribute to the
appearance of anonymity from which other possibilities emerge. Secrets
are revealed, a history of criminality unfolds, and the corruption at the
basis of authority exposed. Issuing from anonymity, the spectral nation
is populated by ghosts of the unmourned dead who travel between the
Noli and *Fili* and beyond any particular interpretation of the two.

Herein lies Rizal's success. In recording a history of failure and misrecognition, he comes close to taking on the communicative power that
had long been monopolized by the Spanish fathers. But he does so
without returning language to its putative source. That is, he does not
appeal to God for salvation, nor even to the church and state. Speaking
beyond a crowd immersed in the language of authority, he establishes a
line of transmission to as yet unknown and unnamed others. This is the
radical event inaugurated by the *Noli*. It seeks redemption not from
religion but from a history of the future whose coming to pass is already
foretold by the ghostly remainders of nationalist figures.

Rumors, Secrets and Other Residues

Rumors and gossip pervade the world of the *Noli*. These circulate among
and between those on top and those below the colonial hierarchy, cutting across Castilian and Tagalog. Such rumors trail after the occurrence
of events—for example in the aftermath of the failed uprising or after the
confrontation between Padre Damaso and Crisostomo Ibarra that led to
the latter's excommunication, or in the wake of María Clara's exile into
the convent. Gossip emanates from convents and markets, circulates in
the plazas and homes, spreads during fiestas and after church services.
We can think of rumors as attempts to lend events a certain syntax,
converting unexpected and novel appearances—or at least, those that are
taken to be such—into narratives that can then travel between tellers
who are simultaneously hearers of rumors. Within the circle of rumor,
one receives, then passes on, something that necessarily comes from
someone else. The fascination with and anxiety over their content, whatever these might be, is thus linked to the scope of their circulation.

By passing on rumors, Rizal puts himself in the midst of a circuit. The author is then also a relay, acting as a node in a network of unauthorized and ungrounded communication. He is neither the origin nor the destination of rumors, but merely a conduit, like a telegraph cable that transmits whatever messages are sent through it. Authorship in this case has to do with becoming part of the chain of hearers and tellers through which rumors pass. It means becoming part of an anonymous mass, carried along by its expressive force. The persistence of rumors and the author's compulsion to relay them would seem to indicate that Rizal could never completely draw himself away from the pleasures of anonymity afforded by the crowd. As much as he sought to address it by translating its language and transmitting it to another site past its reckoning, still he found himself returning to the chatter and idle talk that filled the crowd's everyday life.

Rizal's fascination with the crowd as reflected by his eagerness to relay rumors and gossip suggests another way of understanding the question of anonymity. In gossiping, the crowd appears in the novel as a series of voices barely attached to the bodies of their speakers. Rumors tend to be uttered by "someone," "a young man," "simple peasants," "old women," or by no one in particular at all. At times, they are attached to names, "Capitan Martín" or "Sister Ruffa" or "Don Filipo," whose identities remain attenuated and shadowy, as if they were fleeting points on which to temporarily anchor the course of gossip. The anonymous and often speculative nature of gossip makes it seem as if rumors simply pop in then out again, one opinion easily replacing the next, without one becoming dominant over another. Lacking the systematicness of socially sanctioned discourse (e.g., that of evangelization, folk tales, or the laws of the Indies), rumors come across as equivalent to one another, displaying what we might today call the same difference.

However, while all rumors are alike, they are not so in the same way. What distinguishes rumors is not their truth-value—for their nature as rumors is such that they have none—but their social effects. Certain rumors are more or less damaging, more or less trivial than others. In the novel, we saw how rumors about the revolt had a catastrophic effect not only on Ibarra but also on others who were said to have been part of his plans. On the basis of rumors, many people were rounded up, many of whom were tortured, exiled, and killed. Rumors of a violent conspiracy reached Spanish officials, and they responded with their own violence.[18]

To hear a rumor about someone is to imagine him or her as someone else. It is at the very least to see him or her as outside the circle of gossip insofar as she or he is its object. Put another way, it is to place the other in a scene that unfolds elsewhere, invisible to oneself, acting in ways that one cannot see but can only imagine. It is to think of someone as an other who bears a secret. Rumor then relays a fantasy about secrecy: that someone has it, and by holding on to it, places him- or herself at a remove from authorities.

In one of the *Noli's* chapters, Spanish officials and their native lackeys torture the prisoners who had been implicated in the uprising in San Diego, seeking to extract secrets. They ask for the names of coconspirators, for the kinds of promises Ibarra made in exchange for their participation, for their motives and aims (310–11). They want to confirm rumors and thereby control their circulation. In response, they receive only curt replies, stoic silence, and contemptuous smiles from one of the prisoners, a peasant named Tarsilio. The Spanish military officer, with the parish priest looking on, orders him to identify a pile of dead bodies on a dirty cart.

"You know them?" the lieutenant asked, lifting the matting [that covered the bodies]. Tarsilio did not respond; he looked at the cadavers of the husband of the mad woman [Sisa] with two others, that of his brother riddled with bayonet wounds, and that of Lucas with a piece of rope still around his neck. He took on a somber look and a sigh seemed to escape from his breast.

"You know them?" they asked him again. Tarsilio remained silent.

A whistle cut the air and the whip struck him on the shoulders. . . . The whippings were repeated, but Tarsilio remained impassive.

"Come on, talk!" the director told him; "They're going to kill you anyway . . ."

"Do you know that one?" Padre Salví asked him.

"It is the first time I've seen him!" Tarsilio answered, looking with a certain compassion at the others.

The lieutenant gave him a sharp blow and a kick. (310–11)

This scene of torture is reminiscent of earlier exchanges: in return for speaking up to authority, one receives blows. Tarsilio's silence and his terse response at the end keep authority from extracting the secrets that it seeks and the submission it requires. The peasant in this case speaks out of place as he refuses the terms of exchange prescribed by his torturers. For the Spaniards and their native sympathizers, violence is a kind of language. There is nothing spontaneous about its use. It is rather employed methodically and for specific reasons. Torture, with its elaborate rituals of questions and threats, depends on a grammar of violence to carry out its task.[19] Violence in the context of torture is the language used for responding to perceived insolence just as it is the language used to redirect the circulation of rumors and uncover the secrets they bring to mind.

In the prisoner Tarsilio, the Spaniards sense the bearer of something unknown to them. It is as if they see him as someone who is in contact with another realm of potency that they are barred from. Sensing this, they feel threatened. Demanding that he speak, they seek to claim what they think is his secret power and use it for their own purposes. Tarsilio refuses. He recognizes the corpses on the cart but resists revealing his knowledge. Keeping their identities to himself, he frustrates Spanish attempts at tracing the route of conspiracy that would lead them to its author. For the Spaniards, a plot must be made to yield a singular leader to whom all blame can be placed. Dead bodies are then simply signs of something else at work set loose by an identifiable figure. Behind every rumor, there must be truth. But without identification, the corpses remain merely corpses, like rumors that cannot be confirmed or denied and hence laid to rest.

Tarsilio's power as it emerges in the process of interrogation thus lies in his ability to recognize in death a realm outside the language of colonial authorities and to keep the knowledge of that realm in reserve. We in turn recognize this potential when we read that the sight of the corpses moved in him a feeling of compassion. Looking at their faces stirs in him thoughts of the dead when they were alive. Seeing them, he is moved by a sense of something missing. He thus finds himself in a place analogous to that of Ibarra identifying with the convicts on the street. Tarsilio recognizes in them the call of death. Seized by this call, he takes on a second language emanating from the corpses, one that coming from outside colonial society is able to encapsulate and surpass the language of violence addressed to his body. In this way, we see how someone from the crowd can emerge in the place of Ibarra, the ilustrado. Like Ibarra, Tarsilio discovers another locus of recognition in death, finding a pathway outside of the linguistic hierarchy and the colonial order. In the face of torture and threats of death, he holds on to his secret. Not only does he keep the identity of the corpses hidden within himself, he also holds the knowledge of death in reserve, its language signaled by the traces of compassion and grief that we, the novel's future readers, see but which remains unavailable to Spanish authorities.[20]

We can thus begin to understand why rumors interest Rizal. They return the author to the crowd in a state of heightened expectations. In relaying rumors, he puts us, his readers, in the midst of other possibilities. He shows, for example, how rumors have the power to spread and reach the hearing of authorities, provoking them to respond, testing their ability to control rumors' circulation and failing to manage their effects. But he shows as well how rumors as an expressive force detached from any singular origin or destination can also arouse the masses. As such, they also open up the possibility for converting at least some among the crowd into those capable of recognizing and then translating the call of death into a lingua franca held in reserve for the future. Rumors in this sense work in tandem with but are distinct from ghosts. Images of the dead haunt the living and move them to mourn: that is, to remember what they have forgotten, to return to obligations, to seek revenge, and/or to offer sacrifices as ways of finding for themselves a place on the social map. The failure of mourning and the inability to put the dead in its place results, as we saw, in the return of specters.

Rumors follow in the wake of such events. They have the potential to travel across social boundaries, connecting those within and outside different groups. They do so to the extent that rumors produce phantasms of secrecy that, once they reach authorities, incite a violent response. The crowd, in turn, responds to such violence in at least two ways: it mimics its language of blows and insults and so extends the reach of colonial power, in effect becoming its agent; or, as in the case of the peasant Tarsilio, it holds on to its secret, reserving something from the demands of authority. Possessed of his secret, Tarsilio sets himself apart from the crowd. In his case, as in Ibarra's and María Clara's, that which is kept apart and hidden is that which can then be used for the future, for example in the formation of secret societies, future revolts, and eventually revolution.

Rizal, however, posits a third possibility, one that is neither the extension of linguistic terrorism nor the turn to the language of death. It involves a residual speech that is assimilable to neither ghosts nor rumors. Toward the end of his description of the torture and murder of

Tarsilio, Rizal inserts what seems like a gratuitous story about another peasant, Andong. After witnessing Tarsilio's fate, the peasant eagerly volunteers to talk. He appears "like one completely crazy" (*como un loco a todos partes*). Asked who ordered him to join in the attack of the military headquarters, the hapless Andong replies:

"My mother-in-law, sir!"

Laughter and smiles followed these words. The lieutenant stopped and looked with his severe eyes at the unfortunate one who, thinking that his words had produced a good effect, continued more animatedly.

"Yes, sir: my mother-in-law did not give me anything to eat other than the most rotten and unserviceable food; last night, when I came home, my stomach hurt, I saw the patio nearby in the headquarters, and I said to myself: it is night, no one will see you. I went in . . . and when I got myself up, lots of shots started to resound: I was tying my underwear."

A whip cut off his words.

"To jail!" ordered the lieutenant; "This evening to the capital."

(314–15)

The humor in this incident arises from seeing the Spanish officer duped. He expects to learn the identity of the author of the plot and is stunned when he is told by Andong that it is his mother-in-law. At first, the "imbecile" peasant is so scared that he cannot even recall his own name. But encouraged by the laughter and smiles he gets back, he is relieved that his reply does not meet up with blows. But that relief is momentary. For when he reveals his secret—the reason for his presence at the military headquarters during the attack—it turns out to be an entirely different sort. We can say that what he reveals is a kind of secret, but one which is not meant to be shown, much less shared. Shit is precisely the foreign part of one's self destined for the outside but not for circulation.

Andong's story, however, brings it back to view. What should have been normally repressed returns as a narrative about letting loose what had been kept in. Releasing himself from his mother-in-law's bad food, Andong finds himself instead a prisoner. The joke then is also on the peasant. He expects relief but gets back more trouble. The Spanish officer demands secrets; instead he gets back gross secretions. Both are duped, caught in a spiral of reciprocal confusion. The Spaniard finally responds with the usual blows and orders the peasant imprisoned. His crime, presumably, is one of telling a story that leaves behind unassimilable residues. This is, in a way, Rizal's "crime" as well. He leaves behind foreign traces that cannot be fully domesticated. His stories release remainders that cannot be accounted for and can hardly be taken up for nationalist uses. They deposit a surplus of pleasure that is also a source of befuddlement and thereby eludes domestication.[21] They thus keep open still other lines of interpretation past those that lead to revolution, counterrevolution, and collaboration.

4

THE COLONIAL UNCANNY
The Foreign Lodged in the Vernacular

Castilian and the Possibility of Literature

The *Noli me tangere* attracted attention from all readers of Castilian, Spaniards and Filipinos alike, though for different reasons. Within a year of its publication, the novel was roundly denounced by Spanish friars and their allies in the colonial bureaucracy even as it was avidly sought and surreptitiously circulated by Filipino readers and their non-Filipino sympathizers. By 1888, after being condemned by the archbishop of Manila, the novel was banned by the colonial censors.[1] Official suppression brought with it even greater interest among those who did not read Castilian. It was as if by banning the novel, colonial law saw in the book and its author intimations of a power that challenged its rule. Spanish friars and officials thus invested the *Noli* and its author with a potentiality neither originally had. They sensed, among other things, that Castilian could be used against the interests of its native speakers. Their first language could be inappropriately coopted by someone under and other than them. The author was thus guilty of a kind of theft, making him a filibustero.

Rizal sought to respond to these charges of filibusterismo in ways similar to other nationalists such as Graciano Lopez-Jaena, Marcelo H. Del Pilar, and Antonio Luna. In letters, pamphlets, and newspaper articles, he reversed the charges against him. It was not he, but his accusers, the friars and the inept colonial officials, who were the real criminals. Their reactionary policies and gross racial insults fostered deep disaffection among Filipinos that, if allowed to go unchecked, would lead the Philippine colony to separate from Spain. Rather than a filibustero, Rizal claimed that he was the real patriot, concerned with the progress and happiness of his patria.

But as with other nationalists writing in Castilian, what he got back was misrecognition. Spaniards accused him of being ungrateful. They spread rumors that he was a German spy, which explained his enthusiasm for the German educational system and German science.[2] Rather than applause, he met with suspicion and scorn. In reading his Castilian, Spaniards saw not a fellow citizen but another, dangerous figure. Castilian, however fluently spoken and written, did not remake a native or mestizo speaker into a Spaniard. Instead, he was seen to alter the language, using it to express notions and sentiments at odds with those of its original speakers. The Augustinian friar José Rodriguez, for example, issued a pamphlet castigating the novel's bad writing: "It is a book, as they vulgarly say, written with the feet, which on every page reveals the crassest ignorance of the rules of literature and especially of Spanish grammar. The only thing notable that can be seen in the author is a stupid hatred of everything connected with religion and with Spain."[3] Using his feet rather than his hand, the native is accused of bad grammar, which is linked to harboring hatred for its native speakers. Just as Spanish missionaries had seized upon native languages, refashioning them to contain foreign concepts and retain alien words, so Rizal returns the favor three centuries later. He mobilizes Castilian for the transmission of other kinds of messages. Spaniards who read him now see their own language pressed into a different service. Castilian no longer expresses only their thoughts. It now comes to express those of another subject but no less alien race. As with the native vernaculars used to transmit the Word of God and the earthly power on whose consolidation it depended, Castilian used by Filipino nationalists now comes across to the Spaniards as the same, yet a different language.

Put another way, the *Noli*, like other nationalist writings, repeats *and* displaces the historical relationship between translation and conversion established by the Spanish missionaries. The novel's novelty consists in defamiliarizing the language of the Spaniards it seeks to address. Amazingly enough, Spaniards hear the indio and they respond, even if only to accuse the latter of being stupid and subversive. The former misrecognizes the latter. But such misrecognition is still a form of recognition. It is still a mode of acknowledging the indio's capacity to use Castilian. It is thus to see in the native a certain ability to speak outside of his or her socially ascribed position. To recognize by way of misrecognizing such a capacity is to invest the native with a power to become other than who or what he or she was supposed to be.

How does nationalism manage to win this victory, one that appears to be nonetheless dependent on colonial recognition? To answer this, let us turn briefly to one of Rizal's better-known defenses of the *Noli*, his response to the critic Vicente Barrantes.[4] A prominent colonial official and scholar, Barrantes, like other Spanish critics, claimed that the *Noli* was as badly written as it was full of contradictions. In his judgment, it mischaracterized colonial society in ways that ultimately did more harm than good. He also asserted that the sentiments and ideas expressed by the major characters, especially Ibarra, corresponded to those held by the author. Rizal wrote back, saying he felt "obligated" to respond to the "language of the schoolmaster" (*lenguaje de domine*):

> Your doctrinal tone and your advice move me, and I encounter them as natural in someone like Your Excellency, who is a member of the Royal Academies of Spanish and History, two summits from where mere writers such as I must appear like pygmies and ants, who in order to write have to make do with a borrowed language [*un prestado idioma*]. . . .
>
> I don't know, Your Excellency, if Academics *ambarum denorum* have yet settled as law that the ideas expressed by the characters of a novel have to be precisely the convictions of the writer, and not those suited to them by virtue of their circumstances, beliefs, habits, instruction and positions. (182, 184)

Rizal begins with a hyperbolic show of deference, signaling his putative place in relation to the one he addresses. But unlike Lopez-Jaena's earnest deference to his Spanish audience, Rizal's gesture is obviously a ruse, mocking the exalted status of his interlocutor. He acknowledges his place below, as one who must borrow the very language with which to address those above. But such an acknowledgment is meant to situate him elsewhere, beyond the position he occupies. He questions Barrantes's assertion that the characters of a book can only mirror the ideas of its author. Such ascribes to the author a position of absolute authority. Rizal repudiates this absolutism, writing,

> Until now, I am unable to give freedom to my country, and so I give it to my characters and I give to my Governor General to say what he wants to, without caring if he reciprocates and [gives me back the same]. I have learned, furthermore, from the Authors of Rhetoric and Poetry the laws of genre that they call mixed, wherein diverse characters intervene along with the author himself. Attribute to the charac-

ters what they say themselves, and to me what I say in the narrative. To Caesar's what is Caesar's! . . .

Why then does Your Excellency say that Ibarra and Rizal are the *same*? . . . Your Excellency is a consummate literati [*literato*], you possess a great style and an irreproachable pen. . . . Your Excellency abounds in maturity, experience and honors, and is from a superior and privileged race. I am a pariah, a poor expatriate, a bad writer, with a terrible style . . . an inexperienced youth and from an enslaved race, and nevertheless, I am going to dare to give you advice in exchange for that which you have so paternalistically given to me. When one has titles and high aspirations like Your Excellency, one has to write with more good faith and more sincerity. One must not cling to the antics of the café polemicists. . . . Or is it because Your Excellency does not know how to read . . . and that now you want to pose as a defender of the indios which Your Excellency remembers so well? . . . Your Excellency, who in all of his writings breathes a bitter hatred of my race and my country? Your Excellency, who has always enjoyed seeing us suffer? Your Excellency now places himself as a defender of the indios? How great is our misfortune when the very same ones who have been insulting us are now the ones who have to defend us! (185–87)

Rizal implies that he knows something Barrantes does not: the "laws of genre." Like the friars he associates with, His Excellency can only understand a text in terms of their absolute adherence to their author's intentions. In this view, all words are traceable to an origin outside the text. By contrast, Rizal invokes the laws of classical poets and rhetoreticians that precede the Spanish empire—laws that have in a sense a precolonial, even pre-Spanish origin, and that allow characters to speak and live independently of their author. Unlike the colony, the novel conjures a world where characters are free to behave in ways appropriate to their background and circumstances. The author may intervene, but he does not violate the essential freedom of the characters. Just as the world of the novel runs parallel to but at a tangent from colonial society, so the words of the author and characters are separable and distinct from one another. The Spanish critic does not see this, and it is the indio who has to point this out to him.

What is worth pointing out is Rizal's manner of pointing. In effect, Rizal tells Barrantes: You are superior and I am inferior, yet I will address you directly without the mediation of another figure—the friar, for example. And I will do so in your own language, which I have borrowed and which I now return to you. But I also give it back with a message: you are wrong and, even more important, you do not know that you are wrong. I know something about you that you do not know yourself. This is how I fulfill my obligation to you. I repay you by revealing a secret that you did not know about yourself, one that other natives already know about. I thus turn your insults into signposts that lead to the revelation of something you have borne without knowing it: your own ignorance. This ignorance is epitomized by the fact that you do not know about the laws of genre. Indeed, it seems like you cannot even read at all.

Rizal disavows any immediate correspondence between the protagonists of the *Noli* and its author. He denies, that is, what the Spaniards see in him: the animating force and sole authority responsible for the words of his characters. Instead, he insists on the incommensurability between his ideas and those possessed by the book's characters. In doing so, he holds on to the enduring fictionality of subjects who exist alongside but are never wholly assimilated into the author's social world. There is a gap, Rizal in effect tells Barrantes, between the novel and the world, one that can never be closed. We can imagine him saying to the Spaniard: I see and acknowledge this gap while you don't and won't. Thus you show yourself, without realizing it, to be a poor reader despite your academic reputation and political rank. Without knowing it, you expose yourself as someone other than who you claim to be: neither learned nor protective of the natives, but ignorant and cruel. You think they cannot see through you because you cannot see through yourself. Like them, though, I see your inability to see, your ignorance of your ignorance. I do so from my lowly position and in a second, borrowed tongue. Seeing you from below and seeing what you cannot see are one and the same process. Knowing about that otherness you keep but are not aware of, I show it to you in your own language. His Excellency fails to see what I know about him: his possession of an ignorance about reading and about the world, and about reading about the world. He does not know about this possession until I bring it to his attention.

Through Castilian, the Spaniard will come to know a secret about himself. The Spaniard hears about an otherness he harbors thanks to the native writer. The native announces a secret in print. Such exposure, like a photograph, is mechanically reproduced and disseminated both outside and inside the colony. It reaches different parts of the world, this news that His Excellency cannot read properly. In this way, the native who says he is "nothing" in a second language acquires something and momentarily overcomes the mastery of the Spaniard.

But doing so does not mean Rizal can overcome his reliance on the Spanish language. In fact, this dependence deepens, for without it, Rizal would not be heard by those above. Without recognition from above, he can have no way of influencing those below him. This attachment to Castilian is inseparable from, if not constitutive of the promise of communication even and especially beyond one's death:

> My work . . . cannot be judged nor can it judge, because its effects are still being felt. . . . When the men who have lashed out and the abuses they have fought have disappeared from the politics of my country; when a generation comes that does not make common cause with crimes or immoralities . . . in sum, when we have all disappeared and with us our self-love [*amor propio*], our vanities and little passions, then will Spaniards and Filipinos be able to judge it in tranquillity and with impartiality, with neither enthusiasm nor rancor. (191–92)

The *Noli* is an untimely book, as Rizal understands it. It cannot be judged by the present, only by the future. It can thus be understood only retrospectively, from the vantage point of generations yet to come. Every attempt at reading the *Noli* is thus prone to error, since only a future reading can do justice to it. The *Noli* belongs to the future that reaches beyond death, because it is in a language that invariably survives, like all languages, the passage of its individual speakers and writers even as it anticipates the arrival of new ones. Castilian in this case serves as an archive of nationalist writing. As with any archive, it acts to preserve the novel from present misreadings and bad judgments and keeps it for the future. This safe keeping allows the book to survive and spread beyond the point of its initial emergence. Even if it is neglected or suppressed, Castilian assures that the *Noli* can be discovered yet again. Language, in conserving the traces of literary expression, underwrites its institutionalization as literature, which is to say, the ongoing possibility of its continuous translation and transmission.

The conservative function of language is thus related to its disseminative power. Language allows literature to form and endure, just as literature exemplifies and complicates the sociopolitical salience of language. In the context of the late-nineteenth-century colonial Philippines, however, Castilian is the language that makes nationalist literature possible.

While ilustrado nationalists might, on occasion, write in their native languages, their primary interest lay in Castilian. As we saw in the earlier chapters, they saw in a second language the means with which to communicate vertically with those on top of the social hierarchy and across linguistic, social, and racial divisions. The foreignness of Castilian brought with it the promise of communicating at a distance, traversing social and physical space. Such a belief invested Castilian with the qualities of a lingua franca. To those who could use it, Castilian seemed capable of drawing what was far away—places, people, and events—near, while transmitting what was close at hand to distant places.

It is important to note, however, that the fascination with Castilian was not limited to the first generation of elite nationalists. There also existed a popular, mass interest and investment in the capacity of Castilian to furnish a kind of lingua franca that predated the rise of ilustrado nationalism and arguably shaped its contours. Given their facility and fluency with the language, it is easy enough to understand ilustrado attachments to Castilian. But how do we explain the belief in the telecommunicative capacities of Castilian among those in the lower rungs of society who had only the most rudimentary knowledge of the language? How was the foreignness of Castilian understood among the masses of who could not speak it and yet eagerly sought it out? What were the sites of this popular encounter with a language whose allure was predicated on its opacity?

One way we can begin to answer these questions is to turn to what might at first seem an unlikely source: vernacular theater. As we shall see, vernacular plays expropriated Castilian, mobilizing its potential for amplifying communicative power across geographic and social distances. Plays in the different local languages began to be performed in the eighteenth century and became increasingly popular by the nineteenth. Ironically, vernacular plays, as I will argue, depended for their popularity on their use of untranslated Castilian words. They commanded wide attention because of their ability to convey something of Castilian's opacity and therefore its capacity to communicate at a distance in and through local languages across the broad spectrum of social classes. I turn now to the historical significance of such a genre in popularizing the telecommunicative power of Castilian.

Comedia: The Recurrence of Untranslatability

Vernacular plays came to be known by a variety of names: *corridos, linambay* (in Cebu), *moro-moro* (at least by the later nineteenth century). However, they were most widely known as *comedia* from the Spanish *comedia*, metrical romances with roots in the sixteenth century. By the eighteenth century, comedias had become staple features of lowland Christianized communities. They were performed on makeshift stages in conjunction with the celebration of the town's fiesta, which commemorated the feast day of the local patron saint. Actors were taken from among the town's populace, though by the nineteenth century professionals, who were contracted by nearby towns to perform, emerged, especially around Manila. Professionals, however, at no point displaced local performers and writers. Comedias continued to enjoin popular participation and support, especially in the provinces, until their gradual eclipse by other entertainment forms such as the *zarzuela* (a kind of operetta) and the cinema (both foreign and local) in the early twentieth century.[5]

Comedias were one of the earliest forms of mass entertainment in the Philippines. Literary historian Nicanor Tiongson, following nineteenth-century Spanish writers such as Wenceslao E. Retana, points out that the earliest comedias date back to the late sixteenth and early seventeenth centuries. Written by Spanish clergy in Castilian and in the vernacular, these had explicitly religious themes dealing with the lives of saints meant to promote piety among viewers. Reference is also made to at least one comedia from 1637 based on an actual historical occurrence: the victory of Governor General Sebastian Corcuera over Sultan Kudarat's forces in Mindanao. Such themes, however, were relatively marginal. The most popular kind of comedia that emerged by the eighteenth and throughout the nineteenth and early twentieth centuries involved the fictionalized and formulaic recounting of the "lives and loves of royal characters" from Moorish and Christian kingdoms of medieval Europe and Persia in the various vernacular languages. It is this most common and widespread comedia, often referred to in Tagalog as *moro-moro*, which will be the focus of this chapter. Such plays were sanctioned by the Catholic Church and performances had to meet the approval of the parish priest. However, the writers and actors did not, as we shall see, merely reproduce the logic and interests of the colonial-Christian order. For the very popularity of comedias suggested, as I shall argue, other interests at work which, while appearing to reaffirm the social and ideological boundaries set by colonial authorities, also tended to redraw these.[6]

Performances of comedias drew large crowds from within as well as outside the town. Such plays were amalgamations of the various motifs, characters and geographical settings derived from European, mostly Spanish, metrical romances. Their titles suggest as much: *La guerra civil de Granada, Reina encantada o Casamiento por fuerza, Los dos vireyes, Principe Baldovino, Don Gonzalo de Cordoba,* and so forth.[7] Plots revolved around the forbidden love between a Christian prince or princess and his or her Moorish counterpart. Disrupting the filial relationship between royal parents and their children, such love invariably led to a series of abductions and searches, highly choreographed battle scenes, magical encounters with monsters, extended discourses on love lost and regained, vows of vengeance, and boasts of physical prowess. After stretching more than three or four hours through each of the several nights of the town fiesta, performances ended abruptly with the hurried, almost casual conversion of the Moors to Christianity and the reconciliation of the warring families.

Comedias were translations of such stories into Tagalog, Cebuano, Ilokano, and other local languages. However, no Spanish text was ever translated as a whole. Rather, comedias were composites of various metrical romances and their prior translations. They are translations of translations for which literally no original existed. Yet, as with missionary translations of God's Word into the native languages, comedia writers and performers also retained a notion of untranslatability. They kept certain words and appearances in their original Castilian form. These included proper names of persons and places, titles, stage directions, and other words for which there were no local equivalents. Costumes were made not so much as faithful copies of their original forms but in ways that suggested their alien origins. As with untranslated bits of Castilian embedded in the vernacular, costumes draped on native bodies sought to evoke foreign places. In the absence of an indigenous precolonial classical tradition of royalty and court literature in the Philippines, kings, queens, princesses, and dukes could be depicted only in ways that suggested vaguely European, vaguely medieval fashions. Similarly, musical accompaniments, when these occurred (especially by the later nineteenth century), were also foreign in origin. Battle scenes for instance featured the "Himno de Riego," derived from a Spanish military march from the later nineteenth century.

Untranslated words, "European" costumes, and Spanish military music in effect announced the recurring appearance of the foreign in the familiar. Indeed, it was precisely the repeated return of what came from the outside and which now lodged itself inside the local language that constituted the literary specificity of the comedia. As we shall see, it was what gave the plays their vernacular quality and lent to them their wide appeal. Audiences with little or no knowledge of Castilian and Europe found themselves periodically exposed to a spectacular surplus of foreign signifiers. We could think of performances as scenes of translation occurring around the appearance of untranslatable elements. In this sense, they remind us of the missionary translation of Christianity into the local languages. Missionary translation localized Christian discourse while at the same time retaining certain Castilian and Latin words deemed sacred in their original forms. Certain foreign terms thus came to have a privileged status within the local languages. Such terms transferred but did not translate from one language to another. Translation predicated on untranslatability instituted a linguistic hierarchy that made it seem as if local languages were naturally subordinate to Castilian and Latin. Thus did a second language come to rule over the first. Foreign words left untranslated came to inhabit and punctuate the flow of native speech within a Christian-colonial order.

Comedias in some ways recapitulate the missionary logic of translation premised on untranslatability, of the vernacular coming to be by bearing the traces of a foreign arrival. The foreign, whether by way of costuming or language, lies at the basis of colonial literary expression in the vernacular. As with Christian discourse, the prospect of coming into contact with the foreign and witnessing its arrival in the vernacular drew people toward performances of plays and rituals alike. A colonial public was shaped in large part by this anticipatory relationship to alien appearances in local contexts, whether these happen in churches or on the streets during theatrical shows. Yet, as much as comedias may have reiterated missionary logic, they also differed significantly from their ends and by extension from their politics. Such a difference, I want to suggest, comes to foreshadow nationalist understandings of language and power.

The origins of the comedia in the Philippines remain largely speculative. Wenceslao E. Retana, a Spanish journalist and historian of the
colonial Philippines, claimed in 1909 that the first comedia in Castilian
was introduced by Spanish friars in the early seventeenth century. A
Spanish-language comedia featuring Christians battling Muslims was
performed in Manila in 1637 to celebrate Governor General Corcuera's
victory against Sultan Kudarat of Magindanao two years earlier. Retana
also indicates that as early as 1609 a Spanish Jesuit had written in the
Visayan language of Bohol a comedia that dealt with the martyrdom of
Santa Barbara.[8]

By the first half of the eighteenth century, such religious and historical
themes had become less prominent. More widespread were vernacular
plays written by native authors based on Spanish metrical romances set
in medieval kingdoms featuring "Moros y Cristianos." Written in verse
structured into quatrains of eight- or twelve-syllable lines, these plays
were divided into many acts, featured large casts of characters, and ran
for a number of hours for the duration of the town fiesta. While most of
the comedias were written in Tagalog, almost every lowland Christianized area witnessed the rise of similar dramas in local languages. In
Cebu, they were called *linambay*; in Pampanga, *kumidya* or *kuraldal*; in
Leyte, *hadi-hadi*; in Hiligaynon and other parts of the Tagalog regions,
moro-moro.[9] "Natives are fond of comedias and farces," wrote the Augustinian Fray Gaspar de San Augustin in 1720, "and there is no fiesta of
consequence unless there is a comedia."[10]

From early on, the pattern of vernacular dramas seems to have been
set. Mixing Castilian with the vernacular, "it unfolds," writes Resil Mojares, "a highly elaborated story of war, love and supernatural enchant-
ments against the abstracted background of distant foreign kingdoms."[11]
In this regard, vernacular dramas never made references to Muslim slave
raiders targeting coastal Christian communities or to Spanish attempts
at conquering Muslim-held portions of Mindanao and Sulu through the
centuries of Spanish rule. Instead, they referred only to what Retana
called "faraway places," such as, "Spain, Portugal, Granada, Turkey,
Jerusalem, Hungary, Albania . . . and the names of characters: Florante,
Laura, Pelayo, Doña Inés . . . Infantes de Lara, Doce Pares de Francia . . .
And I ask: to what must we attribute the fact that in the artistic produc-
tions of Filipinos, there exist hardly a note that is genuinely Filipino? . . .

Why this migratory enthusiasm [*afán emigratorio*], why this systematic exoticism of the artistic concepts of Filipinos?"[12]

Retana stumbles into something curious about comedias that other scholars have echoed in his wake: there is not a single reference to the Philippines, to Filipinos, Chinese, Spaniards, or to local Muslims in the entire range of vernacular dramas. Unlike Rizal's novels, which are anxious to portray the social realities of their time, comedias are more interested in foreign scenarios. They appear to be spurred by a "migratory enthusiasm" to escape their social context. They invoke a past that is utterly fanciful and geographies that are wholly imaginary. "Princes, dukes, counts . . . extraordinary adventures, incredible tragedies, all of them lavish . . . and *all of them outside of the Philippines,*" Retana notes of the comedias.[13]

Comedias conjured a phantasmagoric "Europe." Social types such as Christians and Muslims were decontextualized into alien figures speaking local languages about the most distant locations. In the world of comedias, there were neither *sangleys* nor indios, *frailes* nor mestizos, but only Moros and Cristianos ruled by sultans and kings, dukes and queens, rather than *gobernadores* or *alcaldes*. Populated by characters and scenes foreign to the Philippine colony, comedias nonetheless present such foreignness in a familiar idiom. Regardless of religious differences or geographical settings, all of the characters in a comedia spoke a common language.

"Europe" in the vernacular dramas thus came across as a collection of appearances and signs that were lifted from their putative origins and grafted onto native bodies and speech. To Spanish observers, such a process created absurd juxtapositions of the foreign and the local that rendered comedias barely comprehensible. Vernacular dramas estranged "Europe" from itself, splintering it from any unitary concept as a distinct place with its own history. Translation placed European identity in motion, as it were, so that it surfaced in odd ways on colonial stages. Staging comedias meant, among other things, bringing both spatial and temporal distances up close. The unknown regions of the Western past now suddenly became accessible to native audiences. As fragments attached to non-European bodies and speech, "Europe" and its past were converted into spectral signposts from which issued a native present.

But even as comedias brought the foreign up close, hosting it within the limits of the vernacular, they also rendered the vernacular other than itself. They did so first of all by virtue of their prosodic features. All plays were set in verse. They were recited with the rhythmic regularity demanded by eight- or twelve-syllable lines organized around an invariant caesura on the fourth or sixth syllable. For example, from the comedia *Princesa Miramar at Principe Leandro*, written in 1920 but based on earlier nineteenth-century texts, we hear the princess addressing her absent lover:

> Walang kailangang mabuhay pa ako,
> Kung ikaw ay wala mahal kong Leandro,
> tapos na ang lahat, tapos na irog ko,
> ang kaligayahan layaw ko sa mundo.

> No longer do I need to live,
> If you are gone, my dear Leandro,
> everything is over, over my darling,
> the happiness that I enjoyed in this world.[14]

As with all verse, comedias recast ordinary speech into another form. The style of theatrical speech sets language apart from everyday discourse. The latter is usually meant to serve as a means for conveying messages or forging connections outside of what is said. The former, by contrast, calls attention to the act of saying itself. Language comes across as material artifice, palpable and audible apart from any instrumental function. In other words, speech in verse demands to be attended to as if it were another kind of language, one split between a regulated relationship between rhythm and rhyme on the one hand and a range of references crafted by layers of tropes on the other. The very form of the comedia then gives to the vernacular the sense of being two languages, not one. And to speak or hear lines from a play is already to be caught up in a practice of translation with neither beginning nor end.

Coupled with the recurrence of untranslated bits of Castilian along with references to unknown regions, the declamatory style of the comedia makes for the estrangement of the vernacular as well. A double translation was involved. Not only did comedias entail the prosodic transformation of everyday speech, they also entailed the transfer of foreign words into the local idiom. Tagalog, Cebuano, Ilongo, and so on now bore the traces of alien presences of indeterminate origins and destinations. Bearing the recurrent passage of the foreign, the vernacular becomes other than itself: not exactly a wholly different language, but not the same either.

Escaping reference to colonial society, vernacular dramas instead bear witness to another history. It is one that is largely unremarked upon but everywhere present in colonial (and postcolonial) society: a practice of translation that expects the vernacular to forebear the untranslatability of certain words. Hosting such words, bringing their foreignness up close, vernacular plays, like vernacular prayers, hold the local language in reserve for the coming of that which is alien to it. We see in the comedias a double estrangement. They displace fragments of the foreign into the local. But in doing so, they also dislocate the local, denaturalizing the native speech and rendering it beholden to foreign signs and appearances. Through translation, what comes from the outside is given a place inside. And it is this giving place that converts both the outside and the inside into something other than what they were.

Calling attention to the materiality and malleability of languages, comedias also staged the arbitrariness of appearances in colonial society. They showed that it was possible, for example, for a native to speak as if he or she were the embodiment of European or Persian royalty. Addressed as "Duke" or "Your Highness" by actors who were in turn referred to as "Prince" or "Sultan," natives on stage appeared to be other than who they were in everyday life. Just as vernacular speech came to possess and be possessed by foreign words, so the highly stylized manner of moving and costumed appearances of actors suggested the presence of someone else alongside the speaker. It was as if the speaker were two "I"s. There is the "I" who speaks within the plays, addresses others, and is addressed by them; and another "I" that exists underneath his or her role, concealed by layers of clothing and rhetoric. Comedias in this sense enacted something of the fundamental capacity of language, whether foreign or local, not only to reflect the world but also to separate itself from it.

Of course, this simultaneous ability of language to refer to and peel away from the world also lay at the basis of Christian conversion predicated on translation. For missionaries, all words spoken here on earth found their way to a final destination in the otherworldly sphere, where they were received by God. He is regarded as the privileged locus of address, and for that reason, the sole respondent to all appeals.

By contrast, comedias had no interest in reaching a divine address, much less construing a providential source of all responses and responsibility. Their locus of address was more problematic and uncertain, and this is perhaps what gives them their secular quality. Comedias were directed to an audience at large. Those who attended performances did not all necessarily know each other. While local actors would have known some members of the audience, it was more likely that there were many others with whom they had no prior dealings. A degree of anonymity characterized the crowd qua crowd at any given performance.[15] The keen Augustinian observer of colonial society, Fray Joaquin Martínez de Zuñiga, for example, describes the crowd attending a performance in the southern Tagalog province of Batangas in 1799 in the following way: "We went for a stroll and saw innumerable natives of both sexes coming into the pueblo from different directions, some on foot, others on horseback, all of them coming to the fiesta. The comedia had attracted many people. All of the houses were swarming with people and it seemed as if everyone in the province had gathered in the pueblo of San José."[16]

Given the large crowds that came "swarming" to the pueblo to watch the plays, there was no way of determining from the outset who saw and heard the comedia except to say that they came from the town and its surroundings, and that they occupied different social positions in colonial society. Their social identity, even if that could be ascertained, did not exhaust the question of who they were. Similarly, the comedia could not be and was not interested in controlling what was actually received and registered by the audience. With the comedia, we begin to see the possibilities of translation unhinged from evangelization. Less concerned with the identities of those it addressed beforehand, while explicitly playing out the possibilities of speaking and appearing as someone else, comedias opened a way to reconceptualize conversion in more worldly terms.

We can better appreciate the significance of the comedia by going back to the question of its popularity, its ability to call forth a mass of people in anticipation of a performance. For one the most instructive accounts in this regard we can turn once again to that of Fray Martínez de Zuñiga, written in 1800. Fluent in Tagalog after spending over a decade and a half in the country, Martínez de Zuñiga traveled in the company of the Spanish admiral Don Ignacio María de Alava to investigate social conditions in the various Tagalog towns at the turn of the eighteenth century. Arriving in the town of Lipa in the province of Batangas in 1799, the Spaniards and their entourage were welcomed by "a multitude of people." Everyone was well dressed, especially the young ladies, who were waving colorful handkerchiefs. The natives had put together a makeshift stage, where they "performed literary homage [*loa*] to the admiral; they had also assigned seats to us. We dismounted from our horses, sat down, and the performance started with a homage to the guest of honor, similar to what is usually given by the natives on such occasions" (1:60).

Here the appearance of foreigners is greeted by an elaborate show of hospitality. It entails the outpouring of surplus resources and the exhibition of all that is usually held in reserve, from good clothes to young women. Hospitality sublates any possible hostility toward what comes from the outside. Confronted with outsiders, townspeople play host to them, enfolding them in a familiar presentation. They are given a place in front of the stage and in view of the crowd. The foreigner enters and finds itself engulfed by a welcoming crowd. The former is assimilated, however, not as part of the town but precisely as one who comes from elsewhere. Martínez de Zuñiga continues, "The person chosen to present the loa to the guest of honor moves to the center of the stage is well dressed as if he were a Spanish nobleman." He is reclining on a chair, as if asleep, until he is roused by the "lugubrious" song of a choir singing in the back of the stage. He appears puzzled, wondering if he is dreaming or awake. Finally, he is persuaded that these voices are telling him that a "hero has arrived." At this point he "begins his eulogy" with a certain exaggerated propriety, "acting like the comedians in the coliseum and tossing out stories in the local idiom in high praise" of the visitors, to the delight of the guests and the crowd (1:60).

Set in place, the guest is treated to an image of himself. The image speaks but does so in the local language and in a way that is exaggerated. The actor gets back laughter as a way of recognizing his efforts. Dressed in Spanish garb, the native speaks nonetheless in his own language. The separation of language and appearance becomes part of the conventions dealing with the foreign and domesticating its arrival. After the performance, the guests are led to the local convent. Young ladies lead the way and "innumerable people" follow. Foreigners appear and a crowd invariably gathers around them. They stir attention, compelling those who see them to go outside and become part of a crowd of onlookers. Undoubtedly, it would not be the first time some had seen Spaniards, for after all they would have had contact with the Spanish priest and the occasional Spanish official. Rather, their interest in the admiral and his party follows on the trail of a prior concern about the appearance of figures of authority. As Martínez de Zuñiga recounts:

> The admiral had gone hunting [the next day]. When he returned, he was visited by many of those who had come to attend the fiesta. Through the comedias, they had formed an idea of what an admiral looked like, a man far superior to what we are usually given to think. And they were further stimulated to see a man that they regarded superior to everyone else and almost the equal of the king of Spain. ... They were entranced and filled with admiration for him. (1:76)

Vernacular performances prepare the natives, it would seem, to encounter figures of authority. Comedias provide a way of rehearsing such an encounter with the arrival of those who come from elsewhere. Authority becomes locatable, its otherness construed as something that can be apprehended and addressed. Such figures of authority become the aliens who can be copied and converted into surface appearances situated within the ambit of one's own language. The power of that which comes from beyond can thus be seized and transferred into the vernacular. It can be cited and reiterated out of context, even eliciting laughter. A Spanish admiral can appear in a native play and speak Tagalog. Martínez de Zuñiga remarks that the native actor, in eulogizing the admiral, made extended references to the expeditions of Ulysses as well as other allusions to classical antiquity (1:60–61). Not only does he quote the appearance of the foreigner, he begins to call on its pagan past, as if to evoke the foreign within the foreigner. Dressing up as a Spaniard, the native can address the latter and even reach beyond him, back to his pre-Christian origins. The foreigner, reflected in the native, is thereby estranged from himself. He, the Spanish admiral, is assimilated at the same time that he remains someone irreducibly other. He remains, that is, untranslatable in the very process of being translated. In the native actor, the Spaniard becomes a quotation of himself. Placed in quotation marks within the vernacular, Spanish authority becomes conventionalized. It is converted as that which, having already been seen, continues to arrive from outside. But it is an arrival that is announced from within the native language. The recognition of authority is predicated, as Martínez de Zuñiga's account suggests, on its prior citation as the image of an alien figure who transfers but does not translate.

Untranslatability, it bears repeating, was an essential attribute of colonial authority within a regime of translation ordered toward evangelization. Like the foreigner whose appearance stimulates native interests, untranslated terms induce the flow of translation in the vernacular. Castilian, for example, is given a place in Tagalog or Cebuano prayers or plays, but nevertheless retains a discernible Castilian form. As Mojares points out with regard to the Cebuano comedia, plays "are replete with [such] Spanish words as *potencia, batalla, causa, criado, ejercito*" and so on.[17] The same holds true for other vernacular plays. In them, Castilian becomes a part by being set apart, encrusted and hence visible and audible on the surface of the vernacular. The comedia, as I have been suggesting, stands in historical relationship to the missionary logic of translation. The former mimics even as it slides and skids away from the latter. The chief agent for evoking this sense of untranslatability in evangelization is the priest. In the vernacular plays, it is the actor.

Actors, or the Fetish of the Foreign

Actors were recognizable in the first place by virtue of their attire. It was common for them to dress up in costume and parade around the streets accompanied by a band publicizing the evening's performance.[18] European travel accounts remark on the fascination such costumes held for both actors and onlookers. Martínez de Zuñiga notes that before and after the play, actors were seen going about in their costumes, "which by Spanish standards are very elegant. They strut about, adopting an affected manner [in their walk and in gestures] so that they seem to consider themselves above their countrymen because of the roles they were playing that day" (1:75). The Spanish journalist Juan Alvarez Guerra remarked in 1879 that in provinces like Albay, comedia costumes were made at great expense. The more prominent actors might have as many as five to seven costumes, each as lavish as the next.[19] Regardless of whether they pertained to a Moro or a Cristiano, such costumes tended to be "adaptations of European dress, brightly decorated with sequins, beads, embroidery, fringes, and feathers" that signaled a kind of aristocratic splendor.[20]

Dressed in such extraordinary attire, actors were often compared to images of patron saints (*santos*), which were always draped in regal clothing. Both actor and santo exuded an otherworldly sight that attracted attention. They seemed to stand apart from everyday appearances. It was as if they were in touch with another realm from which they acquired an abundance of things signaled by what they wore. The lavishness of their costumes meant that they stood in close proximity to a source of gifts. Among those who saw them, they triggered fantasies of benevolence and generosity even when these might be at times tinged with envy. What we today might refer to as their glamorous appearance connoted their connection to a powerful channel for the circulation of possibilities, including possibilities of being other than what one was supposed to be.

Like the texts of the comedia, costumes were translations for which no original existed. They did not mean to accurately copy medieval European fashion but rather worked to disclose something beyond the limits of colonial society.[21] That is, they were technics for bringing distances up close. What they brought, of course, was an image of that distance the way a photograph, for example, would convey the sense of nearness of what was absent. Their eccentric appearance made it seem as if costumed actors were in contact with someplace else. They became citations of foreign figures and kingdoms in an unseen and indeterminate past. Hence, they, too, became a way for bringing distances up close as much as rendering distant what was close at hand. In costume, actors assumed a telecommunicative capacity. They drew audiences into proximity with imagined sources of colonial power even as they contained colonial authority within the boundaries of vernacular forms.

Costumes allowed native actors to leave behind one identity and assume a second. Colonial law regulated identity by way of racial classifications and dress designed to limit movement within the colony and facilitate the collection of taxes.[22] In the comedia, as we saw, racial categories ceased to matter. Identity no longer becomes subject to the law but now becomes a matter for popular recognition. Actors came to be recognized by audiences both during and outside of performances as figures capable of retaining the traces of a foreign authority. "The natives are very fond of comedias," writes Martínez de Zuñiga, noting that "the most prominent persons in the towns are the actors" (1:300). One can speculate that the popularity of actors had to do with their ability to embody something of the linguistic capacity of the Spanish missionaries. They managed to divorce language from appearance, looking one way yet speaking in another. In doing so, they made explicit the arbitrary relationship between language and identity. They thus seem to possess the power of translation that brought with it the insistent presence of untranslatable elements.

Other European observers, however, note the peculiar nature of this possession. The Spanish journalist Juan Alvarez Guerra, for example, remarked on the sound of actors' voices during a Tayabas comedia in the late nineteenth century. To someone like him who did not speak Tagalog, they all seemed to speak in the same uniform fashion. The rhythmic delivery of their lines worked to flatten the tone of their voices and, at least to a foreign ear, drained their words of affect.[23] About a century later, Filipino scholars would hear something similar. Resil Mojares, for instance, writes that actors in a late-twentieth-century Cebuano comedia delivered their lines in a "stilted recitative manner which allows for limited tonal variations for such situations as boasting and lamentation. Verses are also delivered segmentally, line by line to the rhythm of the dictation of the prompter (*dictador*) in his makeshift cubicle at the foot of the stage."[24]

The flatness of their tone was matched by the "immobile" and "expressionless" faces, Mojares further notes, so that

> the players are subordinated to the play itself. They do not, as in some forms of modern theater, develop the expressive potential of their personalities, faces or voices. They do not aspire to give an individual coloring to their voices nor do they exploit the semiotic qualities of the face (for in this they could as well be wearing masks . . .). In this type of play, the dissolution of personalities into flat characters enhances the play's overall expressive power.

The sonic quality of the actors' voices made it seem as if the language of the play were mechanically reproduced rather than organically produced by the speakers. That is, their voices did not seem to express a self behind and in front of its words. Instead, no one in particular inhabited their speech. The words they spoke belonged neither to them nor to the characters they portrayed. Rather, they served as the media for the passage and transmission of language that they received from the prompter or *dictador*, literally one who dictates. In most cases, the dictador was also the playwright, who composed the play by way of stitching together scenes and characters from other plays. Given that comedias were translations for which, as we saw, no originals existed, the author of the play could not properly be considered its origin. His authorship was a function of translation, as provisional as it was derivative. In this sense, the author-dictador was like the actor. His language was not his own, but always something taken from elsewhere: a second language, as it were, that lodges in his first.

Language passes through the author-dictador as much as it is passed down to him. He then gives it to the actors, who in turn disseminate it to the assembled crowd. What audiences hear is their own language, of course. However, given its provenance and style of delivery, it comes across as a language that also belongs to no one in particular. It is in this sense like a lingua franca: common to all by virtue of being native to no one. In the context of the comedia, the vernacular takes on a foreign quality. It is heard in the same way that it is spoken: at a remove from everyday speech and unlike Christian discourse, traceable to no ultimate source. The flatness of the voices and expressions on faces make it appear as if expression is divorced from intention. Actors come across as figures bearing a language they do not own but which they nonetheless body forth. That is, they embody an estranged vernacular, appearing to possess what in fact possesses them.

As a medium for broadcasting the vernacular now rendered uncanny by its emanation from somewhere else, actors gain a peculiar sort of recognition. Accounts of comedias from the eighteenth to the twentieth century consistently remark on the absence of applause before and after performances. "People drift in and out of the crowd as the play progresses,"[25] eating, sleeping, playing games, gambling, and on occasion addressing actors on the stage. There was then no "audience" in the sociological sense of a group that consciously sees itself to be separate from the actors on stage, constituting itself by judging what it sees, most immediately by way of applause.[26] Instead, people watched comedias in a state of distraction. The length and episodic repetitiousness of the plays seemed to demand this kind of fragmentary attentiveness.

Distracted attention, however, did not mean indifference. Other accounts report the widespread belief that great misfortune would befall a town that failed to host a comedia during its fiesta. Comedias were regarded as offerings, like food dedicated to the town's patron saint in the hope of soliciting his or her protection. Similarly, the performance of a comedia required the active patronage of the town's local elites who provided materials and money for rehearsals, costumes, musical bands, and food. Just as the staging of a comedia was meant to perform a town's submission to its patron saint, it also staged the workings of patronage in colonial society. In some places, even rehearsals drew large crowds that gathered with "great interest and anticipation."[27] Food was served for both actors and audiences during rehearsals and was of course in abundance during fiestas. One observer in 1899 noted the lively interest shown by audiences. They seemed aroused "by the shouts and threats, by the sweet diction, by the mourning of pain . . . these things the audience watch, hardly able to breathe in anticipation."[28]

Audiences alternated between distraction and concentration when confronting the stage. Like native converts attending Christian rituals and mass, they shifted between alertness and relative boredom.[29] The recognition they accorded to actors was thus sporadic. They assumed their position as the addressees of the play and therefore as the recipients of a gift of words and images. But they also drifted in and out of this position, leaving it yet to be consolidated and institutionalized. Similarly, audiences come to witness what we have been referring to as the history of translation predicated on the persistence of untranslatable elements. We can imagine them identifying not so much with the particular actors as with the latter's ability to embody translation. They see, that is, the possibility of claiming for themselves the capacity to keep the foreign in reserve, bringing it up close yet keeping it distanced and contained. They responded, however sporadically, to the call of a vernacular whose reach was now enhanced by the supplementary potency of foreign terms and scenes.

Spanish accounts note how actors were treated with great interest and deference off stage. "Princesses and queens were addressed as 'señora' and they were treated like royalty," Martínez de Zuñiga observes (1:75).[30] Even those who played the roles of clowns, regardless of their humble origins, were treated with respect. Their demands were readily granted during the days of the performances, from "a house to stay in, a horse to ride, an umbrella to shield him or her from the sun," to sumptuous meals and drink.[31] In some cases, actors even had police escorts to protect them from being robbed of the jewelry they wore as part of their costumes. Actors thus were treated in ways reminiscent of visiting Spanish officials that we saw earlier: as the recurring figures of what remains eccentric and unassimilable. For this reason, they were able to galvanize attention across social divides.

We can see then how comedias rehearsed what we might think of as the colonial uncanny, but also furnished a context for domesticating its recurrence. Before the consolidation of ilustrado nationalism, comedias broached the possibility of intermittently imagined communities founded on the recognition of the foreign lodged in the vernacular. Preceded by the drama of Christian conversion, comedias were also products of translation. They furnished venues for expressing and conventionalizing fantastic identifications with alien places and alien sources of power that lay at the basis of colonial-Christian authority. But unlike vernacular prayers, which were directed to God, vernacular plays relied on the recognition of an audience that was yet to consolidate its position as such.

Along with Christianity, colonized subjects thus came to share something else in the form of the comedia. Holding something in common—an interest in vernacular plays—they could conceivably begin to think of themselves as other than who they were. For example, as an audience called forth by the appearance of a second, foreign language amid their first, an appearance which incited translation. In this sense, translation is a response to a prior call which, passing from writer to actor, gathered forth a crowd. But it did so *not* in the name of the Father. Addressing the crowd as an audience not always conscious of itself as such, the comedia anticipated nationalist attempts to invest a second language with the capacity to recast vernacular languages and local identities into something other that could then be commonly shared. Thus does the fetish of the foreign introduced by evangelization run through vernacular plays and, later on, nationalist discourse. Appropriating the inappropriable, both repeat even as they rearticulate colonial-Christian antecedents, borne by the promise of reaching beyond a colonial order to which they nevertheless remained fatally bound.

5 MAKING THE VERNACULAR FOREIGN

Tagalog as Castilian

Responding to the Comedia

Despite its popularity, the comedia was never regarded by colonial authorities to be a subversive force that challenged the church and the state. It was not seen as a source of filibusterismo, as in the case of nationalist writings. Thriving in the shadow of the colonial-Christian order and sustained by dominant notions of patronage, the comedia seemed politically benign if not complicit with colonial authorities. Vernacular dramas drew the attention of European travelers and Spanish writers for their ability to stimulate native interests and call forth large crowds unmatched by anything else in the colony. As I suggested earlier, the popularity of comedias meant that a nascent public formed around the recurring appearance of the foreign in the familiar, along with the defamiliarization of both. Vernacular plays based on colonial notions of translation and untranslatability constituted disparate individuals into audiences of sorts not wholly within clerical or state control. Gathered by the uncanny appearance of actors and stage effects, audiences became habituated to witnessing the arrival of the alien and the unexpected that announced itself as such from within their own language.

Notwithstanding the seeming harmlessness of the comedia, some Spanish observers found in it something vaguely illegitimate. They regarded such plays as mere corruptions of European metrical romances. They accused native writers of producing garbled and nearly incoherent versions, taking the bad qualities while leaving out all that was good from European sources.[1] The Augustinian friar Toribio Minguella, for example, says of the comedia in 1878 that "It has characters and scenes produced by the poet's wild imagination: situations are improbable and stereotyped. For so long as the characters are imaginary, it is all right; but when it uses as characters historical figures, heroes and saints, both the story and theology are objectionable. The bad trends of the times and the anti-Christian ideas [figure] in the works."[2] Fray Minguella finds in the comedia a curious mix of the "improbable" and the "stereotyped." Given the native authors' "wild imagination," anything could conceivably appear in a comedia. It made what seemed like a limitless array of references to European history and mythology. But it also converted such references into "stereotypes." That is, it fixed them into a series of images that in time became predictable through the conventions of prosody, costuming, gestures, and music. In doing so, vernacular plays rendered images detachable from their origins so that they became citable and available for mass circulation. Such applied for both imaginary and historical figures. Comedias engaged in a practice of citation and in the circulation of foreign images that evaded, to the friar's dismay, the oversight of clerical authorities.

Other Spanish writers in the late nineteenth century faulted comedias for their lack of "realism." Compared to the Spanish dramas performed by touring companies from the Peninsula as well as creole and mestizo actors in Manila, vernacular dramas came across as backward. They were mired in impossible fantasies that, if left unregulated, might threaten to ruin native lives. The Spanish journalist Juan Alvarez Guerra, for instance, wrote in 1887 of the supposed dangers posed by comedias, especially among natives who acted or aspired to act in them:

They know nothing of the world except the two hundred *brazas* of land they cultivate or the blue sky that stands over the spread of their nets and the threshing of their abaca. Their thoughts, so deep in slumber, are suddenly awoken and they find themselves in the middle of a world that is totally alien to them . . . Their ears hear verses that in the beginning they do not understand, but in the end poison the mind. During these months of [rehearsals and performances], they are surrounded not only by praise, but also by riches they have never seen. Their short and rough clothes become blouses of thick cotton. Their feet are wrapped in dainty satin boots, their ankles are covered with thin embroidered socks, and on their shoulders, amid the thick black threads of hair, are spread pearls and jewels. It is shocking to awake from this beautiful dream of youth; after wearing those kinds of grand costumes, the return to the sad truth of rags for clothes and poverty becomes truly pathetic. The play that we described . . . has resulted in multiplying the number of prostitutes and criminals. Before she wore lace and jewels, a girl of fifteen of the type we were referring to would be so difficult to tempt; but once she is given these things, what was difficult is now easy.[3]

For Guerra, the comedia is not only bad art, it is also a corrupting influence on native youth. It makes them think that they can be other than who they are. Instead of being poor and simple, comedias give them illusions of being wealthy and regal. Turning them into something they are not, comedias in turn encourage audiences to treat native actors differently. People lavish attention and gifts on those who do not deserve them and thereby fill native actors with expectations impossible to sustain. As a result, actors are eventually tempted into other kinds of acts in order to keep acquiring material goods and favors. Comedias raise false expectations, according to this account. They allow for fantastic identifications and open the way for a loosening of inhibitions that leads to criminal acts. For the Spanish writer, comedias threaten to erode social order as youths are led to think of themselves outside of who and where they are, while audiences are brought to value their conversion into other beings. Like the friar who regards indios who speak Castilian as alien to colonial society, the Spanish writer sees natives appearing in comedias as figures dangerously displaced from their proper identity.

Guerra marks one extreme of Spanish thinking about the comedia. Few other colonial accounts took it to be a social threat. More common among Spanish writers was the notion that vernacular plays were aesthetic abominations that reflected the innate inferiority of native thinking. Vicente Barrantes, for example, cites what he regarded as the lack of historical veracity and narrative coherence in the plays matched only by the excess of bombast and mistaken use of Castilian.[4] Wenceslao Retana faults comedias for their confusing plots and interminable scenes. "Truly absurd" in their use of historical figures, such plays had "neither head nor feet."[5] They thus appeared to be literary monstrosities. That they enjoyed immense popularity is simply a reflection of the fact that among natives,

in general, fantasy reigns, one that refuses any sort of investigation, and for that reason it is rare to see among them observant writers while more common are those who rhapsodize about what they read, particularly about the exotic and pompous, the extraordinary and the tragic; in a word, those things that they have themselves never seen; and that after reading some fantastic work, they recast them according to the caprice of their exalted imagination, coming to feel as if they had actually seen them.[6]

Given to excessive fantasizing along with the refusal of empirical reality, the natives were consumed by all things strange in their grandness and grand in their strangeness. Comedias placed them in the ambiance of what was not there, yet was felt to be arriving from somewhere else. It was thus a genre that induced mass hallucinations. In spite of his condescending tone, Retana nonetheless touches upon an aspect of the comedia that we had earlier seen. As a technic of translation, it also produced telecommunicative effects. It called upon the foreign, bringing distances up close and broadcasting these in a language accessible to those who heard it. In this way, the comedia stole upon something of Christianity's capacity to transform the vernacular into a carrier of foreign words and concepts designed to signal the imminent coming—one that was simultaneously desired and dreaded—of the nonhuman and profoundly foreign. If the comedia appeared to traffic in "absurdities," it was perhaps because, we might respond to Retana, it was always already caught up in the messianism and paradoxical historicity of colonial Christianity.

Ilustrado nationalists responded differently. They viewed Spanish critiques of the comedia as part of the colonizer's attempt to embarrass Filipinos. Spaniards merely wanted to show the world that Filipinos were an abject race in possession of a primitive literary tradition. Nationalists claimed that such assertions only proved Spanish ignorance about the Philippine conditions. They took exception to Spaniards' judgments of vernacular dramas, the language of which they, the Spaniards, could barely understand. In ridiculing the comedia, Spaniards were passing themselves off as authorities on matters they knew little about.[7]

Yet nationalist responses at no point defended the comedia form. In most cases, they implicitly acknowledged the Spanish view of the comedia's "backwardness" and lack of "realism." In the *Noli*, for example, one of Rizal's more enlightened characters, the philosopher Tasio, is asked if he intended to stay for the performance during the town fiesta of San Diego. He replies:

"Thanks, but to dream and talk and act foolishly, I prefer to do alone," the philosopher answered with a sarcastic smile. "But now, I am reminded, does it [the comedias] not call attention to the character of our people? Peaceful, they like bellicose spectacles, bloody battles; democratic, they adore emperors, kings and princes; irreligious, they ruin themselves with pompous cults. Our women are sweet of character yet they go wild when a princess brandishes a sword . . . Do you know why that is? . . . Well . . ."

The arrival of María Clara and her friends cut short the conversation.[8]

The philosopher Tasio implies that vernacular plays involve no more than a sort of dreaming that amounts to foolish talking and acting (*disparatar*). At most, they shed light on what appears to be the contradictory character of "our people": that what they seek out is at odds with who they otherwise are. Put another way, comedias do not reflect "our real selves," nor do they take into account our "true conditions." They do not depict "our own" customs and faults so that we might understand and seek a cure for them (as the *Noli*, for example, attempts to do). Rather, they spawn delusions, spurring audiences to imagine themselves as kings, queens, sultans, or dukes engaging in battles that never actually took place. Comedias were inadequate modes for representing the life of the colony. Their popularity only retarded the spread of nationalist enlightenment.

Indeed, ilustrado attitudes toward the comedias would take an even more negative tone in the wake of Spanish rule, the defeat of the Revolution, and the subsequent consolidation of United States hegemony. By the early twentieth century, vernacular plays, condescendingly referred to as *moro-moro*, in reference to the choreographed battle scenes, were regarded by ilustrado nationalists as the baneful legacy of an imagined feudal past. Writers such as Lope K. Santos and Severino Reyes decried comedias as obstructions to "literary progress" headed toward more "realistic" portrayals of the country's conditions. Moro-moros merely mystified the masses and should be swept aside.[9] Nationalist intellectuals such as Epifanio de los Santos were dismayed by what he referred to as the superstition and stupidity propagated by comedias.[10] And even those who defended the comedias, such as the folklorist Isabelo de los Reyes, called for their "modernization." He argued for the need to preserve the genre as an expression of local cultures, along with folk tales and myths. Rather than abandon them, he urged their reform, shortening their length and correcting historical and geographical inaccuracies. He thus tacitly agreed with the assumption that the comedia was an outmoded genre and its anachronisms called for correction under elite supervision.[11]

A number of local elites also sought to curtail performances by charging license fees, convinced that comedias had little to teach the people. In Cebu, at least one critic echoed earlier Spanish warnings regarding the dangers posed by comedias as they provided occasions for the illicit and unsupervised mingling of the sexes.[12] Steeped in their own phantasmagorias about modernity and reality, nationalist elites saw in the comedia's fantasies of things European a cause of embarrassment. Some imagined American observers watching comedias and thinking that Filipinos must still be captive to feudal forms and thus unprepared for independence. "We ought to be embarrassed by the moro-moro because it is noticed by Americans who say, 'Así, pilipino mucho buang' [Thus are Filipinos very crazy]. . . . Moro-moros have nothing good to teach us."[13]

Faced with the comedias, nationalists imagined themselves being seen by colonial authorities, Spanish or American. The latter watch them watching the comedias and judge the entire race to be crazy. From the ilustrado point of view, literature and art were meant to represent the nation.[14] Such representations were invariably addressed to colonial authorities who would see them as reflections of their producers. Constituted by a practice of translation predicated on hosting the untranslatable recurrence of foreign terms and images rather than the direct representation of demands and desires, comedias did not conform to such notions.

Recall Rizal's character Filosofong Tasio. He saw in the comedias something anomalous. He says in effect that it does not reflect who "we" really are. We have no kings and queens, and our women and Muslim population do not act that way. In this, he departs from the rest of the town attending the play. It is as if he places himself on the side of European observers, seeing the play as they do. At the same time, he is not European; he is still an indio who belongs to the town. Sensing this predicament, he turns away from the performance. His "sarcastic" tone indicates that he feels himself to be divided, split between one who is part of colonial society, and another who watches from a distance and has another perspective. He is about to explain that other perspective when he is literally cut off by the arrival of María Clara and her friends. Had Tasio been able to speak further, he, like the book's author, might have sought to account for the peculiar popularity of the comedias. But whatever he may have said, it would have been undoubtedly addressed not so much to the locals of San Diego, and certainly not to the actors and writers. It would have been directed to those who were perplexed by the comedia and may have been led to make wrong assumptions about the race as a whole.

That Tasio, like other nationalists, felt compelled to furnish an explanation meant that he expected at some point to be asked for one. He was in a sense responding to a prior question that could have come only from a foreign observer mystified or misled by what they saw of the comedia. To embark on an explanation is to respond to a prior call even when the source of that call is absent. Tasio, like Rizal, sensed the proximity of the foreign, primarily European and Spanish observers whose language he knew and writings he read. He would have thus anticipated their questions, prepared to parry their summary judgments. As with other ilustrados like Antonio Luna in Paris and Madrid, or Graciano Lopez-Jaena in Barcelona, he would have felt them even and especially in their absence, observing him, looking at what he was looking at. To be seen watching a comedia risked being mistaken as one who was as stupefied as the natives. Such would be a cause for embarrassment. It implied that one was not sufficiently enlightened for being mired in older forms.

A source of shame, the comedia had to be disowned, or at least reformed. From the point of view of ilustrado nationalists, if it could not be abolished, the comedia had to be subordinated to more "realistic" and modern forms of theater, as well as other genres such as the novel. In other words, translation and citation, which were integral to the production and dissemination of the comedia, were to give way to representation and critique. Ilustrados singled out one particular comedia writer who in their estimation anticipated this shift and paved the way for the remaking of Tagalog vernacular for nationalist purposes: Francisco Baltazar, also known as Francisco Balagtas (1788–1862).

In 1838, Balagtas wrote what nationalists have long regarded as the crucial touchstone of Filipino literature and the most important Tagalog epic poem, *Florante at Laura*. While borrowing from the conventions of the comedia, Balagtas's work also differed from them in significant ways. By the late nineteenth century, it came to be regarded by nationalists as a political allegory for the woeful state of the colony held captive, like the poem's protagonist, by oppressive and illegitimate rulers. Late-nineteenth- and early-twentieth-century nationalist commentators saw in *Florante at Laura* a protonationalist quality that radically set it apart from the tradition of vernacular plays. Such a difference was related to the poem's stylistic innovations. These ranged from the use of footnotes in prose to explain classical allusions in the poem, to a pronounced preference for detailing "inner states" of characters in lieu of repetitious battle scenes and spectacular magical effects. For nationalists critical of the comedia tradition, Balagtas's epic was taken to be the aesthetic and political threshold to more "modern" and "urban" sensibilities.[15] At stake, as we shall see, was Balagtas's attempt to bring Tagalog into equal and complementary footing with Castilian and thereby redraw the hierarchical relationship between the two.

Balagtas and the Possibilities of Tagalog

Francisco Baltazar/Balagtas was born in 1788 in Bigaa, Bulacan, a province north of Manila, son of indios Juan Balagtas, a blacksmith, and Juana Cruz, about whom little else is known. Like most indios, his early education consisted of memorizing prayers and the catechism in the vernacular at a parish school presided by the priest and his local assistants. At age eleven, he moved to Tondo, outside of the Walled City of Manila, to work as a servant for a wealthy family.[16]

Balagtas's chief biographer, Herminigildo Cruz, paints a picture of a checkered life. In 1812, he enrolls in the Colegio de Letran, learning Castilian, Latin, arithmetic, and geography. Later, he studies at the Jesuit-run Colegio de San José, where he comes in contact with the native priest Maríano Pilapil, best known for editing an "official" version of the Pasyon, the verse narrative of Christ's passion and death sung in Tagalog during the Lenten season. He also finds a mentor in José de la Cruz, popularly known as Huseng Sisiw, then the best-known comedia writer and poet around Manila. Balagtas supports himself in part by writing love poems for fellow male students and accepting commissions to write comedias (11–18). He sees early on the exchangeability of money for poetry at a time when Bourbon reforms were putting an end to the Galleon Trade and opening up the colony to foreign merchants. Thanks to British, German, and North American merchant capitalists, along with Chinese entrepreneurs, the colony had been going through an agricultural revolution through the late eighteenth and early nineteenth centuries. As we have seen in the previous chapters, beneficiaries of these economic developments included Chinese mestizos as well as a smaller group of indios from whose ranks would emerge the first generation of ilustrado nationalists later in the 1870s.

Balagtas was the rare indio who managed to gain fluency in Castilian though he wrote primarily in Tagalog. In the late 1830s, he falls in love with María Asunción Rivera but finds himself in competition with another, more influential man for her affection. The rival saddles Balagtas with false charges (the nature of which remain vague) and the poet lands in jail. There, he writes his greatest work, *Florante at Laura*, dedicating it to Rivera, whom he refers to as "Celia." He thus turns to writing to mourn his loss and it is this relationship between language and loss that will figure prominently in the epic poem.

In 1840, Balagtas leaves Manila and takes a job as a clerk interpreter in the colonial court in Bataan. There, he marries his second wife (his first having died), Juana Tiambeng, a wealthy Chinese mestiza, in 1842. He continues to work in a series of low-level jobs in the colonial bureaucracy as a translator. Around 1856 or 1857, he again finds himself in trouble with the law, accused of cutting the hair of some servant—the circumstances are again unclear from his biography. He serves what seems like an inordinately long sentence of four years, finishing out his term in Tondo. While in jail, Balagtas writes prodigiously, though nearly all of his works have been lost. He leaves prison a destitute man. On his deathbed in 1862, his children recall that he wished only that they would not take up writing poetry, and that may their hands be cut off should they follow his path (18–32).

Throughout Cruz's biography of Balagtas runs the wish to see him as a representative figure in the history of Filipino literature. At several points, Cruz refers to Balagtas as a "genius" (*genio*) whose appearance signaled a "revolution or overturning" of literary tradition. Going against the grain of convention, the genio, Cruz claims, is utterly original. He owes nothing to his predecessors but instead places everyone else in his debt (31–32). This perhaps is what confers to his work a "revolutionary" value: the fact that it breaks from all prior obligations and instead reorients the flow of indebtedness toward him.

What "we" owe to Balagtas, Cruz says, is our recognition (*pagkiki-lala*). We who come after him are obligated to acknowledge the poet's transformation of the Tagalog language as a medium for displaying a Tagalog civilization in the midst of Spanish and now, at the time of Cruz's writing in 1906, U.S. colonial rule (2–4). The strength of Balagtas's work is taken to be an index of the strength of the vernacular and its capacity to serve as the lingua franca of the future. The ilustrado interest in literature then was indissociable with the possibility of arriving at a common language for the nation. In the wake of revolutionary defeat and in the midst of the return of colonial rule under the United States, Cruz refers to Balagtas's writing as the "proud flag of a beautiful language in the poetry of the Orient" (*matayog na watawat ng isang marikit na wika sa Dulaang Silangan*, 4). As a kind of flag, Balagtas's poetry becomes a model of Tagalog writing, an exemplar of the vernacular's expressive powers.

With Balagtas, Tagalog achieves for the ilustrados a kind of aesthetic perfection and political eloquence lacking in the comedias and Christian literature in the vernacular. Rizal, for example, singled out Balagtas's work in a short essay written in German for the Ethnographic Society of Berlin on the art of Tagalog versification. He referred to *Florante at Laura* as "a work in the Tagalog language in its apogee and full magnificence" and thus "a model way of speaking for the Tagalogs."[17] It is perhaps not surprising that Rizal carried a copy of Balagtas's poem with him while traveling in Europe, and the *Noli* makes a number of allusions to the poem. Among postrevolutionary ilustrados, it became commonplace to see what came to be called simply the *Florante* as the precursor of Rizal's novels. Cruz and Epifanio de los Santos, for instance, detail the correspondences of character and plot between the two works.[18] Rizal himself unsuccessfully sought to bring out an edition of the epic poem along with illustrations by Filipino artists.[19] He regarded the poem to be engaged in a project similar to his, for it provided a "picture of our own customs, in order to correct our vices and defects and extol our good qualities."[20] In Balagtas, Rizal saw a kind of critical ethnographer of Tagalog "customs" engaged like himself in furnishing materials with which to respond to Spanish claims of Filipino inferiority.

The urge to idealize Balagtas as an ilustrado precursor, to see him as representative of a certain mode of representability, one that stands in contrast to the translation and citational practices of the comedia, becomes even more pronounced in later ilustrado writings. At the height of the Filipino-American war in 1901, the nationalist Manuel Adriatico wrote:

In *Florante*, a noble heart weeps with the profound and delicate sentiments of our race. . . . In it, every grief has its rhyme; a strophe for every cry of our unfortunate people, a truth from the father and a teaching for the child of the family. And in these ill-fated days for the nation, *Florante* offers us a faithful description of our social and political scenes [*cuadros*], in such a way that we can say that the author had foreseen from half a century ago our actual misfortune. . . . With a vigorous accent and an incomparable diction, he has told us that in this vile world, inequity and infamy sit on the throne of injustice in order to condemn the virtuous and drown out the good, just as it exalts treachery and rewards crime.[21]

Read in the midst of war, *Florante at Laura* is regarded as a "faithful description" of our "social and political scene." Adriatico writes in Castilian, lauding a Tagalog poem, and the word he uses for "scene" is *cuadro*, which can also mean "picture" or "painting" as well as the frame around a picture or window. *Cuadro* denotes both the frame and what is enframed. Balagtas's poem thus conveys "faithfully" both a realistic content and an exemplary mode of representation. It is as if the author had foreseen what was to become of the country at the close of the century. His poem is thus invested with a prophetic quality and so represents "our" future becoming present. It is a picture of the present taken from the past. In this sense, the poem is like a photograph of Philippine conditions. It is an accurate recording of reality, a documentation of what is present but one that was taken in an earlier time. As with every photograph, the poem can transfer but cannot wholly translate into another medium. Epifanio de los Santos in his introductory remarks to his Castilian translation of *Florante* in 1916 writes of the "impossibility of a version of the poem in any other language." Further, he says that "the best translation, even more, in prose will never reflect the real beauty of the original. The reduction, though attempted in one's own language, of poetry into prose results in hyperbole and cliché, to the point of being stupid, when in verse it is graceful, elegant, and original."[22]

De los Santos sees what many other translators before him have: that translation entails losing the original. Certain idiomatic expressions, tropes, and diction in one language do not have exact equivalents in another. Any attempt to "reduce" these features of the poem to another language is bound to miss the "beautiful reality," the "grace," and the "elegance" of the original. Because the poem is seen not only as a faithful representation of reality but also as the representation of the power of representation, it cannot be fully translated. The original always escapes, exiled from and foreign to every translation. It disappears in the process of being disclosed, withdrawing at the very moment of being brought forth. Nonetheless, de los Santos feels an obligation to translate that which, in eluding translation, is in the end untranslatable.

He decides to translate at least the content of the poem, even if it means he cannot duplicate its form. He does so, he says, "in order to give some slight idea of the content of the poem to those who do not know Tagalog and provoke among them the study of the language, so that they might directly enjoy the beauties of the poem."[23]

De los Santos's translation of the Tagalog original into Castilian is meant to give foreigners ignorant of the vernacular an idea of the poem's content, not the poem itself. There is a sense then that something essential about the poem—what gives to the poem its uniqueness—remains untranslatable. Like a photographic image that can only be reproduced but can never be made to yield the thing that it represents, the translation of the Tagalog poem could allow for the transfer of only a part, never the whole. At best, translation can deliver only a representation of the poem, not the poem as such, to those who cannot read the vernacular. Translation here enframes the poem as if it were made up of two parts—content and form, idea and reality—and then seeks to split one from the other. Representing the poem, translation also holds it back, keeping the original in reserve. Ironically, as ilustrados like de los Santos knew too well, translation only highlights the Tagalog poem's untranslatability. For this reason, one can begin to think of Tagalog as sharing in the qualities of Castilian.

We can see this effort to claim for Tagalog the power of Castilian in postrevolutionary ilustrado attempts at comparing Balagtas with Miguel de Cervantes. "He is the Cervantes of Filipinos," Hermenigildo Cruz writes in 1906. *Florante at Laura* is to Tagalog as *Don Quijote* is to Castilian. Both broke with outmoded literary genres—comedias in one case, *libros de cabellarias* in another—and set their languages on the path to modernity.[24] Just as Castilian is referred to as the "language of Cervantes," and English the "language of Shakespeare," so Tagalog has come to be known as "the language of Balagtas," notes Lope K. Santos in 1905. In this view, Balagtas brings out in Tagalog what had been obscured by the "crude" and "empty" poetry of the comedias.[25] As "king" (*hari*) of Tagalog, Balagtas endows the vernacular with a new kind of literature. His name becomes synonymous with the Tagalog language itself insofar as it now shares with Castilian and English the ability to communicate across vast distances around the world. Rendered into a contemporary of Cervantes and Shakespeare, Balagtas becomes the master of Tagalog. That is, he is seen by ilustrados to command the vernacular in a way that transforms it from a subordinate language into an equal of other global languages. For this reason, he is lord over Filipino writers who follow in his wake. By the early twentieth century, his name is seen as that to which the vernacular answers, and in answering, it becomes amplified, surpassing its local reach.

Balagtas is thought to place the Tagalog language in his debt insofar as he gives to it what others have been unable to: a literature comparable to and not merely derivative of Castilian. In this way, he is seen by ilustrados to have rescued Tagalog, as it were, from older forms. Tagalog had been fated to translate Castilian and host its untranslatable terms in vernacular prayers and plays. But with Balagtas, nationalists claimed, Tagalog now demanded translation while at the same time remaining untranslatable. Through Balagtas, Tagalog poetry could be representative and represented but could not be reduced and subordinated by being fully translatable into another language. It is this demand for translation alongside the insistence of an essential untranslatability that places Tagalog in the eyes of ilustrados on the same level as Castilian and other global languages like English. Thanks to Balagtas, Tagalog appears modern. That is, it is freed from a linguistic hierarchy and achieves a new kind of expressive power thanks to its untranslatable singularity.

Were the ilustrado nationalists correct in their estimation? What was it in the works of Balagtas that led them to such views about the equality of Tagalog with Castilian as well as the comparability of the vernacular with global languages? How did Balagtas, especially with *Florante at Laura*, recast the question of translation and untranslatability? Did his work differ significantly from the comedia or simply extend what was already in the genre? We turn to these questions in the following chapter with a consideration of Balagtas's poetry, especially his noncomedia comedia, *Florante at Laura*.

6

PITY, RECOGNITION, AND THE RISKS OF LITERATURE IN BALAGTAS

Poetic images are imaginings in a distinctive sense:
not mere fancies or illusions but imaginings that are visible
inclusions of the alien in the sight of the familiar.

MARTIN HEIDEGGER

The Amplification of Tagalog

In the historiography of Philippine nationalism, the work of Francisco Balagtas represents a watershed in the unfolding of vernacular literature. The strength of his writing is such that it is credited for reconceptualizing the place of Tagalog within the colonial linguistic hierarchy. Balagtas is credited for revising comedia conventions, stripping them of their more spectacular effects and elaborate stagings. Battle scenes were narrated rather than acted out, and recurring encounters with demons, monsters, and other magical figures were reduced if not wholly eliminated. His plays then are seen to be more "realistic" when compared to the more fanciful comedias. Though still set in exotic locales like Albania, Persia, and Greece, they allude to colonial conditions of political oppression and local customs such as child rearing, courtship, and modes of friendship and enmity.[1] In this sense, his work has long been regarded, rightly or wrongly, to be protonationalist with no less than national heroes such as José Rizal and Apolinario Mabini claiming kinship with Balagtas's writing.[2]

In addition to revising the comedia tradition, Balagtas is also regarded by nationalists to have altered the very nature of Tagalog literature. The language of his plays is thought by contemporary Filipino critics to be more "sophisticated and refined." They eschew formulaic compositions in favor of innovative rhymes. To nationalist scholars, the tropes in his writing come across as more imaginative, and their characters suggest the existence of "inner subjective states" rather than mere surface appearances.[3] His only surviving epic play, *Florante at Laura*, even contains footnotes in prose that explain the classical allusions in the text. A melancholic mood pervades the entire poem in contrast to the flatness of affect that characterizes the comedia. In the 1970s, Resil Mojares summed up a long tradition of Balagtas scholarship by writing that in *Florante at Laura*, "new ground is broken in the amplification of the resources of Tagalog as a literary medium, in the creative adaptation of the comedia as a vehicle for socially relevant expression and in the artistry of the literary work itself."[4]

In this view, not only did Balagtas change the comedia, he altered the very nature of the Tagalog language, allowing it greater reach. Mojares refers to it as a matter of "amplification," as if Balagtas had electrified Tagalog, allowing it to be carried further from its original location. Such amplification was consonant with what other scholars see as the rise of a "new urban sensibility." As we saw in the introduction of this book, the nineteenth century marked an era of remarkable changes in the colony. Bourbon reforms initiated in the late eighteenth century led to the liberalization of trade, and subsequent liberal reforms emanating from Spain hastened the spread of market relations and the commercialization of agriculture fueled almost exclusively by British, German, and North American merchant capital and Chinese entrepreneurship, especially by the second decade of the nineteenth century. These developments spurred socioeconomic changes linked to the growth of towns and the development of higher education. Though clerically controlled, universities in Manila selectively admitted mestizos and indios. A few of the students joined the secular clergy, barred as they were (with rare exceptions) from joining the ranks of the Spanish regular orders. Prevented from holding their own parishes by the friars (again with a few exceptions) and reduced often to the position of lowly coadjutors, many of these Filipino priests would early on form protonationalist inclinations and forge uneasy alliances with antifriar ilustrados later in the nineteenth century and through the revolution of 1896.[5] Other students, like Balagtas, went on to low-level jobs in the colonial bureaucracy, using their knowledge of Castilian to serve as translators for Spanish officials and the courts. Still others who had the means managed to study abroad. With the opening of the Suez Canal in 1865 shortening the distance between the continent and the colony, travel back and forth to and from Europe increased and would lead, as we saw earlier in the case of Rizal's generation, to momentous developments. In all cases, the possibility of encountering what was new and unknown took place within an imperial context that insisted on the purchase of a second (and belated) foreign presence—the church, the state, Castilian—over local conditions and languages.

The increasing movements and extended contacts among peoples, ideas, and commodities doubtless had an effect on language and literary forms. The "amplification" of Tagalog meant that as literature it could travel more widely, transmitted by print technology and distributed not simply by the Catholic Church, but increasingly as commodities in the marketplace. In this way, we could think of Balagtas's poetry, like that of the comedia, as part of a technological complex for the transmission of Tagalog. This transmission, however, did not mean a decrease in the interest in or influence of Castilian. On the contrary, as I will argue below, Balagtas's writing, like that of Rizal, would draw on Castilian as the basis for Tagalog expression. The amplification of Tagalog thus occurred in relation to the assimilation of that which was thought to be unassimilable. The basis of its literary power, as Balagtas's works would show, lay precisely in its ability to reproduce the effects of the colonial uncanny, one that issued from a translation practice premised on notions of untranslatability.

Vernacular Address

What gives significance to Balagtas's writing is the peculiar way he placed Castilian and Tagalog in touch with each other. Rather than reiterate the hierarchical relationship between the two while locating both in view of a third, overarching language—Latin, God's Word—Balagtas instead flattens the relationship between them. We can see this move in a number of his earlier poems. Written in a ladino style reminiscent of the seventeenth-century poet-printer Tomas Pinpin,[6] the verses alternate between Castilian and Tagalog lines. For example:

1 Inhumano dolor—hirap na matindi,
2 sufre despreciado mi pecho constante,
3 mis tiernos amores—na iyong inapi,
4 destruye mi alma con rigor y fuerte.
5 Adios ingrata!—paalam na irog!
6 Me mata tu desden—pusong dinudurog,
7 recuerdame—kahit isang himutok
8 en la sepultura—kung ako'y mahulog.[7]

Inhuman pain—intense suffering,
My faithful heart suffers, scorned,
My tender love—that you have abused,
Destroys my soul with rigorous force.
Farewell ungrateful one—farewell beloved!
Your disdain kills me—my heart is crushed.
Remember me—even with just a sigh
In the grave—when I am laid to rest.

Here, Tagalog (which in my English translation appears just after the dash) does not so much translate the Castilian, if by that we mean substituting for its terms. Rather, the former completes and comple-ments the latter. The Castilian line "inhumano dolor," inhuman pain, speaks of an existential, qualitative suffering, while the Tagalog "hirap na matindi" refers to a constant and persistent pain, indicating quantity (1). "Adios ingrata," good-bye ungrateful one, does not translate into "paalam irog," farewell beloved (5). Rather each serves as the ironic counterpoint to the other. Similarly, the phrase "mis tiernos amores," my tender affections, is continued, not translated by the Tagalog, "na iyong inaapi," which you are abusing (3), while "recuerdame," remem-ber me, is extended rather than replaced by "kahit isang himutok," even with one sigh (7). In the first stanza, Balagtas even rhymes Castilian with Tagalog lines so that their sounds begin to blur into one another. There is a sense then that Balagtas transforms the relationship between the two languages. He brings them in touch but does not cast them into a hierarchy. Unlike Spanish friars and native ladinos before him, Balagtas does not subordinate one language to the other but juxtaposes them, allowing them to give and take meaning and rhyme from one another.

In the example above, Tagalog is not reduced to Castilian. Rather one serves to gloss the other in the sense of explicating but also misleading each other's referents. One hears in Castilian a Tagalog signifier and vice versa, such as "adios"/"paalam," "ingrata"/"irog," and "dolor"/"hirap." One complicates the other, amplifying their referents. Expanding each other's range of signifying associations, they come into a supplementary rather than hierarchical relationship. How is this possible?

The flattening of linguistic hierarchy in part has to do with the ab-sence of a third language that would serve as a common point of refer-ence for substitution and equivalence. Neither Latin nor God's Word is invoked as the basis for drawing the two languages together. They are linked, but without the mediation of a third language. In addition, the poem, unlike prayers, does not have a specific addressee. The author writes to a beloved, an "I" to a "you." But the latter remains anonymous. It could well be any "you" who happens by, accidentally hearing the poem and feeling herself called by it. Such is possible because it is not clear who the author had in mind. Conversely, it is not certain that the "you" the poem addresses will hear him; or that anyone for that matter will. He writes but does so with no assurance of being heard or, equally significant, getting a response.

By contrast, the writings of Spanish missionaries and their ladino converts were addressed ultimately to God and His divine intercessors, including the Virgin Mary and the saints. Thus did they have a definitive locus of address. Their words were meant to be heard by a transcendent authority to whom all messages were sent and from whom a response of some sort was guaranteed to arrive at some point in time. For example, a popular Pasyon from 1814 depicts Mary, the model of all converts, speaking to God the Father. She asks Him to spare Jesus from His suffering. Hearing her, the Father responds "immediately":

> Marami pa't madlang bagay
> ang sa Virgeng caraingan
> agad siyang pinaquingan,
> at sinagot capagcouan,
> nang Dios sa calangitan.
> Narinig co nang magaling
> María ang iyong daing
> di co nangyaring tangapin
> na icao,i, acquing sagutin
> ang Anac mo,i, timauain.[8]

> There were many other things
> that the Virgin pleaded for
> and immediately she was heard,
> and in no time was answered
> by God in heaven.
> I heard clearly
> Your plaint, María
> but I cannot accede
> and grant your wish
> that your Son be freed.

We see in this as well as in other Christian literature the fantasy of direct communication between God and those who pray to Him. Mary asks and she is assured of a hearing right away. She and God communicate in the same language, which in this colonial context is, of course, the vernacular. Thanks to the vernacular, everyone both inside the Pasyon text and outside reciting and listening to it can hope to speak up, be heard, and receive a response from above. In the Pasyon and other vernacular prayers, Tagalog (or any other local language for that matter) gains a certain capacity. Used as a lingua franca between God and converts, the vernacular would seem to share in the power of Castilian and Latin. It becomes capable of shaping one's thoughts and transmitting these across great distances toward one's intended addressee. Its power is such that it can compel God to respond. Christian discourse thus invests any and all vernaculars with a power they did not originally have: that of reaching across the gulf that separates humans and God, life and the afterlife, in addition to delivering a response from Him. As a telecommunicative technology, the Pasyon in the vernacular brings distances up close, converting what is beyond language into an authoritative voice speaking in the local idiom.

As we saw earlier, the comedia highlights the telecommunicative quality of the vernacular. But rather than address God (which would necessitate going through formulaic language and ritual forms presided by clerical authorities), the characters in a comedia turn to address one another. In addition, they also reach others who understand the language and in reaching them compel their attention. The difference is that the others who gather round the comedia remain anonymous to the playwright and actors, who do not have the audience's particular identities in mind when they write and perform the play. Neither do they seek to convert those identities into a single universal identity. In this sense, the comedia addresses a third party, but one that remains unknown. By being unknown and anonymous, this third party constitutes itself as an audience whose position, as we saw earlier, was still formative and far from being fully consolidated in the nineteenth century.

Herein lies a crucial difference between vernacular prayers and vernacular plays. It has to do with the third party that registers the transmission of messages. In the Pasyon, God receives all appeals and sends back responses. His Word recognizes and redeems all others, giving them value and determining their meaning. In this sense, the incarnation of God's Word in the person of Christ places all other words, along with their speakers, under Him. In exchange for being heard by the Father, one must accept the authority of His response. Hence Mary, despite her initial reluctance, falls silent and accepts God's decision that her son go through the suffering and death that have been laid out for him:

> Nang matanto at mabatid
> nang Inang Virgeng may hapis
> na yao,i, loob ng Langit,
> munti mai,i, hindi umimic
> nag bata nga,t, nagtiis.
> Mahapdi mang ualang hanga
> mapait man at mapacla
> gayang hirap ay binata
> nang PoongVirgeng María,
> pagsunod sa Dios Ama.[9]

> When the grieving Virgin
> heard and understood
> that this was the will of Heaven
> not a word she uttered
> in silence she bore her pain.
> Though the pain was deep and without end
> bitter and raw,
> that suffering was endured
> by the blessed Virgin Mary
> in obedience to God the Father.

There is then a price for direct communication with the Father: submission to His will. It is a submission that takes a specific form. Again: His Word, as human as it is divine, rules over all others. He has both the first and the last word. In the Pasyon, the vernacular gains in telecommunicative reach at the same time that it is conscripted to reproduce a linguistic hierarchy.

In the vernacular plays and poetry of Balagtas, by contrast, the identity of the third party remains unspecified. It is no one and anyone at all who happens to hear what is said between a first and a second person. The audience attends distractedly to the flow of language and so cannot be counted on to give a response. Indeed, insofar as the play or poem can be heard by everyone in general, and thus no one in particular, there cannot be any guarantee that any response will be forthcoming at all. Balagtas's poetry shares this much then with the comedia (and perhaps with all nonritual literature): by necessity, both take on a risk, dwelling in the radical uncertainty of what sort of response, if any, they might get to the calls that they make. They take on this risk because they assume—in the sense of presupposing, forbearing, and suffering—the anonymity of those who might hear and read their words.

If we can speak of vernacular plays as popular, it is perhaps because they leave open rather than foreclose the location and identity of their addressee and so differ decisively from Christian-colonial discourse. They leave the audience free from any prior determination outside of the vernacular. The audience, when it forms, acts as a contingent and shifting presence responding to the call of the vernacular now transformed into a kind of second language galvanizing their interests. In the position of a third person, they attend to the play in a state of distraction, picking and choosing sections to remember and recite. By quoting sections of the play, they repeat the gesture of the writers and actors who themselves quote from other plays. They thus extend the life of the vernacular beyond any particular literary performance. In this sense, we can think of audiences as those who give to vernacular literature a kind of afterlife. They, too, redeem what was written and said, but do so in language. That is, they do so in the materiality of speech and writing that dwells in the world of mortals rather than in a divine sphere. Additionally, reciting lines from a poem or a play converts audiences, haphazardly to be sure, into authors themselves of texts that originated not from them but from someone and somewhere else. Not quite a nation, neither are audiences simply Christian-colonial subjects subservient to the language of recognition emanating from those above. With vernacular literature, they find themselves called occasionally to step into a space left vacant, a space where there is always a vacancy: that of the position of the third person. Neither an "I" nor a "you," it is an "it" momentarily capable of granting recognition to what appears and resounds before it. These ways of writing and speaking, of hearing and responding, predicated on risk and the absence of guarantees in a time and at a place where notions of authorship and audiences are in flux and have yet to be institutionalized form the context for my reading of Balagtas's epic poem, *Florante at Laura*.

Biographers of Balagtas believe that *Florante at Laura*, which went through many editions during and after its author's lifetime, was first published in 1838.[10] I have yet, however, to come across a record of its performances while Balagtas was still alive. My discussion of the poem will thus primarily treat the written text while keeping in mind the fact that it was meant to be recited and acted out.[11] Made up of 399 dodecasyllabic quatrains, the poem is set somewhere in the Greek Empire. It tells the tale of Florante, prince of Albania, who as the play opens has been left to die in a forest by the evil Adolfo, his rival for the hand of Laura, daughter of King Linceo. Tied to a tree, Florante laments his fate, calling out to Laura, then to the heavens, and finally to anyone else who will hear him. He speaks of his suffering and asks for pity that he may be saved from captivity and returned to Albania to reclaim his kingdom and Laura. By chance, his call reaches the Moorish warrior Aladdin, who has been wandering in the forest after being exiled by his father, the Sultan Ali-Adab of Persia who seeks to wed his son's beloved, Flerida. Aladdin responds to Florante and saves the Christian prince from being devoured by a pack of advancing lions. Formerly enemies, the two become fast friends.

Florante tells Aladdin his life story: his carefree childhood (*laqui sa layaw*) full of parental indulgence, followed by a period of separation when he is sent off to Athens to study. There, he excels in school but also earns the enmity of his fellow Albanian, Adolfo. Jealous of Florante's success, the latter tries to stab him during a school performance of what would have been a revised version of *Oedipus at Colonus* (where Adolfo plays the role of Polynice to Florante's imaginary Eteocles). Adolfo is promptly expelled for his attempt at killing Florante and is sent back to Albania.

One day, Florante receives news of his mother's death. Distraught, he goes home to his father, Duke Briseo, and while grieving he meets Laura, daughter of the king. The two fall in love as Florante finds in Laura a focus for transferring the affection he had felt for his mother. Meanwhile, Adolfo plots to ruin Florante and carry off Laura. Adolfo lays a trap for Florante, who is off doing battle against the Persian Moors. When Florante returns home, Albania is in chaos. Adolfo has laid siege to the throne, inciting the populace against the king. He shows no mercy, beheading both the king and his trusted advisor, Florante's father, Briseo, then seeks to have his way with Laura. He imprisons Florante and leaves him to die in the forest until Aladdin finds him.

Moved by Florante's tale, Aladdin shares the tale of his own misfortune. His father, the sultan, covets his own son's fiancée, Flerida, and has tried to have Aladdin executed. Flerida pleads for mercy, and Aladdin instead is sent into exile. He curses his fate yet realizes that he could not bring himself to wreak vengeance on his father. Florante and Aladdin are interrupted by the sounds of voices coming from another part of the forest. They belong to Laura and Flerida. By sheer coincidence, the lovers are happily reunited. Flerida tells of escaping from Persia disguised as a male warrior looking for Aladdin. She stumbles instead on Laura trying to free herself from the advances of Adolfo. With a deft move, the Moorish princess shoots the villain with an arrow and rescues her Christian counterpart. In the midst of their joy, the lovers are found by Menandro, trusted friend of Florante. He has led a countercoup that has managed to oust Adolfo's forces. All of them return to Albania, where Florante and Laura take up their rightful place as king and queen. A perfunctory baptism is performed on Aladdin and Flerida, though by whom we are not told, since no clergy appear in the poem. News of Sultan Ali-Adab's death reaches Albania; now Aladdin and Flerida can return to Persia. Do they return to being Muslims too, or do they embark on the Christianization of Persia? Again, we are not told. The poem then ends abruptly, with Balagtas begging his muse to take this poem to his own lost love, "Celia" (María Asunción Rivera), to whom he has dedicated this work.

The plot of *Florante* proceeds through the triangulation of desire. Florante loves his mother but is forced by his father to give her up and go away to school, where he can learn to be a man of the world. Florante's love for Laura is challenged and blocked by Adolfo, who kills both their fathers and seeks to take their place. Aladdin's father seeks to displace his own son in order to lay claim on Flerida, Aladdin's fiancée, and it is only her resourcefulness that saves the son from the murderous designs of the father. In all cases, women by their inaccessibility compel men's attention and stimulate them to act. Men's desire for women leads to deadly confrontations between fathers and sons, and between countrymen. War, regicide, exile, and social chaos follow, triggered by the competition of two men for the same women.

The poem is in a sense about the consequences of desire out of control. Love is thus shown to have two aspects: destructive and productive. On the one hand, it leads to the violent break of filial ties. Aladdin's father loves too much, to the point of breaking the law. In pursuit of Laura, Adolfo beheads the king, his potential father-in-law, and the duke, his rival's father. He takes their place, making regicide the basis of his rule. Love run wild leads not only to gross injustice, but also to the very destruction of the basis of social relations.

On the other hand, love also has a productive aspect in the play. Such comes in the form of pity, or *aua*, and compassion, or *habag*. Former adversaries become intimate companions as they hear about one another's lives. They take on each other's suffering, holding one another in tender regard. Aladdin, the Moor, and the Christian Florante are drawn into a relationship of mutual pity after hearing about each other's misfortunes. Flerida saves Laura from Adolfo, and the two women find themselves sharing each other's fate. Love as pity can thus convert enmity into friendship. It allows for the recovery of what has been lost, for the destruction of evil, and for the restoration of a benevolent order. In the poem, compassion sublates competition and contains oedipal rage.

One of the most eminent authorities on Balagtas, Bienvenido Lumbera, has argued for an essential continuity between *Florante*'s notion of pity and that in Christian-colonial literature such as the Pasyon. In both cases, pity is a dominant mode of recognition that, Lumbera claims, simply reiterates a colonial ideology that stressed deference to those above. "Religious poetry from San José to de la Merced constantly spoke of the necessity of suffering for the Christian. . . . [*Florante*] gave suffering a secular coloring, but the end result was the same—pain brought about perfection."[12] To suffer is to be in a position to solicit pity from above. To be pitied, in turn, is to receive recognition as a subject within the ambit of divine or secular authority. It is to become the recipient of gifts, spiritual and worldly, with which to ease if not eliminate one's pain. Suffering attracts pity and provides an occasion for those in power to display their generosity. Once pitied, one who suffers becomes empowered, gaining a connection to a higher source capable of great compassion.

It is difficult to argue with this analysis that sees an ideological complicity between *Florante* and Christian-colonial discourse. However, we can see from the sketch of the poem's plot above how the agencies of recognition and sources of pity in *Florante* tend to come horizontally from the enemy or the beloved, rather than vertically from God, the saints, the king, or the father. *Florante* unquestionably bears a resemblance to the other genres of colonial literature. It is especially indebted to the comedia and the Pasyon. Still, the nature of this resemblance and the trajectory of this indebtedness are worth asking about, especially in view of translation and the risks of communication we have been pursuing.

We can begin by looking at the full title of the poem as it appears in the 1861 edition: *Pinagdaanang Buhay ni Florante at Laura sa Cahariang Albania. Quinuha sa madlang cuadro Historico o pinturang nagsasabi sa manga nangyayari nang unang panahon sa Imperio nang Grecia at tinula nang isang matouain sa versong tagalog*, or *The Coming to Pass of the Life of Florante and Laura in the Kingdom of Albania. Taken from diverse historical and painterly scenes that tell of what happened in the olden days in the Greek Empire and rendered into verse by one who is fond of Tagalog verses*. Although the poem, like other comedias, is not based on a particular European metrical romance, it nevertheless presents itself as a translation of sorts. It is a poem "taken from diverse historical and painterly scenes." The poem proclaims itself to have a multitude (*madla*, diverse, various, numerous) of sources other than the author. Indeed, Balagtas's name does not even appear on the title page; his initials, worked into one of the verses in the dedication, are the only traces of his name. The poem in this sense is left unsigned if we think of the signature as the mark an author leaves behind to guarantee the originality of his or her work. Signatures stand for the author in his or her absence. Unsigned, Balagtas's poem seems to have no definitive origin. Rather, it is said to have been "taken" (*quinuha*) from different historical scenes or pictures —*cuadro*, as we saw earlier, is Castilian for both. The poem does not purport to be a telling of actual events but a retelling of earlier tellings. The unnamed author passes on what he has not seen but only heard or read from different sources about a somewhere else—here, the Greek Empire.

The title thus presents the poem to have had an origin beyond that of the author and readers of Tagalog. The author's role consists of rendering these foreign sources into verse. Again, the author appears anonymously as part of the poem, right in its title (*ysang matouain sa versong Tagalog*, one fond of Tagalog verses), rather than separate from it (and by inference, outside of the text as its controlling agent). By taking on the task of setting the story in verse, the author comes across as a figure who is both inside and outside of his writing. He appropriates the story from other, foreign sources and translates it into the vernacular in order to be transmitted by way of print and presumably public performances.

We thus begin to get a sense of how authorship and translation are inseparable in the poem. One who writes always does so between or among different languages and historical "frames" (yet another meaning of *cuadro*). Note, as a further example, how Balagtas uses the Tagalog and Castilian words for verse, *tula* and *verso* respectively, in the same phrase to indicate his identity (*tinula nang isang matouain sa versong tagalog*). As in his ladino poems, Castilian and Tagalog supplement and amplify one another, adding to the poem's reach. The author comes across as a figure suspended between languages, capable of drawing upon both, just as he is suspended between the inside and outside of the text. He translates into Tagalog, taking historical scenes from foreign sources, while at the same time trafficking in untranslated bits of Castilian. The title of *Florante* features Castilian words lodged either in their original form (*cuadro historico, imperio, grecia*, etc.) or inflected by Tagalog affixes but still recognizably Castilian (such as *versong*). Like the comedia, *Florante* takes on the non-Tagalog as an essential element of Tagalog writing. It responds to the call from the outside; in that responding, it becomes a vernacular poem. Put another way, the vernacular specificity of *Florante at Laura* is founded on what is foreign to it yet resides within its textual body. Balagtas is explicit on this point. His authorship of the text, as with his authority over Tagalog and Castilian, is enmeshed in what we have been calling the colonial uncanny, whereby the familiar emerges in the process of hosting the foreign, while both become other than what they may have been originally.

In one sense, Balagtas can be said to be reiterating the Spanish missionary practice of translation based on a notion of untranslatability. He acknowledges that the origins of his poem lie elsewhere. He then comes across like the missionary as a medium for conjuring that elsewhere, bringing it closer in the language of his readers. It is, of course, a language that has itself been changed by virtue of its prosodic structure and the presence of Castilian words. Converting the vernacular, the poet acts as a medium in a way analogous to the Spanish priest-translator.

But in another sense, Balagtas differs from the missionaries. He does not translate stories into Tagalog verse as a gesture of faith in the ever-approaching presence of a Divine Father who had always already heard and responded to all messages at all times. Like the comedia playwrights, his task is underwritten by the uncertainty of its reach. The locus of his address, like the social and linguistic basis of his authority, is persistently open-ended. He does not ask the saints or the Virgin Mary to intercede on his behalf and witness the poem as an offering to the Father. Instead, he invokes fictitious, imagined readers to receive his words. One such reader is "Celia," the pseudonym he gives to a lost lover, María Asunción Rivera, to whom he dedicates the poem. The dedication in part reads:

> Cong pagsaulang con basahin sa isip
> ang nangagcaraang arao ng pag-ibig,
> may mahahagilap cayang natititic
> liban na cay Celiang namugad sa dibdib. (st. 1)
>
> . . . .
>
> Sa larauang guhit ng sa sintang pincel
> cusang ilinimbag sa puso,t, panimdim,
> nag-iisang sanlang naiwan sa aquin,
> at di mananacao magpahangang libing. (st. 6)
>
> . . . .
>
> Parang naririnig ang lagui mong uica
> "Tatlong arao na di nagtatanao tama"
> at sinagot co ng sabing may toua
> "Sa isa cataua,i, marami ang handa. (st. 12)

> When returning to read the memory
> of days of love gone by,
> are there any other letters to be found
> except those of Celia nesting in the heart?
>
> . . . .
>
> Your picture drawn by love's paintbrush
> imprinted on the heart and mind,
> the only heirloom left to me
> that won't be stolen till death comes.
>
> . . . .
>
> It is as if your words are always heard
> "Three days and we've not seen each other,"
> To which I respond with knowing gladness
> "For one guest, much will be served."

The poet addresses not so much "Celia" herself but his memory of her. That memory is both "drawn" (*pincel*) and "imprinted" (*ilinimbag*) on his mind, and like an heirloom, it will never be taken until his death. She comes across as an image, the "visible inclusion of the alien (because absent) in the sight of the familiar."[13] Rendered into an image, the woman herself is out of reach. The poet imagines hearing her voice only to realize that she is no longer in his midst. He cries out to no one in particular, "Nasaan si Celiang ligaya ng dibdib? / ang suyuan nami,i, baquit di lumauig?" ("Where are you Celia, joy of my heart? / our days of love, why did they end?" st. 14). The poem calls up her memory. But her memory, set as a series of images, simply confirms her absence, which the author will take to his grave. Memory only intensifies the sense of loss. It seems no one is available to answer for "Celia" and respond to the poet's lament. He concludes his dedication with a plea: "Cong binabasa mo,i, isa nang himutoc /ay alalahanin yaring nag hahandog," ("If you read this, with one sigh / remember the one who offers this to you," st. 19). The poet hopes that should she read it, "Celia" might let out a sigh and so signal her memory of him. He hopes his words will reach their destination and produce a particular effect. But given the recurring absence of "Celia," he cannot be certain. The author addresses a reader whose response he cannot count on, a "you" whose location he can only imagine but cannot determine.

Similarly, Balagtas invokes an anonymous readership in his prefatory remarks to the poem, titled *Sa Babasa Nito*, "To Those Who Will Read This." As in the dedication, the poet turns to address us, the readers, directly. We, like most readers in the past and yet to come, are unknown to the author. We come from the future and so remain essentially foreign to his text. Yet he calls out to us, not knowing how we will respond, much less whether we will even heed his appeal. He begins by assuming a tone of deference: "Salamat sa iyo, o nanasang irog, / cong halagahan mo itong aquing pagod" ("Thanks to you, oh beloved reader / should you come to value what I have labored on," st. 1). He apologizes if the poem, like unripe fruit (*hilaw*), may not look as attractive outside, but assures us that what lies inside will make for "delicious" reading (*masasarapan din ang babasa pantas*, st. 2). He bids the reader: do what you will with the poem. You need not love it, you can laugh or hate it, he says. But I ask you, whoever you are, not to alter the verses (*houag mo lamang baguhin ang verso*). When coming upon an "incomprehensible word" (*malalim na uica*), rather than avoid it, he asks us to consult the explanations he has provided below the text (st. 3–5).

Florante at Laura is the only vernacular Filipino poem that comes with footnotes. It is unusual in that sense. More important, however, is the fact that Balagtas felt compelled to furnish them at all. Such a move underlines the author's uncertainty about the nature of his readership and its possible responses. He tries to safeguard what might appear unclear in his work, defining Castilian words along with a number of Greek and Roman allusions. In both his prefatory appeal to his readers and his dedication to "Celia," Balagtas acknowledges the uncertain identity of those to whom his poem is addressed. Will his words reach anyone, much less elicit a response? What will be heard of the poem? Who, if any, will hear it, and what, if anything, will they say back in return? These questions of calling, responding, and the risks of failing to do so are opened up in the title, preface, and dedication, then haunt the rest of the poem.

Calling Long Distance

Well over half of Balagtas's poem is taken up by the lamentations of Florante. His voice dominates that of other characters and it is his story that frames those of Laura and the Moorish couple, Aladdin and Flerida. This narrative dominance, however, is counterpointed by the fact that he speaks from a position of physical helplessness. We see him tied up in the forest, weakened not only by the lack of food but by thoughts of having been betrayed by Laura. He cannot save himself but must count on someone else to do so. The protagonist here is not so much a heroic figure of great physical prowess as he is an abject figure, abandoned by all those he loves. Like Christ in the Pasyon, Florante is set apart by virtue of the great pain he undergoes. But unlike Christ, Florante suffers alone. Where the former is always accompanied by his mother and friends, seen by sympathetic strangers and watched over by God the Father, the latter is for the most part cast off. There seems to be no one who can receive his call and bear witness to his grief. Not until Aladdin accidentally wanders into the forest nearly midway through the poem do Florante's words reach someone. Held captive, he finds himself for the most part talking to himself.

I say "for the most part" because Florante's words of course do reach someone—one who is no one in particular, the anonymous reader or listener of the poem. Like the author, the reader hears Florante but cannot as yet respond. Instead, she or he is initially drawn to attend to Florante's appearance. Balagtas describes it as "pitiful" ("dito nagagapos ang cahabaghabag / isang pinagusig ng masamang palad," "here is held captive one who is so pitiful / one who has been tormented by misfortune," st. 18). He writes:

> Bagong tauong basal, na ang anyo,t, tindig
> cahit natatali ang camay paa,t, liig
> condi si Narciso,i, tunay na Adonis,
> mucha,i, sumisilang sa guitna ng saquit. (st. 9)
> Maquinis ang balat at anaqui bulac,
> pilicmata,t quilay mistulang balantoc,
> bagong sapang guinto an culay ng buhoc
> sangcap ng cataua,i, pauang magca-ayos. (st. 10)

> One in the prime of life, from his appearance and stance
> even with his hands, feet and neck tied
> if not like Narcissus, then like a true Adonis,
> his face shining through his pain.
> Smooth was his skin like silk,
> his lashes and eyebrows were arcs
> like newly minted gold was the color of his hair
> the parts of his body in perfect symmetry.

Florante's appearance is at once pitiful (*cahabaghabag*) and beautiful. Balagtas compares him to Narcissus and Adonis and details the smoothness of his skin, the golden color of his hair, and the symmetry of his body. Despite his pain, his face shines through. It is as if his captivity allows the author and reader to regard Florante's body not only as an abject entity but also as an object of aesthetic contemplation. His appearance counterpoints his experience suggested by his shining face, which, unlike his hands, feet and neck, seems to resist the effects of imprisonment. Left to perish, something of Florante nonetheless persists, asking to be noticed. His appearance is reminiscent of the images of Catholic saints based on European features popular in Philippine churches. The appearance of his face is thus legible within the grammar of a certain colonial iconography familiar to Christian Filipinos. It is a familiarity built on the visibly intractable foreignness of saintly icons. What is given to be seen in Florante's body, then, is the persistence of a certain untranslatability: an element or appearance that cannot be wholly subsumed by the experience of suffering. The endurance of the recognizably foreign, which resists assimilation into pain, comes across like a message of sorts in and through the prince's captive pose. We are shown this recalcitrant appearance, indeed an image of recalcitrance itself made over into something pitiful and beautiful.

We can see that Florante's abjection is conjugated by his beautiful appearance. In the midst of his abandonment, parts of his body speak, asking to be seen. His beauty, based on foreign models, constitutes an appeal that reaches past his imprisonment. It gives itself to be seen and, as with any gift, solicits a response. By doing so, his appearance opens up a channel for the transmission of other messages. Sure enough, the author portrays Florante raising his head as he begins to speak. He embarks on a long soliloquy, at first addressing the heavens:

Mahiganting langit, bangis mo,i, nasaan?
ngayo,y, naniniig sa pagca-gulaygulay
bago,i ang bandila ng lalong casam-an
sa Reinong Albania,i, iniuauagayuay? (st. 13)

Vengeful heavens, where is your wrath?
now you seem shaken and weak
while the banner of evil
in the Kingdom of Albania waves.

Florante calls out to the vengeful heavens, asking them to strike back at the evil that reigns in Albania. He paints a vivid picture of the world turned upside down, where the good are despised and put to death, where the dead go unmourned, where injustice rules and the bad are rewarded (st. 17). Despite his weakened position, he gathers the rhetorical force with which to send a message to the heavens. He is barely able to live, he says, but still manages to bear witness to the chain of events that led to the "pitiful" (*cahabaghabag*) conditions of his kingdom. The heavens, however, remain silent. Much to Florante's dismay, they are deaf (*bingi*) to his pleas.

Unable to reach the gods or God, he tries another line. He reaches out to Laura. He thinks of her thinking of him, each dwelling in the other's absence. Imagining Laura remembering him as he remembers her seems to lighten his suffering (st. 14–15). The thought of her sharing in his pain fills him, however briefly, with a measure of happiness (st. 30), for it means that she acknowledges his loss. She recognizes his call and with her tears returns something in kind ("ang pagluha niya cong aco,i, may hapis / naguiguing ligaya yaring madlang saquit," "Her crying over my sorrow / makes for happiness amid all this suffering," st. 30).

But the fact remains that Laura does not answer Florante and does not ratify his appeals for pity. Failing again to reach his intended address, the prince begins to hallucinate his beloved's betrayal:

> Sa sinapupunan nang Conde Adolfo
> acquing natatanto si Laurang sinta co,
> camataya,i, nahan ng dating bangis mo?
> nang dico damdamin ang hirap na ito. (st. 32)

> Resting on the chest of the Count Adolfo
> I can see Laura, my love,
> Death, where now is your former fierceness?
> [Come] that I may stop feeling this pain.

His pleas for pity left unanswered, Florante comes to think of Laura leaving him for Adolfo. Feeling utterly abandoned, he now calls on death, hoping that it will come to rescue him from his misery. In effect, he says: Death, where are you? Come and put an end to my pain.

Who is this "I" that calls out to Death? Implicit throughout Florante's lament is the copresence of two "I"s. His captive state splits him into an "I" that is helpless and close to death; and another "I" that speaks about its abject condition. This second "I" comes to encapsulate the first. It converts the misery and vulnerability of the first "I" into an appeal that can then be sent out to anyone who would listen, including Death itself. For example, it turns to address the reader, summing up the prince's pathetic state:

> Alin pa ang hirap na di na sa aquin?
> May camatayan pang di co daramdamin?
> Ulila sa ama,t, sa inang maganquin,
> walang kaibiga,t, nilimot nang giliw. (st. 63)

> What other suffering have I not owned?
> What deaths have I not gone through?
> Orphaned, with no father or mother to call my own,
> with no friends, and forgotten by my beloved.

Florante speaks as a divided "I," a self beside itself, moving between an abject body on the verge of death and a subject who represents the former, between a second "I" that sends out messages and a first "I" whom the message is about. The poem makes no attempt to suture this split. Instead, it highlights such a division. The doubling of the self into one who speaks and another who is spoken about recalls the linguistic conditions in colonial society whereby a second, foreign language recasts the first, vernacular idiom into a language other than what it was originally. Here in *Florante at Laura*, the second "I" speaks for the first and so takes on a certain authority. The second translates, as it were, the sufferings of the first into a language that carries beyond its initial point of formulation. Balagtas describes this process:

> Sucat na ang tingnan ang lugaming anyo
> nitong sa dalita,i, hindi macaquibo
> aacaing biglang umiyac ng puso
> cong uala nang luhang sa matai,i, itulo (st. 36)
> . . . .
> Halos buong gubat ay nasasabugan
> nang dinaingdaing na lubhang malumbay
> na inuulit pa at isinisigao
> sagot sa malayo niyang alingao-ngao. (st. 38)

> It was enough to see the pathetic appearance
> of one unable to move from suffering
> the heart would cry out
> until the eyes ran out of tears.
> . . . .
> Nearly all of the forest exploded
> with sobs and sighs so melancholy
> that was repeated and shouted
> by resounding echoes answering from afar.

On the one hand, we witness a body that is deadly still; on the other, we hear a voice that issues sounds of sadness, a keening sweeping across the forest. It is a sound that echoes, extended and amplified by its surroundings. In this way does the voice broadcast the fate of its speaker beyond its prostrate body. Just as Florante's appearance exceeds and so signals something beyond his abject condition, his plaintive voice issues a call that travels far beyond the point of its enunciation. Amplified by echoes, his voice takes on a telecommunicative potential, reaching the remote corners of the forest. That it does not seem to reach God or Laura or even Death does not necessarily vitiate its capacity to communicate at a distance. Asking for pity from anyone who will answer, Florante's voice (and by extension, Balagtas's writing) keeps open the possibility of a response. All it takes is for another party to hear this call and return it for the potential of Florante's voice to be realized.

Indeed, one particularly loud and frightful cry ("himutoc na casindac sindac / na umalingao-ngao sa loob ng guhabt," "a cry so startling / it resounded throughout the forest," st. 67) draws Aladdin into the scene. Surprised by the sound he hears, the Moorish warrior turns to its source. He does not yet see Florante, but Florante's voice reaches him, calling him forth and triggering in him a rush of thoughts. Hearing but not yet seeing Florante, Aladdin is reminded of his own sorrows. Like the prince, Aladdin begins to talk about his own sad state: his exile and the impossibility of taking vengeance against his own father. Tears running down his face, Aladdin repeats Florante's gesture, turning to address no one in particular.

But something else happens. By coincidence (*nagcataoun*), Aladdin's lamentations are echoed in Florante's cries: "Nagcataoun namang parang isinagot / ang buntung hininga niyaang nagagapus," ("by chance it was as if he was answered / by the sighs of he who was tied up," st. 83). It is not that Florante hears Aladdin, only that Florante continues talking about his fate without realizing that someone else is actually nearby, listening. Aladdin thus assumes the position of the anonymous audience. We see him drawn to Florante's words as he begins to sympathize with his position. Aladdin, too, grows sad, allowing the sadness he hears to overtake him. Receiving the prince's words, the exiled warrior feels his own heart bursting with pity ("naauang morong naquiquinyig / sa habag ay halos nagputoc ang dibdib," "the pitying Moor listening / his heart almost bursting with compassion," st. 98). Identifying with Florante's plight, Aladdin is contaminated by his sorrow and continues to tell of his own.

In Aladdin, Balagtas puts forth his ideal interlocutor. He or she is someone who suddenly comes into contact with a prior transmission from an unseen presence. The audience here is the unexpected recipient of words. Surprised, he or she is led to respond.[14] Being surprised and responding are parts of a single process of being held up, in all senses of that term, by the sudden soundings of a voice. Responding, one is taken out of oneself and drawn to seek the source of what one hears. In tracing the path opened up by the voice, Aladdin is led to Florante. As he approaches the spot where Florante is held, he sees two ferocious (*mabangis*) lions approaching him. But such is the power of Florante's cries that not only do they draw the Moor, an enemy, into compassionate identification, they also momentarily detain the lions from killing him. Seeing Florante's pitiful appearance and hearing his pathetic pleas, they, too, are filled with pity ("nanga-aua mandi,t, maualan ng bangis / . . . nanga-catingala,t, parang naquinyig / sa di lumilicat na tingis-tangis," "[they] also felt pity and lost their fierceness / . . . looking up as if listening / to the never ceasing cries," st. 109). Seeing the lions approach Florante, Aladdin moves in to chase them away. He unties the prince and takes care of him. At first, Florante is surprised to see Aladdin, thinking Aladdin would kill him. But he is soon reassured by his rescuer's words. Time passes as Aladdin nurses (*aruga*) Florante like a mother tending to a child. Eventually, they are heard by Laura and Flerida, then rescued and returned to Albania by Florante's friend, Menandro.

Surprised by the sound of a voice he did not expect, Aladdin allows himself to be carried away to its source. Responding to a call, he takes responsibility for the other's pitiful state. Florante's cries constitute a demand for pity. Heeding this demand, one who receives this call moves toward its source, drawn to identify with its condition. One begins, that is, to imagine oneself in the other's place, taking on its desire and sharing in its burden. For Aladdin to identify with Florante's plight means that he steps out of a prior identity and takes on another. This second identity, however, does not displace the first so much as it keeps it in reserve. It is not an identity that forms from the violent negation of what it confronts as in the Hegelian parable about the master and slave. Rather, this second identity—one that is more than "Aladdin the Moorish warrior" but not quite "Florante, the Christian prince"—is precipitated by language. Despite their differences, Aladdin and Florante have Tagalog in common. The vernacular, embedded with Castilian terms and classical allusions, brings the two together, turning enemies into friends. In Balagtas, as with other comedia writers, we see how the vernacular allows for Persians, and Albanians from some Greek Empire dating back to a vaguely medieval era to appear simultaneously on a Tagalog stage. Florante's cries in Tagalog move Aladdin to a state of pity signaled by the copious flow of tears. Weeping itself, so plentiful in colonial and postcolonial literature, is a kind of protovernacular: a shared idiom as much as it is the proof of reciprocal caring. It is thus the privileged sign of and for pity. The sight of tears flowing in response to other tears is the sign that a common language of recognition based on compassionate identification is already at work.

To pity is to join the other in its sorrow, as in mourning or *damayan*.[15] It is to grant recognition to the other's pain and partake in its grief. That granting is a response to a prior call. And that call, in turn, issues from the translation of a first "I" into a second, alongside the transformation of an abject condition into a narrative of loss and a demand for pity. In reaching someone he did not expect, Florante, or more precisely, the Florante that translates and thereby makes its other captive self heard—gains recognition in the form of compassion (*habag*). Making himself available to the arrival of someone he did not and could not have counted on, Florante begins to regain his freedom.

Who exactly recognizes the prince and comes to his rescue? Just as the Florante that is heard is a second "I" distinct from its first, so the Aladdin that hears and arrives to save Florante is not selfsame. Rather, the Aladdin that comes is one who, in exile, is stunned by the sound and moved by the appearance of a foreign presence speaking in the vernacular. Taking on the agency of recognition, the Moor is himself transformed. Formerly an enemy, he becomes a friend of Florante. More than a friend, he even takes on the role of a mother caring for her child. For what Aladdin is drawn to recognize—what he feels compelled to receive and partake in—is not only Florante's suffering. Just as significant, Aladdin, like Balagtas and the readers of the poem, identifies with Florante's ability to communicate. Such entails, as we have seen, the translation of experience into expression, whereby an abject state is converted into an appeal for pity that can traverse great distances. Identifying with Aladdin's identification with Florante's telecommunicative capacity, the author himself periodically enters into the text. Balagtas, for example, finds the scene of Florante's helplessness at the approach of the lions so affecting that he says he is unable to continue with his narrative:

> Di co na masabi,t, luha co,i, nanatac,
> na-uumid yaring dilang nangungusap,
> puso co,i, nanglalambot sa malaquing habag
> sa ca-aua-auang quinucab ng hirap. (st. 111)

Sinong di mahapis na may caramdaman
sa lagay ng gapus na calumbay-lumbay. (st. 112)

I could no longer speak, my own tears fall,
my tongue that speaks has grown still
my heart melted by enormous compassion
for the pitiful one harbored by grief.
Who would not feel sorrow
at the sight of such a melancholy captive?

Located outside the text as an omniscient narrator, Balagtas in this and other highly charged occasions finds himself addressing readers from within the text. We see him seeing Florante as Aladdin does and similarly being moved. Florante's call pulls in not only Aladdin but also Balagtas. Both come from outside the space of Florante's captivity and thanks to the power of his call are drawn inside to identify with him. That is, they move from being passive listeners to being active witnesses, interceding on Florante's behalf. Just as Aladdin saves Florante from death, so Balagtas turns to the reader and speaks for the prince. It is as if Balagtas says to us: "How can you, whoever you are, not pity him? How can you not be moved to respond to his pleas?"

From occupying the position of a third person outside the text, Balagtas assumes in this and similar instances a position analogous to Aladdin: that of a second person, a "you" that attends to the demands of Florante. As a second person, Balagtas registers the prince's words, assuming the latter's loss but also confirming his ability to translate and transmit messages. Such messages seek to open the way for the arrival of someone unknown and unexpected—Aladdin or Flerida, or Laura, or even Balagtas himself, for example—and anyone else who might find him- or herself addressed. This anyone else, held up by Florante's call initially takes the position of an anonymous audience, a third person outside the text, but who, if he or she were sufficiently receptive, could just as easily slide into the position of a second, quoting the poem and taking up Florante's call. The poem thus formulates the position of the third person as one that is always on the way to being filled, then vacated, only to be filled again and so on. If the popularity of the poem is any indication, the he or she who reads and listens finds itself like Balagtas, Aladdin, or even the lions, sporadically converted into the position of a you, obligated to recognize the "I" that speaks. It is an "I," furthermore, that is already a function of translation and is therefore invested with a certain telecommunicative power. Moving inside and outside the text, the reader, like the author, takes on the responsibility of mourning Florante's loss. But they also assume the promise of the poem: that of a language reaching out and going beyond the time and place of its enunciation to reach not God, the saints, or the colonial state and church. Rather, it seeks to reach those who hear in the vernacular the possibility of an afterlife among fellow mortals. In Balagtas's own time, this afterlife made conceivable by a new kind of vernacular literature outside of clerical control had as yet no singular name. With the emergence of nationalism, it came to be called the patria, the nation steeped in the history of deaths recalled rather than eternal life deferred.

We can think then of *Ang Pinagdaananang Buhay ni Florante at Laura* —the coming to pass or history of Florante and Laura (*pinagdaanan* from the root word *daan*, meaning a road, a path or an opening)—as part of a technic for altering and enlarging the imagination of colonial subjects. Like other comedias, Balagtas's work instigates as much as it dramatizes the possibilities of translation that dwell in the midst of untranslated words. It mobilizes the vernacular to conjure the foreign and brings it to lodge in the familiar. In the comedia, the foreign lives on, surviving in and through the hospitality furnished by the vernacular. And in *Florante at Laura*, the vernacular harbors the foreign understood not only as the fetish of Castilian, but also as the promise of that which is always yet to come, of others who are always yet to hear, and in hearing, respond.

Before the comedia, the technology for conjuring the colonial uncanny was monopolized and regulated by the Spanish clergy. But as we have seen, a different interest informed vernacular plays, which represent neither the church nor the state. It was an interest in seeing translation freed, even if only momentarily and provisionally, from the imperatives of Christian conversion. Thus do vernacular plays defer to a colonial order at the same time that they reopen its linguistic foundation. They raise, for example, the risks inherent in every communicative act. Messages may not reach their intended destination and translation might fail. But such risks raise other possibilities as well—for example, that of an anonymous audience, forming in response to what they hear and see, endowing plays and poems with a secular afterlife, or the possibility of shifting identifications that allow one to assume a position in common with others whom one would not have previously known.

Assuming the position of a third *and* second person, moving between the two while identifying with a first that is already on its way to being a second, and so forth: all of these possibilities were cultivated by an emergent literature in the vernacular which, while requiring access to a second language, did not depend on the mediation of an overarching, transcendent Word.

Given these possibilities, it is arguable that vernacular literature by the nineteenth century would help pave the way for the emergence of a nationalist imagination. This was because vernacular literature was already a kind of technology. Thanks to the history of colonial translation and the shared belief in the power of Castilian, vernacular literary genres such as the comedia were configured as technical ensembles capable of tapping into and containing the colonial uncanny. As such, the vernacular could become like Castilian. That is, it could take on the telecommunicative agency usually associated with technologies of print, telegraphy, and photography, and with forms of writing such as the newspapers and novels. In this regard, it is not surprising that pre- and postrevolutionary nationalists as well as Filipino nationalist scholars in the 1960s and 1970s were drawn to comment on the comedia in general and *Florante at Laura* in particular, for they saw in these plays the power to call forth a mass response and stir popular interests. Before the introduction of cinema, electoral politics, and other mass entertainment, the comedia was the only genre other than Christianity that could gather people from different social groups. Drawing them from their various localities, vernacular plays placed audiences in proximity with what otherwise remained ineluctably alien. Gathered around performances, crowds came to possess something in common outside of their everyday lives. Their anonymity posited by the uncertain address of vernacular plays periodically became the basis for a new kind of public intimacy. Nationalists acknowledged the comedia's legacy while seeking to take its communicative power for themselves. In Balagtas, they found an ancestor of sorts, one whom they claimed succeeded in taking the power of the comedia for himself and deeding it to a nation whose existence he could not in his own lifetime even begin to imagine.

In time, ilustrado nationalists would seek to consolidate and define the audiences called forth by the comedias. They would reconceptualize them, first as "the people," mobilizing some to become revolutionary fighters in 1896; then, in the wake of revolutionary defeat and recolonization by the United States, as clients and citizens subject to the limits and recognition of laws they themselves had no hand in crafting or administering. The comedia genre would wane, living on as a quaint bit of "folk culture," while *Florante at Laura* would become, like the *Noli* and the *Fili*, required reading in postcolonial classrooms. Thus were all of them consigned to mass amnesia. They would become the traces of possibilities taken up, then abandoned—but always ready to be found again.

7

"FREEDOM = DEATH"
Conjurings, Secrecy, Revolution

The Anxieties of Translation

Nearly a century after Balagtas wrote *Florante at Laura* and fifty years after the publication of Rizal's *Noli me tangere*, Philippine Commonwealth President, Manuel L. Quezon gave a radio address from Malacañang, the presidential palace, on December 31, 1937. Speaking from what had been the residence of the Spanish and later American governor generals, he spoke of the need to develop a national language (*wikang pambansa*) in anticipation of the political independence promised by the United States. Tagalog, he declared, would furnish the basis of this common language of the future. Newspapers reported his speech and the *Tribune* provided an English translation of the Tagalog original (though not the Tagalog text itself). Ironically, Quezon's speech in translation lamented the need for translation. The president referred to the embarrassment he felt when faced with the necessity of speaking through an interpreter, thanks to the persistence of different vernaculars in the country. He continues:

> Today there is not one language that is spoken and understood by all Filipinos, or even by a majority of them, which simply proves that while the teaching of a foreign language may be imposed upon a people, it can never replace the native tongue as a medium of national expression among the common masses. This is because, as Rizal asserted, the national thought takes root in a common language that develops and grows with the progress of the nation. We may borrow for a time the language of others, but we cannot truly possess a national language except through adoption, development, and use of our own.
>
> We must as soon as possible be able to deal with one another directly using the same language. We need its power more completely to weld us into one strong nation. It will give inspiration and

warmth to our popular movements and will accord to our nationality a new meaning to which we have never learned to give full and adequate expression. As president of the Philippines, many times I felt the humiliation of having to address the people through an interpreter in those provinces of the islands where Ilocano, Pampango, Visaya or Bicol is the language used.[1]

With the defeat of the revolution of 1896–1902 and in the midst of American colonial rule, Quezon recalls Rizal's dilemma: how to arrive at a lingua franca capable, like the radio or the telegraph, of communicating at a distance across linguistic barriers. For rather than speak directly and without delay to the people, he must rely on someone else to relay his words. On the verge of Philippine independence, President Quezon was still dependent on translators to reach his own people. He thus felt the weight of language, or more precisely the history of a linguistic hierarchy deeded to the commonwealth by over three centuries of colonial rule. The failure to overcome this hierarchy meant that no common language existed that could subsume all other languages in the country. This lack was a source of shame for ilustrado leaders like Quezon. He imagines himself being seen by those he addresses as someone incapable of understanding or being understood except through the mediation of an anonymous third person, the interpreter. Unable to speak on his own, he requires a linguistic double of sorts to make himself heard. His condition, like those of other elite leaders, suggested that the nation-state could not as yet sublate local differences. Symptomatically, the leader of the country could not directly reach across to those he led. This lack required supplementation in the form of translation that, when performed in public, served only to highlight the weakness of those on top, dependent as they were on the intercession of an other.

In Quezon's case, the sense of humiliation did not come, as in Rizal's novels or in Luna's travel accounts, from speaking Castilian and being misrecognized as a "savage" or a filibustero by Spaniards. Rather, it came from speaking Tagalog, his native language, only to be taken as incomprehensible by those non-Tagalogs below him. Expecting to command his audiences' attention, Quezon, we can imagine, is filled with anxiety, unable to control the transmission of his message and incapable of consolidating his place in his listeners' social lives. Instead, he comes across as a kind of familiar foreigner, with his Spanish mestizo appearance, uttering unintelligible words, in need of a translator.[2] Dependent on the United States for political survival, Quezon found himself just as captive to the hearing of the masses for political legitimacy.[3] But while English enabled him to speak directly with American officials in the colony and in the United States, Tagalog seemed insufficient to link him with the great numbers of non-Tagalog peoples in the nation.

To address this dilemma, Quezon established the Institute of National Language (INL) with the task of developing the wikang pambansa, based, as the phrase indicates, on Tagalog. As conceived by the INL, the Tagalog vocabulary would be transformed and augmented by words from other vernaculars such as Cebuano, Ilocano, and Hiligaynon. More words would come from recuperating lexical items long out of use from Tagalog texts written in earlier centuries.[4] What would emerge, it was hoped, was a new kind of Tagalog, at once more "indigenous" and full of non-Tagalog words no longer tethered to a specific region. It would be a Tagalog that could be pried loose and transported to all parts of the archipelago by means of new dictionaries and a standardized grammar (balarila), literary works, and critical essays, which were to be disseminated and taught regularly in public and private schools. The commonwealth's dream of a common language then saw Tagalog taking on a telecommunicative power. Alienable from its original users, it would reach nonnative speakers who would recognize in the language aspects of their own. As a common language, Tagalog would no longer belong only to Tagalogs. What was native to one group could be reinvented—"adopted and developed"—into a national and, retrospectively, "natural" language for others in the country.

This national language that was yet to come, this Tagalog as wikang pambansa that would arrive from the future, was invested with the "power . . . to weld us into one strong nation." Yet it would also continue to exist in view of two other official languages: Castilian and English. Quezon continues:

The fact that we are going to have a national language does not mean that we are to abandon in our schools the study and use of the Spanish language and much less English which, under the Constitution, is the basis of primary instruction. Spanish will preserve for us our Latin culture and will be our point of contact with our former metropolis as well as Latin America. English, the great language of democracy, will bind us forever to the people of the United States and place within our reach the wealth of knowledge treasured in this language.

For Quezon then, refashioning Tagalog into another language that would serve as common currency among all Filipinos meant two things. It not only entailed subsuming existing linguistic differences into an overarching lingua franca; it also meant maintaining Castilian and English as languages of the state and public education. The latter two would continue to be languages with which to communicate with the world outside the nation for the future. While Tagalog as wikang pambansa would seek to put an end to the need for translation among Filipinos, as official languages Castilian and English would ensure the continuing need for interpreters when addressing state authorities and those beyond. In this regard, it is worth noting that Castilian served as the official language of the Philippine legislature and courts until 1941. With the declaration of independence in 1946, English became the language of the state and the courts, a situation that continues to this day. Filipinos could address the state only in a second language, not in their first. Quezon thus ratified the endurance of a linguistic split between the nation—understood as the people—and the state. Such had a mixed effect.

On the one hand, Quezon's conception of a national language that was yet to come imagined the progressive homogenization of linguistic differences. As with the radio, Filipino leaders would then be able to communicate directly with the people, whoever they were and wherever they might be. And they would do so from great distances, including from the safety and security of their official residence. Thanks to the hoped-for coming of a common language, Quezon and other nationalist elites would in the future no longer need to worry about feeling humiliated, risking misunderstanding and doubts about their authority to rule the nation. Or so it was thought.

On the other hand, the corollary to this notion of an emergent national language was that it would not be permitted to displace the political power of Castilian and English. Rather, the place of these colonial languages would be safeguarded to the point of being mandated by the laws of the land. The coming national language would shelter the colonial languages and so tame them for official use, turning their intractable foreignness into valuable resources. Both Castilian and English would become instruments for making connections: to the past, to Latin culture, and to Latin America in the case of Castilian; to democracy, the United States, and knowledge in the case of English. Through a renovated Tagalog, these languages would become part of a vernacular continuum at the disposal of state institutions. Herein lies the promise of the wikang pambansa: by sublating the vernaculars, it would also preserve and harness the power of colonial languages to link the nation to the world. It would, that is, incorporate the foreign and convert it into an aspect of the nation, but a nation that, in Quezon's case, was beholden to the state. Rather than abolish linguistic hierarchy and the social hierarchy it implied, Quezon, as the last ilustrado leader under colonial occupation, hoped for its refinement and revitalization. Seeing himself as the nexus between the nation and the state and between a colonial past and a postcolonial future, Quezon, like the Spanish missionaries and the ilustrado nationalists before him, sought to appropriate the power of translation.

That Quezon wanted to revitalize the linguistic hierarchy suggests that at some point it had been in danger of being destroyed. We saw in previous chapters how nineteenth-century attempts at appropriating Castilian and rearticulating Tagalog along with all other modes of communication in the colony had the effect of making evident the uncanny power of language over social life. In the work of both Rizal and Balagtas, for example, language brought out what was radically foreign: that which had no place in life but for that very reason insisted on lodging itself there. By responding to that which belonged by virtue of not belonging, by seeking to translate what nevertheless remained untranslatable, novel social formations emerged: nationalist figures, costumed actors, weeping Cristianos and Moros speaking in verse, subversive novels full of terrorist conspiracies, and the like. But such new developments, which we might hastily characterize as the emergence of figures of modernity, could become real historical possibilities only to the extent that they engendered, in turn, other responses from those who found themselves addressed, whoever they were and wherever they may have been.

This question of address—its formulation, conventionalization, disruption, and recuperation—animates the relationship between colonialism and nationalism in the Philippines and perhaps in many other parts of the world as well. "Who speaks?" is always contingent on "Who is spoken to?" Both in turn rest on the technical means with which they are asked and answered. Such technics include, but are not limited to, the hierarchization of languages and the translation practices that enable as well as disable them. In the historical contexts we have been examining, we have seen that whenever the technics of and for addressing the question of address become objects of struggle and reinvention, crisis tends to break out.

Addressing an expectant nation in 1937, Quezon was no stranger to such crisis. He had fought in the latter phase of the revolution and like almost all other ilustrados and local elites collaborated with the American regime as a way of capitalizing on the promise of political independence from above while guarding against the ever-present demand for social revolution from below. As the leader of the colonial legislature and later the commonwealth, he had authorized the suppression of several local rebellions in the 1920s and 1930s.[5] Quezon's wish to reinforce linguistic hierarchy occurs against the context of past and ongoing challenges to it. In this chapter, I want to consider the nature of these challenges, especially on the eve of the most fundamental challenge to the Spanish regime: the revolution of 1896. In particular, I will address the ways by which Spanish writers and officials responded to what they thought they heard in the Filipino demands for separation.[6]

Conspiracy and the Workings of Secrecy

Let us return briefly to Rizal's second novel, El filibusterismo (1891). In a chapter called "Pasquinades," he tells the story of anonymously authored posters appearing on the university's walls a day after the petition of a student association to establish an academy for the teaching of Castilian is denied.[7] We are never told about the contents of the posters, which are judged by the authorities to be subversive by virtue of their presumably satirical nature and their unknown origins. Rumors quickly spread that they are the signs of a secret conspiracy. Perhaps they are the work of students in league with the bandits hiding out in the mountains, some say. Or perhaps not. In any case, their appearance unleashes rampant speculation that, as one character says, "other hands are at work, but no less terrible" (andan otros manos, pero no menos terrible) (221).

The colonial police soon arrest students and other ilustrados who were known to have been critical of the influence of the Spanish friars. But rather than put fears to rest, the spectacle of their arrest incites more talk, adding to anxieties up and down colonial society. Rumors abound of an impending attack on Manila, and of German boats anchored off the coast waiting to lend assistance to such an attack. Mysterious disturbances and noises trigger panic as they are taken to mean "that the revolution had begun—it was only a matter of seconds" (219). The appearance of the posters thus raises the specter of language beyond colonial control. They suggest an origin outside of what can be accounted for. Wild speculations seek to track the path of this mysterious origin but only serve to further obscure it. Arresting the usual suspects, authorities hope to find the source of the posters but discover that there is always something yet to be uncovered.

The posters then are significant less for their content as for what they reveal: the existence of "other hands at work . . . no less terrible." They give rise to the sense of unseen forces working in secret to bring about what cannot be fully known, much less anticipated. Occurring outside of hierarchy, the posters reveal something that defies revelation. This defiant power draws intense interest from everyone in colonial society. That no one can resist hearing, passing on, and amplifying rumors suggests something of the power of this secret as it holds everyone in thrall, endowing them with a commonality they did not previously possess.

Rizal's story about the posters is most likely an allusion to the appearance in October 1869 of anonymous leaflets at the Dominican university in Manila. The leaflets were critical of the friars and called for "academic freedom." Referring to themselves as "we indios," the authors protested the disrespectful practice of friars in addressing them condescendingly with the informal second-person singular pronoun *tú* instead of the more formal *usted*. And they demanded an end to racial insults. Spanish authorities construed the leaflets as signs of a growing conspiracy among liberal elements in the colony intent on launching a revolt. They proceeded to arrest a number of students, while professors and secular clergy thought to be sympathetic allies were removed from their posts. Many others who even remotely advocated reforms in the colony were placed under surveillance, and their mail was periodically intercepted and opened.[8]

Three years later, in January 1872, a local mutiny erupted at the Spanish arsenal in Cavite, led by a disgruntled creole officer and two Spanish peninsular soldiers. The uprising was rapidly put down, but it further stoked the currents of fear among the Spanish residents convinced of the existence of imminent plots to terrorize Spaniards and overthrow the state. Believing that the Cavite mutiny was a prelude to a much larger revolt, Spanish authorities ordered the arrest and exile of a number of prominent Filipinos and indios who had been vocal in their calls for economic and political reforms and were critical of the reactionary and racist views of the friars. These events culminated in the public execution of three secular priests—José Burgos, Maríano Gomez, and Jacinto Zamora—who had been prominent figures in the secularization controversy as they called upon Spanish friars to devolve more control over parishes to Filipino secular priests. Their execution is widely acknowledged as a milestone in the history of Filipino nationalism. As we saw in chapter 2, Rizal (whose brother Paciano had been a student of Father Burgos) was moved to dedicate the *Fili* to the memory of the three priests and vowed vengeance on their behalf.[9]

The Spanish governor general, Rafael de Izquierdo, had presided over the hunt for suspected subversives, relying mostly on "rumor and anonymous communication." It seems he never doubted the veracity of such rumors, which merely confirmed what he was already certain about: that a plot was afoot to overthrow the regime by killing all Spaniards and declaring independence for the colony. So it did not matter how many were arrested, exiled, and executed. Imagining subversives, or filibusteros meeting in secret in the colony and in the metropole, the government continued seeking them out. Capturing and killing one led only to the discovery of yet other subversives and other plots. Like most other friars and Spanish officials, Izquierdo thus believed in the existence of conspiracies in advance of any evidence, relying instead on "public rumors and confidential reports."[10] It did not matter that ilustrados sought to counteract this belief by claiming their innocence and loyalty to Spain. Spanish conviction in the subterranean spread of filibusterismo across different groups in the colony yielded neither to debate nor to demonstration.

What was the nature of this Spanish belief in conspiracies? The word for conspiracy that commonly appears in Spanish accounts is *conjuración*, which the dictionary of the Real Academia Española defines as unlawful gatherings with the presumed aim of overthrowing the state or the prince. Aside from "conspiracy," however, conjuración also translates as "conjuring," "the act of summoning another in a sacred name." It comes from the verb *conjurar*, to "conjure up," "to implore, entreat, to ask anything in a solemn manner." Additionally, it means "to bind oneself to an other through the means of an oath for some end," thereby recalling its Latin origin in *conjuro*, "to swear together, to unite by oath."[11]

To understand conspiracy in the sense of *conjuración* is to imagine previously unrelated individuals coming together in secret to take oaths. It is to think of the remarkable, indeed magical, ability of a linguistic act—the exchange of promises—to establish new forms of being in the world.[12] In taking an oath, one binds oneself to others, thus forming a group that in turn gives to each of its members an identity different from what they previously had. Oaths are speech acts that bring about the very thing they refer to: in this case, a "conspiracy," from the point of view of the state, a new or alternative association from the point of view of its members. It is new to the extent that it is composed of members who, thanks to taking an oath, become other than who they previously were. Freed from their prior origins, they assumed the capacity to move about covertly, armed with double identities, discrete passwords, and encrypted gestures with which to recognize one another and gain access to meeting spaces hidden from official view. Eluding the comprehension of state authorities, such groups were suspected to be in touch with other, alien sources of power. In their calculated duplicity, they operated at a tangent from colonial society.

A prototypical example of these secret associations in the late nineteenth century were Masonic lodges. Though lodges of European Masons had existed in the colony since the late eighteenth century, lodges for Filipinos did not emerge until 1891, after ilustrado nationalists had been accepted into the membership of those in Barcelona and Madrid. Given their liberal politics and antifriar sentiments, members not surprisingly incurred suspicion from colonial officials. Forbidden from meeting openly, they were forced to convene at different houses, often disguising their gatherings as innocuous social events. Women pretended to host dinner parties and dances while men met in backrooms away from public view. In these moveable lodges, members took on fanciful ranks, performed initiation rituals, held elections, discussed political matters, and referred to themselves with pseudonyms (usually in Tagalog) while pledging themselves to the aid and welfare of every member in need. Private spaces were thus transformed into a different sort of public space, one that fell away from official supervision.[13] Constituting a covert public sphere, lodges in the late nineteenth-century Philippines were in constant contact with other lodges in the metropole, effectively bypassing the mediation of the colonial state. Like the telegraph, Masonic lodges were telecommunicative technologies, allowing for discreet transmissions and connections among members across state borders.

Regardless of their aims, such societies compelled the attention of the state not so much for what they did and said but for what they held back from view. Spanish accounts by the late nineteenth century increasingly became concerned with the signs of this holding back. Yet, every attempt to read those signs and assign their origin to particular figures and meanings seemed to draw officials and friars even farther away from the secret locus of imagined conspiracies. In 1896, a royal decree banned secret societies, targeting in particular Masonic lodges. These were widely believed by Spaniards to be the "womb" (*seno*) from which separatist plots were born.[14] Indeed, nearly every ilustrado nationalist had belonged at one point or another to a Masonic lodge. While many members were not even remotely involved in revolutionary activities, it was the form of the lodge itself that was important. At the very least, it furnished the ritual vocabulary and symbols used by other secret societies, such as the Liga Filipina, founded by Rizal in 1892, and its more radical successor, the revolutionary organization called the Kagalanggalangan Kataastaasan Katipunan ng mga Anak ng Bayan (the Most Noble and Highest Gathering of the Sons and Daughters of the Nation), or Katipunan for short (literally, "the gathering") led by Andres Bonifacio. "These societies," the royal decree states, "by the mere fact of being secret, are illicit and illegal, harmful in every state and the source of insidious evil in a territory like the Philippines. . . . It is absolutely necessary to prosecute them with diligence and constancy . . . until this evil is rooted out or at least until those who still persist in the wicked enterprise are made powerless and harmless."[15] From the perspective of state authorities, the mere fact of secrecy constituted a crime. Members were thought to evade recognition from above rather than seek to solicit it. Out of reach, they were able to tap into other circuits of communication beyond the hierarchy of languages. Indeed, by operating under cover, lodges served as networks for the circulation of news, money, and banned books between the colony and the metropole as well as within the country itself. Placed under surveillance, members became even more secretive. For this reason, they were endowed by the state with the foreignness—and thus the criminal status—of filibusteros. They were deemed to be carriers of "evil," because unknown, intentions. Like witches, they had to be repressed, periodically hunted down and exorcized from the body politic.

Suddenly, the Unimaginable: Pacto de Sangre

In responding as they did, Spaniards felt themselves addressed by the secrecy of secret societies. They ascribed to this secrecy catastrophic possibilities: revolution, the destruction of the regime, and the murder of Spanish residents. In short, they were forced to think the unthinkable and entertain the possibility of the impossible arriving suddenly and without warning.

A month before the eruption of the revolution, for example, Manuel Sityar, a lieutenant in the Civil Guard, writes about the growing sense of "a formidable conspiracy against Spain." He notes a change in the faces of the indios. "Insignificant details perhaps for those who were born in another country . . . had made me suspicious that something abnormal had occurred, something which could not be defined, making me redouble my vigilance." He notes the existence of "an atmosphere of distrust and suspicion among the locals whose characteristics had always been those of apathy, indifference, and stoic tranquillity in all other circumstances."[16] In a similar vein, the journalist Manuel Sastrón notes the transformation he sees among different classes of natives once news of the revolution begins to spread. An "atmosphere of pure hatred against Spanish domination" was palpable. Once accommodating to a fault, natives increasingly refused to step aside the road to let a Spaniard pass. In certain Tagalog towns in Laguna and Batangas, natives began to openly insult Spaniards, at times greeting them "in the most cruel and injurious tone: *the Spaniards are pigs (castila ang babui) (sic).*"[17] University students fell under the spell of the Katipunan and thus "catipunized" (*catipunados*) were writing "grossly injurious" things about Spain. Suddenly, servants began to talk back to their masters complaining about their wages, while *cocheros*, coach drivers, felt entitled to haggle in "harsh tones, sometimes punctuated with a few well placed blows (on their horses)," with their Spanish passengers about the fare. Even well-off Filipinos and mestizos thought nothing of cutting off the carriages carrying Spaniards, further evidence of the erosion of deference and the loosening of hierarchy.[18] Meanwhile, rumors circulated of Katipunan plots to poison the Spaniards in Manila by placing toxic chemicals in their drinking water and in the food they were served at home. "What other proofs," Sastrón wails, "were needed that thousands of conjured Filipinos (*conjurados filipinos*) were frantically seeking to gain their separation from the Mother Country, and that they were thinking of accomplishing this by beheading (*degollando*) all of the peninsular Spaniards?"[19]

The thought that equated Filipino independence with Spanish death had existed in official circles since the aftermath of the Cavite mutiny of 1872. It took even firmer hold in Spanish accounts after the Spanish friar

Mariano Gil's discovery of the existence of the Katipunan along with various documents relating to a planned uprising in August of 1896. The Spanish journalist and bibliophile W. E. Retana, for example, reproduces a Spanish translation of a Katipunan document from 1896 stating that "our principal objective is to leave no Spaniard alive in the future Filipino Republic," and that in order to carry out this goal, it would be most expedient to "procure the friendship of these barbarians with the purpose of dispatching them with greater security and promptness once the moment of the cry of independence comes."[20] In another captured document, Retana calls attention to the "monstrous" nature of a plan to kill all friars and burn them rather than bury their bodies. It would be an act of vengeance, according to the Katipunan document, for all the "felonies that in life they committed against the noble Filipinos during three centuries of their nefarious domination."[21] Destined for a double desecration, friars were to be killed, then burned and left unburied.

Another Spanish journalist, José M. Castillo y Jímenez, reproduces a similar document from the Supreme Council of the Katipunan in his account of the early months of the revolution, commanding fighters to attack Manila and "assassinate all of the Spaniards, their women and children, without any consideration of generation, or parentage, friendship, gratitude, etc."[22] It also orders the sacking of convents and the "decapitation of their infamous inhabitants." Once killed, Spaniards were to be buried (except friars, who were to be burned) in graves at Bagumbayan field, the site of public executions. On the graves of dead Spaniards, Filipino independence would then be declared.[23]

It is important to point out that none of these atrocities did, in fact, occur. There is no evidence of Spaniards beheaded, raped, or murdered en masse. Only a very small number of friars were actually killed, and none were burned. Most of the Spanish priests were actually protected from violence by their local parishioners, despite the calls for vengeance on the part of revolutionary leaders. Indeed, it was more common for revolutionary fighters to treat Spanish prisoners humanely, even arranging for Christian burials for those who had been killed in battle.[24]

Still, Spaniards like Castillo believed that these horrible crimes were bound to take place. To clinch his point about the fate that awaited Spaniards, Castillo reproduces a photograph in the middle of his book that illustrates the link between Filipino independence and the death of Spaniards. It is that of an apron, the sort used in Masonic rituals, found buried along with other Katipunan documents in the barrio of Trozo just outside the walls of Manila (figure 2). The apron depicts two upraised arms, presumably belonging to a Filipino. The right hand clutches a knife while the left holds aloft the severed head of a bearded Spaniard, blood dripping from its neck.[25] One thinks of the line from Rizal's *Fili* again: "Other hands are at work, but no less terrible." The terror arises precisely from sensing the otherness of these hands detached from an identifiable body. Working as if on its own accord, its origins remain hidden from view.

Drawn by the workings of a secret power, Spaniards searched after signs of conspiracies and conjurings. They found themselves living among a population "bewitched" or "catipunized" by the workings of filibusteros. Lurid figures kept appearing, predicting the imminent loss of their colony, while calls for their death and dismemberment were turning up with greater frequency. The crime of revolution would begin with subtle acts of disrespect, turning into gross insults and ingratitude for the "debts owed to Spain,"[26] then finally erupt into a frenzy of killing and the decapitation of Spaniards. In seeking revenge and passing judgment on the putative crimes of the colonizers, the colonized would commit even greater crimes. "These are the laws of the Katipunan, their sole and criminal intention," writes Castillo, summing up Spanish sentiment.[27] For the Spaniards, revolutionary nationalism on the part of Filipinos perverted the order of things, making crime the foundation of law. In doing so, it brought forth the unimaginable—for example, death followed by dismemberment rather than remembrance, or death by burning rather than mourning—as the basis for what could be imagined.

How do we understand this notion—the unimaginable as that which insists on shaping the imagination? How can formlessness be the basis for giving form to experience, or the unspeakable as the basis of expression? Let us look once again at this most persistent motif in Spanish accounts of the revolution: that of the equation of Spanish death with Filipino independence. Manuel Sastrón cites what he imagines to be a typical Katipunan slogan, "Death to the Spaniard and long live independence!": (*Muere al castila y viva la independencia*). "This and no other was the slogan that was emblazoned in the banner of the *insurrectos* . . . the cry of the natives led by Andres Bonifacio and his slippery Katipunan gang, all of whom have entered into a pact to exterminate all the Spaniards, conquerors of this land not by brutal force but through the sweet preaching of the Gospel."[28] In response to the "gentle" Word of conquest, Filipinos can only cry: "Death to the Spaniard." Led by Bonifacio's

FIGURE 2

The "horrible apron" and knife used for blood compacts.

From José M. del Castillo, El Katipunan o el filibusterismo (1897)

Katipunan, they become who they are because of an oath (*pacto*) they have taken to "exterminate" all the Spaniards in the colony. It is as though Filipino independence, or better yet *kalayaan*, the Tagalog term for "freedom" used in Katipunan documents, can come only through the "medium" of Spanish death: "That which the people wished to obtain was their independence," Sastron writes, "and the means for doing so was the slaughter of Spaniards."[29] Betraying Spain's generosity, Filipinos had shown a criminal lack of hospitality. This inhospitality was precisely the product of a prior promise. As members of a secret society, Katipuneros as such came into being by virtue, first of all, of the linguistic act of entering into a pact. Spanish writers repeatedly remark on the peculiar nature of this pact and the rituals surrounding it. Called in Castilian *pacto de sangre*, or blood compact, it was thought to be the decisive event in the conversion, as it were, of passive indios and docile mestizos into fierce fighters eager to take Spanish lives.

The putative desire to spill Spanish blood begins, in the pacto de sangre, with the shedding of one's own. By the 1880s, ilustrado nationalists had developed a fascination with the history of the pacto de sangre as mentioned in sixteenth-century Spanish accounts. The Portuguese explorer Ferdinand de Magellan, who landed in the Philippines in 1521 and claimed it for the Spanish crown, as well as Miguel Lopez de Legazpi, the first governor general of the colony in 1565, both entered into blood compacts with local chiefs as a way of establishing alliances with them. Nineteenth-century ilustrados idealized these events. They saw in them nothing less than a contractual agreement entered by equals to come to each other's aid. The renowned Filipino artist Juan Luna, brother of Antonio, depicted the scene in a painting titled "El pacto de sangre" in 1885 to suggest that colonization began with an oath of friendship sealed by the "mixing of blood taken from an incision in the arms" of the Spanish and native leaders.[30]

For Filipinos, the ritual mixing of blood signified a promise of mutual recognition and the exchange of obligations. In return for pledging allegiance to the Spanish king, Filipinos were entitled to be treated as "Spaniards in the full sense of the word."[31] This story about the blood compact thus became an allegory about the promise of mutual assimilation of the descendants of one group into that of the other. The mixing of blood meant a shared genealogy. As the privileged medium for connecting colonizer with colonized, the blood compact established between them a relation of filiation and a history of male-ordered miscegenation meant to mitigate existing inequalities. Though attributed to precolonial practices, the blood compact undoubtedly echoed for nineteenth-century ilustrados the miracle of Christian transubstantiation, whereby Christ's body and blood are believed literally to reside in consecrated bread and wine shared by communicants during mass. By eating His body and drinking His blood, believers acknowledge their indebtedness to Christ and enter into a sacred contract with God. In the pacto de sangre, one gets a secularized version of this Catholic belief. Native and Spanish men (for no women were known to have engaged in such practices) shed their blood for each other. In doing so, they took on a new identity: no longer strangers but friends, and even, perhaps, fellow citizens. Hence does the blood compact, like all other vows, bring about the very condition that it signifies.

However, ilustrado nationalists argued that centuries of Spanish abuse amounted to the betrayal of this ancient agreement. By refusing to recognize Filipinos as fraternal equals, Spaniards broke their part of the deal. In the face of this injustice, Filipinos felt justified in reneging on their promise. They would continue to perform what they construed to be an indigenous custom, but this time in secret and only with one another, to the exclusion of Spaniards. In this way, the pacto de sangre became an integral part of the initiation rituals of the secret society, Liga Filipina, founded by Rizal, and its revolutionary successor, the Katipunan.[32]

In Filipino nationalist historiography, the pacto de sangre tends to be regarded as a relatively minor part of the rites of passage that allowed one to join the Katipunan. Other aspects of the initiation rituals have attracted more attention, such as the formulaic interrogation of candidates about the past and present conditions of the country—that it was once highly civilized and prosperous, then fell into poverty and backwardness with the coming of Spain, but will rise up again with the revolution. Trials by ordeal, the ceremonial concealment and revelation of the symbols of the Katipunan, and the sermons preached by the presiding brother are other aspects that have been described by scholars.[33] The pacto de sangre occurs at the end of the initiation ritual. An incision is made with a knife on the left forearm of the initiate. With his own blood he signs an oath pledging to defend the country to the death, to "keep all secrets and follow the leaders blindly, [and to] help all the brothers in all dangers and needs."[34] Variations of these rites existed in different places, but its basic structure remained the same through the revolution against Spain and later against the United States in the early twentieth century. In Filipino nationalist historiography then, the blood compact came across as a relatively benign oath that had little to do with addressing the Spaniards.

For Spaniards, however, the pacto de sangre took on enormous significance. It was no less the "anchor of the revolution," the very means for "fanatisizing" the masses. By taking the oath, they were driven to hate the "white race." Thanks to this "horrible pact," the native populace had become mad (enloquecido), taking up arms against "la Patria."[35] While Filipinos saw the blood compact as a means of pledging oneself in common cause, Spaniards like Castillo imagined the moment of incision to be a kind of "hypodermic injection" that corrupts the blood and poisons the heart. Once "fanaticized," he writes, Filipinos "live in eternal convulsion, in permanent delirium; they sleep soundly in the execution of their crimes and awake in the fire of their victim's blood; they are afraid of neither death, nor punishment, nor the law, nor conscience, nor the human, nor the divine, because they swear by the following: to conquer or to die [vencer o morir]."[36] By entering into a blood compact, Filipinos become possessed. The oath turns them into monstrous figures. Unable to control their own bodies, they live in a state of "permanent delirium." They thus exceed the boundaries of nature and culture. And because they fear neither death nor the law, they exist outside of the human and the divine. They are therefore beyond social recognition. It is as if the blood compact converts its pledges into agents of a power that outstrips social conventions and political control. Judging from the breathless prose of Castillo—the hyperbolic piling of images, the string of negations that he is unable to consolidate into a single image—it is a power that also eludes narrative description even as it provokes a seemingly endless train of tropes. Its negative force—afraid of neither death nor punishment, nor law, neither human, nor divine—just keeps coming with no end in sight. Lurid images conjured up by the writer fail to bring this power under control, narrative or otherwise. By eluding representation and disclosure, this power instead brings the writer to reiterate the very vow that carries its force: "Vencer o morir."

Beyond articulation, this covert power nevertheless demanded to be heard. It compelled the attention of Spaniards and Filipinos alike, though for different reasons. Just as the Spaniards dreaded what they saw in the "terrible curse" of the pacto de sangre, Filipinos who joined the revolution enthusiastically took to it. In this sense, the blood compact, as it did in the past, brought together the colonizers and the colonized. They found themselves through their enmity sharing something in common: a fascination with the ability of language to bring forth a power that escapes full articulation in the sense of the total disclosure of its origin and meaning. But by defying such attempts, it is also a power that makes articulation itself possible—articulation in the sense of connection and transmission that we have seen in the case of the telegraph, the lingua franca, and the comedia. The oath linked Filipino fighters together in the expectation of a future they could barely begin to imagine. This current of expectation in turn created an experience of fraternal solidarity among men (and the small number of women) from different classes and regions. But where the Spaniards were concerned, the oath transmitted a message whose meaning they could neither absorb nor accommodate.

We can see another moment of this secret power at work if we return to the photograph in Castillo's book we cited earlier. Recall that the "horrible apron" found among Katipunan documents depicts a pair of arms holding the severed head of a Spaniard in one and a knife in the other. On the same page below this photograph, there appears the picture of another knife. Its handle bears the Katipunan symbol and the Tagalog word, *taliba*, or guard. The caption below the picture says that the knife, found in the possession of the Katipunan's "Minister of the Treasury," Enrique Pacheco, was used for making incisions on the arm of prospective Katipuneros during the ritual of the blood compact. By force of association, the writer and reader are led to think of the two knives as if they belonged together. That which decapitates the Spaniard in one photograph becomes the one that cuts the Filipino's arm in the course of the ritual. Following this logic, it would be possible as well to assume that the left arm that appears on the apron as the arm that had been cut by the knife that appears below. Of course, the two knives are not the same instrument. They remain objectively distinct. But by way of juxtaposition, which we can think of as a method of articulation, one thing is connected to another, leading the reader to imagine an equivalence between the two. It is like the cinema, where the technique of montage brings previously unrelated and distinct objects and scenes together to form a narrative whole. Seeing two things together within a common frame, we think they must somehow belong together, where "must" implies the workings of faith: we *believe* they belong together in advance of any explanation or knowledge of the actual facts. What actually connects the two images, however, remains invisible and nowhere explicit in either the photograph or the text. Yet it is a force undeniably at work, shaping not only what Castillo sees and writes but our reading of his book as well. Such a force makes possible the thought, for example, that the knife is a ritual object that not only connects Filipinos with one another by virtue of the pacto de sangre, leading them to form new identities by joining secret societies. The knife is also a kind of transmitter that allows "catipunized" Filipinos to communicate with Spaniards no longer as subordinate subjects but as agents of the latter's death.

The knife can be thought of then as an instrument for realizing the oath in that it is itself, like all ritual tools, a kind of "congealed language."[37] As an integral part of the pacto de sangre, it, too, is a kind of speech that links men together in common cause. For the Spaniards, however, the knife as part of the oath is a medium for communicating Spanish death. It speaks of destruction, not solidarity. The knife appears in these contexts as a powerful instrument for articulating messages, however conflictual and unsettling. It also acts to connect men both as friends *and* as enemies. Yet, as with every communicative media, the source of its power, that which endows it with the capacity to make possible such articulations, remains unseen. It is a power that persists and insists in the world, but as a secret, withdrawing at the very moment when its agents appear and its effects are felt. As a secret, it is a power foreign to every attempt to tame it and make it speak a determined set of meanings. It thus always remains to be seen, even as it promises the arrival of what is given to be seen.

The Promise of the Foreign

Spaniards learned about Katipunan plots and the pacto de sangre from captured documents and confessions (*declaraciónes*) coerced from imprisoned Filipinos. In the available sources, these documents and confessions all appear in Castilian even if they may have been originally in other vernacular languages.[38] Additionally, the text of the confessions is paraphrased in such a way that the captive's speech appears never in the first-person singular but always in the third person, as in "he said that he . . ." As with the Catholic ritual of confession, the language of the Katipunero is translated and made to appear within the linguistic and juridical terms of colonial authority. The voice we hear in these declaraciónes seems filled with the language of the law, ordered to reflect not so

much the singularity of the speaker—his accent, intentions, and inter-
pretations of events—as the capacity of colonial authority to capture and
contain that singularity. In this way, whatever the speaker revealed could
be contextualized and domesticated in ways readily accessible to official
interlocutors. Similarly, the Katipunan documents translated into Castilian were meant to decode the vernacular in terms readily understood
by the Spaniards. Or so it was hoped.

Complications developed almost immediately. Whether they quoted
captured revolutionary documents or wrote about the confessions of
captured Filipinos, Spaniards invariably heard themselves addressed,
yet they could barely account for what came through. Though the confessions and documents were translated into Castilian, they communicated a message that surpassed what Spaniards could understand. The
most significant example is the phrase *pacto de sangre*. Though it is
Castilian, its meaning exceeded Spanish comprehension, for what they
heard in this phrase was a kind of death sentence. Their own language,
returned to them by Filipino nationalists, sounded like it had become a
foreign tongue. In effect, it said, "your death is our freedom." We can
rephrase this into the simplest of formulas: "Filipino freedom = Spanish death." The equals sign that connects one term to the other also
establishes a relation of substitution between the two, to wit: freedom
for death.

The equals sign is neither Castilian nor Tagalog. As with other di-
acritical marks it is not a word but makes possible the legibility of words,
spacing them into some sort of syntactical and discursive order. Such
marks are indispensable supplements of language even if they are themselves nondiscursive. They work to connect and articulate even if they
themselves escape articulation. Similarly with the word *for* in *freedom for
death*: by connecting words and phrases, it allows for predication and the
transmission of meaning while remaining itself freed of reference. We
can think of the workings of these marks as analogous to the copulative
action of the pacto de sangre. The oath, as we have seen, consists of a set
of linguistic acts that join disparate peoples and thoughts and so allows
for the utterance of, among other things, such impossibilities as "freedom for death." The key tool that enacts this joining is the knife used to
make incisions on the forearm. By leaving a permanent mark on the
body—"branding" it, as one historian shrewdly observes[39]—it alters the
person's identity. He becomes and belongs to someone else; he is no
longer a dockworker, a peasant, a student, or a local bureaucrat but a

revolutionary fighter dedicated to the movement. It is a sign that one has taken a vow. As a sort of signature or brand, the incision then is like a piece of writing that marks one as the carrier of a promise: to kill or be killed for the sake of the nation's freedom. From a docile indio or a reformist ilustrado, one becomes through the pact and the mark it leaves behind a new and therefore foreign presence in colonial society. Being new, one is yet to be assimilated and remains unassimilable so long as one is seen to be a medium for transmitting the impossible message, "Filipino freedom for Spanish death."

Hearing the news of their coming death, the Spaniards panic. They hunt down suspected fighters only to realize that thanks to early successes of the movement, people are eager to take the pacto de sangre, and more and more fighters emerge. "Looking for a clever medium to facilitate the conspiracy," writes another Spanish official in a letter to the Overseas Ministry, "they foment it by means of the pacto de sangre, making them swear to a war to kill Spaniards, and placing on them an incision on their left arm, and with their blood, they were made to sign and they signed the frightful oath [espantoso juramento]."[40]

What is frightening (espantoso) about this promise, of course, is that it brings with it a contract to murder Spaniards, or so the Spaniards think. Like the ancient practice of mixing blood to seal an agreement, here blood is drawn and used as ink to sign an oath. One's body is marked and leaves behind, in turn, its own mark. Some of the signatures or their copies still survive, preserved in the Philippine National Archives.[41] Long after their original signers have disappeared and are barely remembered, their traces still persist. They are there to be read as part of a larger historical moment whose effects continue to be felt today. Signatures, as Jacques Derrida has argued, share with all marks the ability to survive the moment as well as the context of their production. That is, they must exist in the absence of their signers, communicating the latter's presence across geographical and temporal divides. In this way, a signature is a kind of prosthetic device, a technic for expressing and transmitting one's presence in the world beyond any particular location to reach the attention of those otherwise too distant or too powerful to care. Testifying to the singular existence of their signer, a signature is nonetheless meant to live on apart from its origin, producing effects beyond the latter's life. It thus extends the life of the signer toward a future beyond the latter's death, a future the signer can never fully control because, like a secret, it cannot be wholly disclosed. By signing an oath, one evinces a trust and a belief in this coming future even and especially if it exceeds what one can know. But at the same time, one accedes to the power of the signature to promise the possibility of *a* future—in effect, the possibility of possibility—in the absence of any certainty of its unfolding.[42] This is perhaps what is meant by one side of the equation implied by the pacto de sangre. Signed in blood, it conjured the possibility of freedom for Filipinos: the promise of an afterlife, if you will, where one's traces would survive and would be inherited by those who were yet to come, though there could never be a guarantee as to what form this survival or this coming would take.

But the other side of the equation meant precisely the opposite to the Spaniards. "Death" implied no future, no life, and no afterlife, for even their corpses, they believed, would be dismembered and left unmourned. This was the substance of the horrible oath they heard, the terms of the contract to which they could not affix their signatures, much less control the wording of the agreement. For unlike the history of Christian conversion predicated on the control of translation, the revolution expropriated the colonial legacies—Christian rituals and Castilian words, for example—and converted them into a message that Spaniards could translate but could not understand. They were faced with a term in their own language, *pacto de sangre*, that when uttered by the revolutionary fighter exceeded what the Spaniards could recognize and recuperate. Coursing through secret locations, the revolution radicalized the very terms of translation and untranslatability in ways that terrorized those at the top of the colonial regime. (And it is arguably the tremors of that terror that could still be felt in Quezon's anxiety about translation some two generations after the revolution.)

We can begin to understand the Spanish obsession with the blood compact as distinct from yet clearly related to the interest of Filipino nationalists. Both were drawn, as we have seen, to the promise of the foreign. Such a promise constituted a kind of telecommunicative power: that of bringing forth what seemed new and for that reason outside of what could be known—death, freedom, and the future, for example. At once hopeful and menacing, it was a power that defied disclosure and representation even as it solicited belief. Various attempts at localizing and containing this promissory power in such loaded figures as the filibustero, friar, Rizal, Balagtas, and so forth were apt to fail, though their failure produced important and long-lasting effects. Similarly, to call this power "translation," or the "untranslatable," "revenge," "telecommunication," "the colonial uncanny," or the "lingua franca," as I have sought to do, or even at its most extreme, the power of death, is at best to hint at its workings rather than disclose its nature, trace its source, and fix its meaning (as colonial and postcolonial authorities have sought to do) once and for all. By invoking a sense of something beyond or amiss, the promise of the foreign provoked the search toward a common language as a technic for arriving at common meanings with which to institute a new kind of community, as in, for example, the nation. Such efforts were necessarily contradictory and incomplete because they were founded on what was decidedly uncommon and thus irreducibly alien. But equally important is the fact that this lack, perhaps even failure, produced those events we have come to regard as truly historical.

As one of the envoys of the promise of the foreign, the pacto de sangre no doubt had magical effects, conjuring up secret societies and new identities while delivering a message of terror that seized the attention of Spaniards. For the performative capacities of the oath could not, as the Spaniards realized, be fully represented and appropriated, not even by the Filipinos themselves, who could act only as its agents. The former saw in this promise a diabolical curse that prophesied the end of their rule and the obliteration of their lives. For Spaniards, the promise of the foreign came across as a menace and threat where once, within the workings of translation and evangelization, it offered the prospect of redeeming the colonial enterprise. For their part, Filipino revolutionaries heard and responded to something else. For them, the promise of the foreign intimated the nearing of kalayaan, of freedom, whose coming would sweep away the colonial regime and bring a future open to all sorts of possibilities. Such possibilities included the prospect of a social revolution that would demolish not only Spanish privileges but also other forms of social inequities, including those on which elite influence rested.

It is this promise of a social revolution and the coming of justice—of that which was new and therefore alien to colonial society—which the pacto de sangre brought forth but which is yet to be realized. For this reason, it points to yet another aspect of what remains foreign to the nation even as constitutes its origins. Such a promise pointed a way beyond both linguistic and social hierarchies. In the nationalist imagination, it has never ceased calling for a common language capable of reaching beyond local idioms and hierarchies. It mobilized Filipinos to seek ways to become other than the colonial subjects that they had been, just as it made possible the performance of oaths and conjurings that frightened Spaniards during the revolution of 1896. The future of that revolution, however, was foreclosed not by Spanish actions, which proved less than effective, but by the recolonization of the nation, first by the ilustrado-dominated First Republic in Malolos, and subsequently by the United States and its ilustrado successors: Quezon's commonwealth and the postwar Republic of the Philippines. They, too, sought to tap into the promise of the foreign, calling it at various times "democracy," "progress," "the modern," "independence," and "national develop-ment," to shore up their domination. But as with the Spaniards, they were unable to exhaust, much less tame, its possibilities. The result is that while the postcolonial Philippines has experienced a series of politi-cal transformations, it has yet to realize a social revolution. As such, it has yet to overcome the colonial legacy of linguistic hierarchy. Nonethe-less, the power of this promise—one which, for example, brings into impossible juxtaposition "freedom" and "death"—endures. It continues to make the unthinkable—for instance, the revolutionary transforma-tion of social life—the ground on which historical thinking can take place. For this reason, it continues to call, periodically issuing from sources that we can never fully locate, in languages just beyond what we are capable of translating, and often at the fringes of what is socially recognizable. It is a call that remains to be heard.[43]

AFTERWORD

GHOSTLY VOICES

Kalayaan's *Address*

*Death speaks in me. My speech is a warning that at this very
moment death is loose in the world, that it has suddenly appeared between
me, as I speak, and the being I address: it is there between us at the distance that
separates us, but this distance is also what prevents us from being separated,
because it contains the condition for all understanding.*

MAURICE BLANCHOT

The conjunction of freedom and death informed both Spanish and Filipino understandings of the revolution of 1896. This thought filled
Spaniards with terror, for they felt subject to a death sentence uttered in
secret pacts by revolutionary fighters. But what of Filipino revolutionaries, or at least those in the Tagalog-speaking regions who were drawn
to participate in the earliest phases of the fighting? How did the promise
of freedom appear? How was the link between freedom and death, both
of oneself and the other, construed? Who or what made this call and
responded to its promise? One way we can approach these questions is
to examine one of the most important documents of the early history of
the revolution: the Katipunan newspaper, appropriately enough called
Kalayaan, or *Freedom,* written originally in Tagalog.

Only one issue of this newspaper is thought to have appeared. By all
accounts, the newspaper's circulation in the Tagalog areas around March
1896 contributed to the rapid growth in Katipunan membership.[1] However, no copies of this first issue are known to have survived, and no
historian has ever laid eyes on the paper. We know of its existence from
the memoirs of Pio Valenzuela, one of the members of the Katipunan,
and we can get a glimpse of its contents from the work of Spanish
bibliophile and journalist Wenceslao Retana.[2] The third volume of Retana's documentary history of the Spanish colony, published a year after
the beginning of the revolution in 1897, features Castilian translations of
three articles from the newspaper. The translations were made by a

journalist, Juan Caro y Mora, who kept the titles in their Tagalog original. Other Filipino historians have since retranslated the *Kalayaan* articles into Tagalog, relying entirely on their Castilian versions.[3] As with the comedia, or for that matter the history of conversion, the first language comes across only through the mediation of a second, foreign idiom.

The masthead of *Kalayaan* identified its place of publication as "Yokohama," presumably in Japan, with the date of January 1896. However, subsequent investigations by the colonial government showed that this was a ruse on the part of the editors designed to disguise the origins of the publications. Retana speculates that the paper was likely printed in a house in Binondo just outside of Manila's walls.[4] Just as *Kalayaan* in the original Tagalog is available only in Castilian translation, so its place of origin remains uncertain, disguised to make it seem as if it came from a foreign city. Consistent with what we have seen in the early history of nationalism, the foreign understood as that which is capable of emerging both from within and outside the borders of colonial society, is regarded as the privileged site from where the unknown and the unforeseen issue forth. *Kalayaan*, the name for the newspaper as well as the term for "freedom," like the revolutionary organization, the Katipunan, literally, "the gathering," dwells in secrecy. Both posit a source outside of and alien to colonial society and the historiographic tradition that follows in its wake. We can see *Kalayaan* recapitulating the communicative logic of the ilustrado propaganda paper *La solidaridad*. Indeed, the editors of the paper greet their readers in a section titled "A los compatriotas" (*Sa mga kababayan*, "To Our Compatriots"): "From here, from across the wide ocean, from the bosom or lap protected by other laws, we address you (*os dirigimos*) with our first greeting, our dearest compatriots" (134).

Kalayaan, while speaking in the vernacular, nonetheless seems to come from elsewhere, calling from far away. It is as if the local language leaves its origins to return as something other, freed from colonial modes of mediation. The message of freedom addressed to distant compatriots comes in a familiar language by the most unfamiliar means. Native speech gains power precisely from its association with foreign locations. What is spoken inside arrives from outside, by way of long-distance communication. Bearing pseudonyms, its authorship remains concealed. And by seeming to emanate from a foreign location, its origins remain enmeshed in secrecy, accessible only by means of translation. But because of its telecommunicative capacities, *Kalayaan* not only transmits messages from afar. Thanks to its articulation in a vernacular that has been estranged and revivified, it can also receive and register the call of all those who are left unheard: "At the point when we heard your sighs, immediately did your eyes appear [telling of] grievances unique and exemplary (*sin segundo o sin ejemplo*) and the innumerable punishments and hardships [visited upon you]; at that moment, a just and great desire was born in our heart to lift you from your [state] of prostration, so that the pain and affliction that oppresses your heart so full of sadness and bitterness will be answered (*se contestará*)" (135). "We" hear "your" sighs of grief and see your sufferings. So powerful, it seems, are the lines of transmission that communication and contact between the two take place "immediately." Hearers and speakers are linked rapidly across distances, allowing for the ready recognition of one by the other. It is this "moment" (*al momento*) of recognition that makes possible the formulation of a response to the state of affliction now shared by "us." *Kalayaan* thus issues a response to a prior call and furnishes a site for assuming responsibility of the one for the other. However, doing so requires that "we lift our heads, long accustomed to being bowed," and realize that "the word of Madre España is nothing more than mere flattery," that she is "no more than a race of robbers, a country that fattens itself on what does not belong to her." Thus "there is nothing else to hope for other than our own strength and defenses" (136). Echoing the words of Simoun in Rizal's *Fili*, the anonymous writers of *Kalayaan* urge separation and self-reliance. Both in turn are borne by an acute sense of betrayal by "Madre España," for unlike a real mother, she fails to keep her word and instead spawns a "race of thieves." Responsibility that flows out of recognition is thus sustained by resentment over broken promises. Such betrayal demands a response in kind: a breaking away from the mother. The promise of revenge, of repaying the (m)other in kind, shadows the response and responsibility constitutive of the "we" conjured up by *Kalayaan*.

A similar motif can be seen in the longest of the three articles translated in Retana: the "Manifiesto" (*Pahayag*) signed by Dimas Alang (literally, "untouchable," 138–44). Though this pseudonym had been used by Rizal in some of his journalistic writings and served as his Masonic name (no doubt in sly reference to the title of his first novel, *Noli me tangere*, touch me not), the *Kalayaan* article has been attributed to another revolutionary intellectual, Emilio Jacinto (though even this remains largely speculative).[5] What is manifested in this "Manifiesto" is no less than the figure of Kalayaan speaking through a newspaper with the same name. The printed words are thus converted into a speaking voice issuing from another land. Its emergence is set during "a dark night." In a room illuminated only by a flickering candle, an indio youth is sunk in despair bordering on rage.

> At the moment of falling into his anger, at that moment, he felt a soft touch on his shoulder, and heard a voice that was suave, harmonious and sad. It asked him:
>
> "Why are you crying"?
>
> He lifted his head and was filled with surprise: he recovered himself as he caught a glimpse of a shadowy figure that appeared enveloped in a white vaporous aura coming close to him.
>
> "Oh, merciful shadow! My sadness has no remedy. It is beyond consolation . . . Why do you still come to relieve my sighs?"
>
> "How long," the shadow replied, "will ignorance and stupidity [continue] to cause the hardships and punishments of the people of this country? Do you know who I am? Listen: I am the principle of all things most grand, most beautiful, and most laudable, dignified and precious from which humanity derives its benefits. Because of me, men unite and forget each and every one of their own interests and think of nothing but the common good. All those who, living under my protection, enjoy and cherish the relief and improvements and abundance of all, are obligated to me, as they are obligated in Japan, America, and other places; because of me, thought is elevated to probe and discover the profundities of science; wherever I reign, tears are dried and chests long drowned by tyranny and cruelty breath with frankness. My name is *Libertad*." (139–40)

Responding to the sorrowful cries of the youth, Libertad, which presumably appears in the original Tagalog as Kalayaan, comes forth as a disembodied voice. At the very moment that the youth is about to cry, he hears a question—"Por que lloras?" "Why are you crying?"—as if he was receiving a response at the instant he let out a call. He sees only a shadowy figure speaking in "smooth, harmonious, and sad" tones. It is tempting (and we will give in to this temptation) to see the youth as an allegory for the suffering nation haunted by the ghost of Kalayaan. As with most ghosts, it comes across as a voice minus a body. To communicate with such specters, one might customarily resort to a ritual specialist, for example a medium or a sorcerer whose task would be to give body to this voice. What is curious in this scene is that the youth speaks directly to the ghost rather than resort to a medium, and does so almost at the same instant that he is addressed. The striking absence of a medium becomes understandable, however, when we consider that the exchange between the two takes place in print. We see rather than hear, or better yet, we hear by seeing their words mechanically reproduced and translated. The ghostly voice of Kalayaan is channeled not through a sorcerer or a priest but by way of print technology, allowing for its broadcast beyond the particular point and moment of its enunciation. Thanks to print, the voice of freedom and that of the youth can be emancipated, as it were, from their temporal and geographical moorings to travel far and wide across space and time. The youth is like the reader of the text, encountering the voice of freedom in a mass circulation medium rather than through the body of a spirit medium. Unlike more traditional ghosts that are tied to specific locations and emerge only on particular occasions, Kalayaan comes across as a kind of technological specter capable of roaming the world and visiting all places at all times.

Kalayaan the ghost, like *Kalayaan* the newspaper, hears the youth without the latter knowing it. The youth, used to being unheard and ignored, is surprised when his cries bring forth a quick response. It is a response that comes from a shadowy figure of indeterminate origins, capable of appearing anywhere in the world. Voice without body, Kalayaan is a force of transmission that leaves benevolent effects wherever it reigns. It consoles and liberates the oppressed, just as it is "the principle of all things grand, beautiful, dignified from which humanity derives its benefits." At home nowhere, Kalayaan can lodge itself everywhere. And because it belongs to no one in particular, it gives itself to be claimed by anyone in general. Hence, "because of me, men unite and forget each and everyone of their own interests and think of nothing else but the common good" (140).

The force of Kalayaan is such that it compels humans to abandon their individual concerns and accede to what is greater and other than them: the "common good." Put differently, it gathers together those who forego and forget what comes to them immediately, one might say naturally, for example, their individual lives. They give up what comes first in order to welcome the arrival of a second, foreign presence. In its spectrality, this presence underlies the very making of all that is valuable in human life. Welcomed by humans, it makes possible the practice of welcoming itself from which spring "grand things," "beauty," "dignity," and compassion. Hence when it says its name, "Mi nombre es *Libertad!*" it announces the very possibility of naming, that is, of referring and signifying, of hearing and speaking to the world. With Kalayaan then comes the possibility of addressing and being addressed in a way analogous to the lingua franca. It brings with it the phantasm of a second language that belongs to no one and thus can be spoken by everyone. Surpassing local vernaculars, it establishes new because unforeseen connections that are imagined to produce beneficent effects for its speakers. As a secret source of rapid and infinite response, Kalayaan is also a figure of inexhaustible generosity, giving itself to be possessed by all those who seek it, no matter who and where they are.

Given an audience with Kalayaan, the youth tells of his sorrows. He talks about appealing to authorities for relief, only to get back more cruelty and debasement. Complaining of his thirst, he is told to drink his tears. Standing stark naked, he receives the response "Now you will be enveloped in chains." Worst of all, when he speaks to the Spanish judge or friar to ask for "a little love, a little clemency and charity," he is told "This is a filibustero, an enemy of God, of Madre España: to Iligan [a place of exile] with him!" (141–42). Like the ilustrados we saw earlier, the youth is one who suffers from misrecognition. What he takes to be legitimate desires are mistaken by authorities to be signs of subversion and grounds for punishment and exile. Misrecognized, the youth is left with only an unremitting sense of loss, unable to complete the work of mourning what he has been deprived of. After narrating his woes, he tells Kalayaan that surely it must feel for him and grant that he has good reason to cry.

Kalayaan responds, but in a way that decisively departs from the "smooth" and "harmonious" tones with which it spoke earlier. Now it mocks the youth's tears:

> "You must feel and cry," Kalayaan responded with a mocking tone. "Cry! Crying is necessary only when there is no more blood running from your wounds, when all those infamous ones (*los infames*, [i.e., the friars]) no longer have life that can be cut, when the shameful execution of Padre Burgos, Gomez, and Zamora and the exile of Rizal no longer asks for just and prompt vengeance. For so long as there is blood in the veins, and there is life in the enemy and there are inequities that ask for revenge, to cry in one's room is inconceivable; no, it is not the most appropriate thing for a youth." (142)

Once again reminding us of the voice of Simoun in the *Fili*, Kalayaan ridicules the youth's despair. Instead it stirs him with the call to avenge those persecuted by the colonial regime. Indeed, one can justifiably cry only when there is no longer any life left to cut (*cortar*) from the enemy, and when the deaths and exiles of other Filipinos are forgotten. One cries only when one no longer hears the call for revenge. For so long as there exist inequities that ask for vengeance and for the death of the enemy, merely crying and asking for pity would be inappropriate. As with Rizal, the work of mourning can be carried out only with an act of justice conceived as giving back what one has received from the enemy: death. As the elementary gesture of seeking justice, the call of vengeance accompanies the message of freedom. Such a call places freedom in intimate association with death by way of sacrificing oneself and killing the other. This terrible and fearsome association would seem to herald the coming of justice.

This, then, is the truth that Kalayaan shows to the youth: "What I have revealed to you, this is the truth" (143). The truth in this case has to do with death. "For he who does not know how to die for my cause is not entitled to my protection and my shelter. You can tell this to your compatriots" (144).[6] Kalayaan tells the truth. In exchange, it wants death— that of the enemy in acts of revenge as well as that of compatriots in the way of sacrifices. In return for its protection, it requires the willingness to give and take death, which is to say to give and take what is beyond all giving and taking, what supersedes exchange itself. It wants, therefore, what is impossible, not just vengeance and sacrifice, which posit the equivalence and substitutability of one life for another. Kalayaan also seeks what lies beyond such calculated acts even if it must rely on the technics of counting and rituals of reckoning. It seeks those who "know how to die" (*sabe morir*) and thus presumably know how to kill, who know the limit to knowing, a limit that opens into the instant of decision —the decision to kill and die—beyond all knowledge. In the context of revolutionary thinking, the truth of Kalayaan is indissociable from death as the impossible source from which the very possibility of justice, of knowledge, and of truth emerges. And so, too, nationhood.

At the end of their dialogue, Kalayaan departs, leaving the youth in darkness as the light from his candle goes out. The next day, the youth awakens and from his eyes something (*una cosa*) shines forth in a low, slow projection (*lento projecto*, 144). This "slow projection" suggests that he has incorporated the truth of Kalayaan, embodying its ghostly message. He becomes a carrier of its impossible demand for death. He is ready to become a revolutionary fighter, shedding blood rather than tears. Projecting the traces of Kalayaan, he becomes a medium for their transmission, possessed by a presence other than himself. Consider the look in those eyes, and think of the Spaniards seeing it. Then we can think of what other Filipinos suddenly saw: Spaniards regarding them in terror and dread. Seen in this new way, revolutionary fighters, we could well imagine, found themselves endowed with a power they did not realize they possessed. Like the youth, they had awakened to the truth of freedom and its exorbitant, terror-filled demand for death.[7]

NOTES

PREFACE

1. Ernest Renan, "Que'est-ce qu'une nation?" 891. I have also referred to the English translation provided by William G. Hutchison, reprinted in Pecora, *Nations and Identities*, 162–76.

2. Renan, "Que'est-ce qu'une nation?" 899.

3. Ibid., 903–5.

4. For a fuller elaboration of the role of mourning and the imperative of remembering to forget in the formation of the nation, which my own understanding is indebted to but also somewhat deviates from, see Anderson, *Imagined Communities*, especially 199–203. Anderson points out that Renan was writing two generations removed from the French and American Revolutions, when the reality of the nation had already become a settled fact, at least in the West. But for the first generation of Filipino nationalists that I will be concerned with, the period from 1860 to 1890 marked the emergence of nationalist sentiments for the first time, and a great deal of what makes their writings so fascinating are the ways by which they rediscover in the fact of nationhood something novel and yet to be understood.

5. See Anderson's enormously influential book, *Imagined Communities*, as well as *The Spectre of Comparisons*; Chatterjee, *Nationalist Thought and the Colonial World*; Cheah, *Spectral Nationality*; Culler and Cheah, *Grounds of Comparison*; Balakrishnan, *Mapping the Nation*; and Bhabha, *Nation and Narration* for some of the more recent work on nationalism. Indispensable references for the recent thinking about nationalism also include Habermas, *The Structural Transformation of the Public Sphere*; Benjamin, "The Work of Art in the Age of Mechanical Reproduction"; and Marx and Engels, *The Communist Manifesto*.

6. For a brief but suggestive meditation on this point, see Anderson, "The Goodness of Nations," in *The Spectre of Comparisons*, 360–68. For an extended and sustained analysis of the transaction between "death" and "history and technology," see James T. Siegel's accounts of Indonesian nationalism in *Fetish, Recognition, Revolution* and *A New Criminal Type in Jakarta*. See also Mrazek, *Engineers of Happy Land*, and Cheah, *Spectral Nationality*.

7. The term *Castilian*, or *castellano*, has been nearly synonymous with *Spanish* or *español* since at least the sixteenth century and increasingly through the nineteenth and twentieth centuries. Before it became a lingua franca of the territory that has come to be known as Spain (at least since the aftermath of the *reconquista* in the late fifteenth and early sixteenth century), Castilian was one among many Hispano-Romance languages spoken in the Iberian peninsula, including *leones, aragones, catalan, gallego*, and so forth. By the ninth century, Castilian was spoken primarily in a small area around Burgos, north of

Madrid. It took on enormous importance and power with the capture of what was then the Moorish capital of Toledo in 1085 by the king of Castile and Leon, Alfonso VI. Subsequent monarchs began using Castilian as the language of the court and administration beginning in the thirteenth century. By the late fifteenth and early sixteenth centuries, overseas expansion coinciding with the rise of the Golden Age of Spanish literature further expanded and consolidated the hegemony of Castilian over other languages in the peninsula. It should thus come as no surprise that by 1611, the Spanish scholar Sebastian de Covarrubias should call his dictionary *Tesoro de la lengua castellana o española*, as if to suggest that the language of Castile was now that of the entire Spanish realm, and that by 1713, in emulation of the French, the Real Academia de la Lengua Española was created by Felipe V with the motto *limpia, fija y da esplendor* (cleanse, fix, and make splendid, referring of course to Castilian, now regarded as *lengua española*).

The fact, however, remains that there has never been a perfect fit between Spain, in either its imperial or its national guise, and Castilian. Other Spanish languages have persisted and to this day continue to be important, most notably Catalan. The tension between national and local languages is in fact acknowledged in the post-Franco constitution of 1978, which states that "El castellano es la lengua española oficial del Estado. Todos los españoles tienen el deber de conocerla y el derecho de usarla. Las demás lenguas españolas serán también oficiales en las respectivas Comunidades Autonomas de acuerdo con su Estatutos. La riqueza de las distintas modalidades linguisticas de España es un patrimonio cultural que será objeto de especial respeto y protección" (Mar-Molinaro, *The Politics of Language in the Spanish-Speaking World*, 88). By using *Castilian* rather than *Spanish*, I try to keep in view the unsettled dominance of *a* "Spanish language" over other languages in the peninsula and in the empire, and therefore its availability to all sorts of investments, appropriations and misappropriations by those subjected to Spanish colonial rule. At the same time, it is useful to keep in mind that among both Spaniards and Filipinos in the nineteenth century, *Castilian* was used interchangeably with *Spanish*, as if it existed above all other vernaculars in both Spain and the Philippines. See Penny, *The History of the Spanish Language*, 14–23; and Mar-Molinero, *The Politics of Language in the Spanish-Speaking World*, 18–39 and 86–92. I am grateful to Kit Woolard and José del Valle for their helpful comments on thinking through the difference between Castilian and Spanish.

8. See, for example, José Rizal's heavily annotated edition of Antonio de Morga's *Sucesos de las Islas Filipinas* for a pioneering example of the nationalist revision of the precolonial and early colonial history of the archipelago. It is worth noting, though, that Rizal can arrive at an alternative reconstruction of precolonial societies only in and through the archival screen provided by a Spanish writer and by means of the Castilian language. Rizal's work, as we will see in chapters 2 and 3, is an instructive example of Castilian's paradoxical role as an essential supplement to the nationalist project of calling the nation into being. For a more contemporary version of this nationalist project, tracing the crucial role of local languages in the vernacularization of consciousness in and through the workings of English and Castilian, see the seminal work of Reynaldo Ileto,

especially *Pasyon and Revolution*. In all cases, one sees in Philippine history the originary contamination, as it were, of nationalism by the language of colonialism so that the former's ability to posit a precolonial past is necessarily mediated by and infused with colonial understandings.

INTRODUCTION

1. Quezon, *Messages of the President*, vol. 2, part 1, 26–27, cited in Robles, *The Philippines in the Nineteenth Century*, 288.

2. Ibid.

3. See for example, Schumacher, *The Propaganda Movement*, rev. ed., 303–4; Schumacher, *The Making of a Nation*; Constantino, *The Philippines*; Legarda, *After the Galleons*; Joaquin, *Culture as History* and *A Question of Heroes*.

4. See Anderson, *Imagined Communities*. For incisive accounts of Quezon's role in the consolidation of U.S. rule, see Cullinane, "The Politics of Collaboration in Tayabas Province," and McCoy, "Quezon's Commonwealth."

5. See Rafael, *Contracting Colonialism*, for a more extended discussion of these points.

6. By the later eighteenth century, Bourbon reforms had the cumulative effect of opening up the Philippine colony to foreign commerce, in particular British and American. By the nineteenth century, the Chinese, who had been expelled due to their collaboration with the British during the latter's occupation of Manila from 1762 to 1764, were allowed to return, and they quickly stepped in to dominate the wholesale and retail trade of agricultural commodities in great demand by foreign merchants and the world market: sugar, abaca, and tobacco, for example. As I will discuss below, the colony went through a veritable agricultural revolution by the 1820s as the character of its economy moved from one of subsistence to one of growing crops specifically for export in the world market. Hence did the workings of foreign merchants and capital link the colony to a world beyond that which the Spaniards could control, much less dominate.

The liberalization of trade was also accompanied in time by the uneven and often unrealized reforms of the colonial bureaucracy and the introduction of new technologies. In the 1830s, along with the opening of the Philippine ports to foreign commerce, the postal system was reformed and expanded. Steamships made their entrance in 1848, originally for use in Spanish efforts to turn back Muslim raiders and unsuccessful attempts to extend colonial rule to the Muslim south. Between the 1860s and the 1870s, improvements in transportation and communication took place. The first telegraph lines linked Manila to Cavite in 1872, spreading to other regions in the years to come. An undersea cable came to link Manila with Hong Kong and the world beyond starting in 1879, "allowing instant communication with world markets" (Legarda, *After the Galleons*). The opening of the Suez Canal in 1869 drastically shortened the way to Europe and direct steamship service between Manila and Spain began in 1873.

Along with attempts to institute a public school system and a normal school for the training of teachers, especially in the Castilian language in 1863, university education was actually expanded through the 1870s and 1880s such that it was possible to get degrees in law, medicine, pharmacy, theology, and fine arts at the Dominican university in Manila. The colonial government also moved from a regressive system of tribute, which extracted payments and forced labor from those least able to pay, to a system of taxation that was determined along racial lines (such that the Chinese were taxed at the highest rate because they were deemed capable of paying the most, while indios were taxed the least). Attempts, not always successful, were also made to replace forced labor with wage labor.

In the 1880s and 1890s, more books and newspapers were published (notably *La solidaridad*, between 1889 and 1895, which served as the main propaganda vehicle of the nationalist movement based in Spain; see chapter 1). The first railroad system was built (by a British company) in 1892, linking Manila with Dagupan to the north. Limited telephone service was installed in the colonial capital in 1890 and electrical lighting first appeared in 1895. Manila's waterworks were modernized in 1882, while San Miguel, one of the first breweries in Southeast Asia, began brewing beer in 1890. The first horse-driven streetcars began to ply the streets of Manila in 1883, soon to be replaced by electric streetcars with the coming of the American rule after 1900. See Legarda, *After the Galleons*, 336–39; Robles, *The Philippines in the Nineteenth Century*; A. Corpuz, *The Colonial Iron Horse*; McCoy and de Jesus, *Philippine Social History*; O. D. Corpuz, *An Economic History of the Philippines*; Fast and Richardson, *Roots of Dependency*; Cordero-Fernando and Ricio, *Turn of the Century*.

7. The section that follows is indebted to the scholarship of Benito Legarda, *After the Galleon Trade*, and to Wickberg, *The Chinese in Philippine Life, 1850–1898*; de Jesus, *The Tobacco Monopoly*; the essays in McCoy and de Jesus, *Philippine Social History*; Owen, *Prosperity without Progress*; Larkin, *The Pampangans*; and Bankoff, *Crime, Society and the State in the Nineteenth-Century Philippines*.

8. Legarda, *After the Galleons*, 32. See also Lytle Shurz, *The Manila Galleon*.

9. Legarda, *After the Galleons*, 181–211. See also Diaz-Trechuelo, "Spanish Politics and the Philippines in the Nineteenth Century." For the Spanish context, see Raymond Carr's mammoth account, *Spain*, 70–388.

10. For a history of the Manila-Dagupan railroad complex, see Corpuz, *The Colonial Iron Horse*.

11. Carlos Recur, quoted in Legarda, *After the Galleons*, 93.

12. Bowring, *A Visit to the Philippine Islands*, 409–10, cited in Legarda, *After the Galleons*, 213.

13. T. H. Pardo de Tavera, cited in Legarda, *After the Galleons*, 213.

14. See Schumacher, *The Propaganda Movement*, rev. ed., 1–18; and Robles, *The Philippines in the Nineteenth Century*, 3–28.

15. For an overview of the religious politics in the nineteenth century, see Schumacher's works: *The Propaganda Movement*, especially 13–16; *Father José Burgos: A Documentary History*; and *Revolutionary Clergy*. See also Arcilla, "Ateneo de Manila"; de la Costa, *Jesuits in the Philippines*; and Anderson, *Studies in Philippine Church History*.

16. T. H. Pardo de Tavera, "Results of the Economic Development of the Philippines," lecture delivered before the Philippine Columbine Association, 1912, cited in Legarda, *After the Galleons*, 215–16.

17. Regarding money as a lingua franca in the marketplace with which commodities come to express their exchange value, the classic argument comes of course from Marx, *Capital*, 1:125–243.

18. Legarda, *After the Galleons*, 215.

19. For important examples of the cosmopolitan, which is to say, foreign, origins of nationalist thought in a Southeast Asian context, see Siegel, *Fetish, Recognition, Revolution*; Anderson, *The Spectre of Comparisons*; and Mrazek, *Engineers of Happy Land*. For a compelling discussion of the cosmopolitan, or better yet, the "cosmopolitical" aspect of nationalism, especially as it stands in critical relationship to the state on the one hand and to global capitalism on the other, see Cheah, "Introduction, Part II: The Cosmopolitical—Today," and "Given Culture: Cosmopolitical Freedom in Transnationalism," in Cheah and Robbins, *Cosmopolitics*, 20–41 and 290–328.

20. I owe these formulations about translation and historicity to Benjamin, "The Task of the Translator," 69–82, and to many of Jacques Derrida's writings, especially "Des Tours de Babel," *Monolinguism of the Other*; "Acts," in *Memoires for Paul de Man*, 89–153; "Faith and Knowledge," in *Acts of Religion*, 40–101. Needless to say, Martin Heidegger's works, beginning with *Being and Time*, also cast their shadows here and elsewhere in this book.

I. TRANSLATION AND TELECOMMUNICATION

1. *La solidaridad*, 1:199. This newspaper began publication in Barcelona in 1889 and later moved to Madrid. It ceased publication in 1895. The translations that appear in this text are mine unless otherwise indicated. It is useful to cite here the stated aims of the newspaper as it appears in its maiden issue of February 15, 1889. In an article titled "Our goals," the editors state that they seek to "combat all reaction, to impede all retrogression, to applaud and accept every liberal idea, to defend all progress. In a word: one more propagandist of all the ideals of democracy, aspiring to make democracy prevail in all the peoples both of the Peninsula and of the overseas provinces." Here, note that while the paper would come to focus overwhelmingly on the Philippine colony, it was also concerned with events in what we might think of as "greater Spain," occasionally publishing news about Cuba, Puerto Rico, Guam, and the Carolinas. Thus did Filipino nationalism from its inception not only bear a certain liberal trait, it also bore, like nationalism everywhere else in the world, a certain cosmopolitan orientation that would continue to be more or less pronounced throughout the history of the Philippines. For a compelling discussion of the cosmopolitan origins of nationalism, see Cheah, *Spectral Nationality*.

2. See Schumacher, *The Propaganda Movement*, rev. ed., for a concise overview of this generation. I am indebted to this work for much of the historical background on the formative years of Filipino nationalism. However, it will also be evident to those familiar with Schumacher's scholarship that my work, though benefiting greatly from his, moves in a somewhat different direction.

3. For details on the economic and political changes of the long nineteenth century in the Philippines, see Legarda, *After the Galleons*; McCoy and de Jesus, *Philippine Social*

History; and Bankoff, *Crime, Society and the State in the Nineteenth Century Philippines*, as well as other sources cited in the introduction of this book.

4. See Grifol y Aliaga, *La instrucción primaria en Filipinas*; and Alzona, *A History of Education in the Philippines*. See also Schumacher, *The Propaganda Movement*, rev. ed., 12–16; and Netzorg, *Backward, Turn Backward* for brief, laconic descriptions of grammar books that were used to teach children Castilian. For an example of ilustrado fascination with Castilian, see Rizal's stories about learning the language as a boy from his mother as discussed in Rafael, "Nationalism, Imagery and the Filipino Intelligentsia in the Nineteenth Century."

5. Given the very small numbers of Spanish settlers in the Philippines—less than 1 percent of the population by the end of the Spanish regime in 1898—the number of criollos was understandably minuscule. A small number joined the Propaganda Movement, but most of them became alienated once the majority made up of mestizos and indios began to espouse more radical separatist goals. Unlike in Latin America, criollos played a minor role in the campaign for reforms and independence in the Philippines. However, it is worth noting that before the 1890s, the criollos were those to whom the term *filipino* with a lowercase *f* was applied to by the colonial state. *Filipino* thus began as a term denoting Spaniards born in the Philippines in the same way that *Americanos* first referred to those of Spanish parents born in the New World. That *filipino* was historically associated with the capacity to speak Castilian as well as a familial link to Spain further underlines the hybrid origins of national consciousness. It was precisely the accomplishment of the first generation of nationalists to convert an ethno-linguistic term into a national one by the beginning of the 1890s.

6. This intense interest in the telecommunicative capacity signified by telegraphy is echoed in the writings of other ilustrados. For example, José Rizal wrote in an essay about the experience of travel and its importance in one's education during his first trip to Europe in 1882, "Modern nations have understood the advantage of . . . multiplying modern means of communication. . . . The good state of its communication and commerce would thus be an index to the progress of a country, just as the health of a man would be indexed by the perfect circulation of blood through his entire anatomy. Because without these routes, there can exist no relations, without relations there can be no understanding of bonds, without bonds there can be neither union nor strength, and with neither strength nor union, neither perfection nor progress will ever come" ("Los Viajes," 22). See also Rizal's essay "Por Telefono" (1889), which similarly foregrounds another telecommunicative medium, the telephone, in satirizing the Spanish friars. Ilustrado fascination with the technics of circulation, the free flow of commerce, and communication as indices of modernity would seem to echo a powerful strain in European enlightenment thinking, especially since Kant.

7. See Schumacher, *The Propaganda Movement*, rev. ed., 105–7; Fernandez, "The Philippine Press System"; Retana, *El Periodismo Filipino*; and Mojares, *The Origins and Rise of the Filipino Novel*.

8. See Schumacher, *The Propaganda Movement*, rev. ed., 15–16. Schumacher points out

that not all friars opposed the teaching of Castilian even if they thought it was impractical given the shortage of teachers (150). Dominicans, for example, established the Universidad de Santo Tomas in the late sixteenth century, along with other colleges that came to admit native and mestizo students, such as José Rizal, and where classes were conducted in Castilian. The Jesuits, upon their return from exile, were also allowed to establish schools and teach Castilian (along with other languages, such as Latin and Greek). Several members of the first generation of nationalists, most significantly Rizal, emerged from these schools.

9. See United States Bureau of Census, *Census of the Philippine Islands, 1903*, 2:78–79. The Census notes that out of a population of about six million people at the end of the Spanish regime, about 20 percent could read and write in some language, and about 1 percent had "received superior education" and so undoubtedly was fluent in Castilian. Out of this small number, males outnumbered females two to one.

10. See Cushner, *Spain in the Philippines*.

11. It is worth noting the gap between ilustrado ideas about the friars and the friars' actual situation in the colony, which, not surprisingly, was more complicated. As Schumacher has patiently pointed out, among the Spanish clergy, the Jesuits stood out as supporting Filipino education in Castilian. Among the friars themselves, there were in fact a few who did not necessarily oppose the teaching of Castilian but were also resigned to the practical difficulties of doing so on a broad scale. And even the Dominicans, as pointed above, taught Castilian to their native and mestizo students at the Universidad de Santo Tomas. See Schumacher, *The Propaganda Movement*, rev. ed. 15–16, 150. For another treatment of the place of the friar in the ilustrado imaginary, see Rafael, "Nationalism, Imagery and the Filipino Intelligentsia of the Nineteenth Century."

12. See Rafael, *Contracting Colonialism*.

13. See ibid., especially chapters 2, 4, and 6.

14. Anonymous, "Enseñanza del Castellano en Filipinas," 8.

15. The Dutch were of course less interested in Christian conversion and far more concerned with commerce. And where Castilian was the first language of the colonizers in the Philippines, in the Dutch East Indies, Melayu as a bazaar language belonged to no one in particular. Finally, the revolutionary salience of Melayu as it was transformed to Indonesian by revolutionary leaders from different parts of the archipelago provided it with a radical pedigree that the postrevolutionary Indonesian state could draw upon in establishing it as the national language. In the Philippines, given the fact that U.S. colonization had the effect of aborting the revolution and replacing Castilian with English as the national lingua franca, neither the Tagalog vernacular nor Castilian could achieve national hegemony.

For the history of Melayu, see Maier, "From Heteroglossia to Polyglossia"; and Siegel, *Fetish, Recognition, Revolution*. My understanding of the history of the language of nationalism in the Philippines has been influenced by the ways it seems to have differed from the history of the Indonesian language, but also the ways by which such differences have produced at certain moments instructive similarities. Maier and Siegel, along with

Anderson's "The Languages of Indonesian Politics," have been indispensable guides for thinking through the topics on language and politics in the Philippine case.

16. See *Si tandang basiong macunat*, a widely distributed tract written in 1885 by a Spanish friar, Fray Lucio Miguel Bustamante, that lays out these charges. See also Rizal's novels *Noli me tangere* and *El filibusterismo*, both of which are discussed extensively in the following chapters of this book.

17. "Los Frailes en Filipinas," *La solidaridad*, 1:228–30, signed "PADPYVH."

18. For a similar and more elaborately sustained critique of Spanish officials and friars who refused to allow Filipinos—in this case, Filipina women—to learn Castilian, see José Rizal, "Sa mga Kababayang Dalaga sa Malolos."

19. I give to the term *native* a somewhat more elastic meaning to indicate those who were born in the colony and claimed a certain attachment to it. They were those who from the perspective of the colonial-Catholic regime appeared to be racially inferior and therefore subject to the rule of peninsular Spaniards: indios, mestizos (both Chinese and Spanish), and to a certain extent criollos. It is a provisional and ultimately unsatisfactory way of designating the ethnic identity of nationalists, and it is not meant, even if it undoubtedly appears to be, to furnish a reductive formulation of the plural identities of late-nineteenth-century nationalists. For a suggestive discussion on the hazards of translating the multiple racial categories of the colony's plural society, see Anderson, "Hard to Imagine."

20. Lopez-Jaena, "Filipinas en la Exposición Universal de Barcelona," *La solidaridad* I: 28–46.

21. "Taga-ilog," "Algo sobre las colonias franceses," *La solidaridad*, 1:550–54.

22. Siegel, *Fetish, Recognition, Revolution*, 180.

23. "Taga-ilog," "Sangre torera," *La solidaridad*, 1:796.

Igorot is the Spanish term for the linguistically diverse non-Christianized peoples from the uplands of Luzon who staunchly resisted Spanish attempts at conquest and conversion, even as they continued to have regular commercial dealings with lowland Christianized communities and Spanish administrators. In 1887, a group of Igorots, along with Muslims and other lowland natives, was brought to Spain to become part of the Madrid Exposition at the Retiro Park. The Igorot exhibit proved to be the most popular, drawing the attention and stirring the imagination of Madrid crowds, who came to look at "savages" performing the rituals and routines of their daily lives. Newspapers covered the event extensively. The queen herself came to the exposition and invited the group to the royal palace.

Designed to showcase what was left of the dwindling remains of the Spanish Empire in the last two decades of the nineteenth century, the Madrid Exposition also infuriated Filipino nationalists living in Spain. The latter were acutely ambivalent about the presence of "savage" non-Christian groups in the metropole. On the one hand, there was some degree of identification and sympathy with their fate as exploited colonials subjected like animals to display and racial insults; on the other, the ilustrados were also dismayed that Spaniards would come to see Igorots as representative of all Filipinos, thereby obviating the nationalist claims of Filipino capacities for assimilation. Thus did non-Christianized "savages" come to stand for yet another foreign presence that nationalists would have to come to terms with again and again throughout the history of the nation. For a detailed and insightful discussion of the Madrid Exposition, see Sánchez-Gómez, *Un imperio en la vitrina*. For an illuminating history of ilustrado racial thinking, especially with regard to non-Christianized peoples, see Aguilar, "Tracing Origins."

24. "Taga-ilog," "Impresiones Madrileñas de un Filipino," *La solidaridad*, 1:682–86.

2. THE PHANTASM OF REVENGE

1. Richard Kissling was actually the runner-up, with his entry "Moto stella." The winning entry had originally been a piece submitted by the Italian sculptor Carlo Napoli, "Al martir de Bagumbayan." But because Napoli could not post the required bond during the construction of the monument (which called for the use of marble from Carrara, Italy), he had to forfeit his prize. The commission then went to second-place winner Kissling. Act No. 243 passed by the Philippine Assembly set aside the land at the Luneta for the Rizal monument. As early as 1901, a subscription committee was organized by the nationalist journalist Pascual Poblete to raise funds for its erection. It was made up of Rizal's brother, Paciano, and other prominent Filipinos such as Juan Tuason, Teodoro Yangco, Maríano Limjap, Maximo Paterno, Renato Genato, Tomas G. del Rosario and Aristón Bautista. Some forty entries from all over the world were exhibited in 1906 in Manila, and the American governor general James F. Smith presided over the jury that evaluated these. Kissling's bronze statue of Rizal was cast in Switzerland and its base was built by a Chinese foundry in Hong Kong. The parts were shipped to Manila in 1912, and on December 30 of the same year, Rizal's remains, which had been buried at the Paco Cemetery, were transferred with much fanfare to the new monument at Luneta. The most important national landmark is thus literally of foreign origins and materials.

There is as yet no social history of nationalist monuments and urban design in the nineteenth-century Philippines. For information relating to the Rizal monument, see Ongpin, *La historia y fotografías del monumento* (a scrapbook of photographs, including some taken by the Filipino artist Félix Resurrection Hidalgo of the Kissling monument under construction, and newspaper articles relating to the building of the monument deposited in the National Historical Institute, Manila); Republic of the Philippines, "The Rizal Monument"; Baliza, "The Monument in Our Midst"; and Avestruz, "Building the Monument." My thanks to Bert Florentino for forwarding the latter article to me, and to Ambeth Ocampo for pointing out certain details regarding the Rizal monument and Rizal's life and work.

2. See Ocampo, *Rizal without the Overcoat*, for a series of perspicacious observations on the oddness of Rizal's officially sanctioned images.

3. It is interesting to note that the first known monument built to commemorate Rizal shortly after the first anniversary of his death, while the revolution against Spain was still being fought, did not bear his figure. It was instead a simple obelisk with "Masonic-tinged abstractions on which only the titles of his two electrifying novels were inscribed—as if to

say, Read Them! Then Fight For Your Country's Liberty!" Benedict Anderson, "Republic, Aura, and Late Nationalist Imaginings," 5. The statue on the official monument is modeled after the last known studio photograph of Rizal, taken in Madrid by Edgardo Debas in 1890. The seriality of Rizal's monuments is thus based not on an original but on a photographic reproduction, just as his books were also mechanically reproduced. They are then copies for which there are properly speaking no originals. See Rafael, "Nationalism, Imagery and the Filipino Intelligentsia in the Nineteenth Century."

4. L. M. Guerrero, *The First Filipino*, is the standard and most lucid biography of Rizal. See also Retana, *Vidas y escritos del Dr. José Rizal*; Craig, *Lineage, Life and Labors of José Rizal*. For a sharp analysis of popular perceptions of Rizal as a messianic figure, see Ileto, "Rizal and the Underside of Philippine History"; see also Marcelino Foronda, *Cults Honoring Rizal*; and Santos, *Rizal Miracle Tales*.

5. The phrase "first Filipino" comes of course from the title of Leon María Guerrero's biography of Rizal.

6. For a discussion of the Rizal law as an example of "official nationalism" at work, see Hau, *Necessary Fictions*. See also Totanes, "The Historical Impact of the *Noli me tangere* and *El filibusterismo*." For a commentary on the legislative battles surrounding the passage of the bill, see Laurel, "The Trials of the Rizal Bill."

7. See Schumacher, *The Propaganda Movement*, rev. ed., 92, 260.

8. Recently, Benedict Anderson has written a series of essays demonstrating the transnational and cosmopolitical context within which Rizal wrote his novels. See his essays, "Nitroglycerine in the Pomegranate" and "In the World-Shadow of Bismarck and Nobel." Suggesting that "Filipino nationalism really had its locational origins in urban Spain rather than in the Philippines" ("In the World-Shadow of Bismarck and Nobel," 92), he argues that the *Fili* in particular was saturated by Rizal's awareness not only of European modernism, but just as important, of the great historical transformations that were unfolding in the world, ranging from revolutionary Marxism to anticolonial independence movements and especially the rise of anarchism. The novel was an attempt, according to Anderson, to transpose (and one could say, translate) these global events into a Philippine colonial setting, as if Rizal was saying that Filipinos, too, were on the same path toward revolutionary modernity. As Anderson puts it, the *Fili* was "written from the wings of a global proscenium on which Bismarck and Vera Zasulich, Yankee manipulations and Cuban insurrections, Meiji Japan and the British Museum, Huysmans and Mallarme, Catalonia and the Carolines, Kropotkin and Salvadar Santiago, all had their places" (ibid., 128–29). In the same spirit, though by a somewhat different approach, I have sought to underline the cosmopolitanism of Rizal's—and indeed, ilustrado—nationalism in its formative stages from the 1880s to the early 1890s. However, I will also suggest vernacular precedents for this ilustrado cosmopolitanism in my discussion of vernacular theater and the works of the great Tagalog poet Balagtas in chapters 4, 5, and 6.

9. Rizal, quoted in Schumacher, *The Propaganda Movement*, rev. ed., 252, 268. Rizal's frustration with Spain grew from a number of other factors: Spanish intransigence combined with the politically volatile situation in the Spanish parliament where control shifted

rapidly between liberals and conservatives between the 1860s and 1890s, and a series of family tragedies—the imprisonment of his mother and sister under false charges, the exile of his brother-in-law, father, and brother, and the loss of the family's lands in Calamba, Laguna, to the Dominicans. Both novels teem with allusions to these events.

10. For details around the life and death of Gomez, Burgos, and Zamora, see Schumacher, *Revolutionary Clergy*, 1–47. See also Joaquin, *A Question of Heroes*, 7–24.

11. Rizal, *El filibusterismo*. I use the facsimile edition published in Manila by the Comisión Nacional del Centenario de José Rizal, 1961. All references to this book will appear in the text. All translations are mine unless otherwise indicated.

12. Schumacher, *The Propaganda Movement*, rev. ed., 33. Rizal was no doubt being fanciful about this last point, since membership into the major religious orders, including the Jesuits, would have been unlikely for Filipinos in the nineteenth century. Natives and mestizos were limited to becoming secular priests.

13. "The first time I heard it [the word *filibustero*] was in 1872 when the executions took place," Rizal wrote to Blumentritt on March 29, 1887. "I still remember the terror it aroused. Our father forbade us ever to utter it . . . [It means] a dangerous Patriot who will soon be hanged, or a presumptuous fellow." See *The Rizal-Blumentritt Correspondence*, vol. 1, fifth and sixth unnumbered pages after 65, cited in Anderson, "In the World-Shadow of Bismarck and Nobel," 89. Anderson also points out that the political usage of *filibustero* as "subversive" originated in the Spanish Caribbean, specifically in New Orleans and Cuba in 1850, and most likely spread to the Philippine colony through Spanish military officials, many of whom had served in the Caribbean. See Anderson, "In the World-Shadow of Bismarck and Nobel," 89–90.

14. See L. M. Guerrero, *The First Filipino*, 271–85, and Schumacher, *The Propaganda Movement*, rev. ed., 260–69, as typical of the commentaries on the *Fili*. See also Mojares, *The Origins and Rise of the Filipino Novel*, 137–50. Note, however, recent important exceptions to this tendency, in Hau, *Necessary Fictions*, 48–93, and Anderson, "In the World-Shadow of Bismarck and Nobel."

15. For an important discussion of the dynamics of blockage and its relation to the sublime, to which the following discussion owes a distant kinship, see Hertz, *The End of the Line*.

16. See Blumentritt, *La solidaridad*, 2:366. Other kinds of pidgin Spanish existed in the Philippines at this time, including Chavacano, which is still widely spoken among residents of the town of Ternate in Cavite, near where the Spanish shipyards used to be, and in parts of Zamboanga Province on the western coast of Mindanao. The contemporary descendent of lengua de tienda is of course Taglish.

17. The friar here not only parodies Chinese pronunciations of Spanish, he also mimics the Tagalog tendency to confuse *f* for *p*, as when he tendentiously mispronounces *afuera* as *apuera* and *puerta* as *fuerta*.

18. The other possibility in this story, of course, is that Julí could have struck back, taking it upon herself to seek vengeance from colonial authority. Instead, she turns against herself. It is in this way that she can come across as a victim whose "innocence" comes to haunt the teller and listener of her story.

Something else is also at stake in Julí's story, however, and this has to do with the gendering of revenge. Among Rizal's women characters, there is in fact one who seeks to exact satisfaction from a Spaniard who has done her wrong: Doña Victorina. Unlike her more prominent role in the first novel, in the *Fili* she makes only the briefest of appearances, mostly in the first chapter, where she is on a boat looking for her crippled Spanish husband who had deserted her after fifteen years of marriage (3–4). Victorina is depicted by Rizal as a native dedicated to denying her nativeness. She tries to speak Castilian—and does so badly—by repressing her knowledge of Tagalog; dresses in what she takes to be European clothing; dyes her hair blond; and cakes her face with cosmetics. She is in this sense someone in disguise, out to seek vengeance from an errant Spanish husband. But rather than approximate the character of male ilustrados, Victorina comes across as their parodic double, one who fails to recognize that others fail to recognize her for what she takes herself to be, namely a "Spaniard." Neither native nor Spaniard, she is described by Rizal as a "renegade Filipina who dyes her hair blond" and whose appearance eludes the racial categories of nineteenth-century ethnologists. Her scandalous appearance might have made her, like the ilustrados, into a filibustero. Yet she is merely avoided by the other passengers on the ship, regarded with bemused indifference by colonial authorities and agitated annoyance by the author. Rather than lead to disruption and conflict, her presence seems to lead only to embarrassment, thus to a sense of shame among those, especially male ilustrados, who see her. She is a figure of mistranslation unable to see herself as such, a foreign presence oblivious to her foreignness. Literalizing for herself the desire for otherness and the linguistic and phallic authority that such desire promises, Victorina construes herself as an agent of revenge. In so doing, she disfigures the self-regard of male ilustrados, which casts men as the rightful authors of such plots. And for this, she is punished with indifference and marginalized by the author. In this comedic vignette about Doña Victorina, Rizal consolidates what he had already laid out in the *Noli* and in other political writings: namely, the secondary place of women relative to men in the nation.

In this connection, see also Rizal's famous letter to the women of Malolos who, like the male students in the novel, in 1889 sought permission to establish a school that would teach Castilian to the women of their town and were subsequently turned down: "Sa mga kababayang dalaga sa malolos."

19. Michael Meeker has made the intriguing suggestion that Simoun is in fact an iteration of the figure of the Jew as filtered through the anti-Semitic imagination of nineteenth-century Europe. Perhaps influenced by the anti-Semitism of the era, it was as if Rizal was accusing the Spaniards of perverting the original goal of conversion, turning the very best Filipinos into Jews (personal communication). There may be something to this hunch, but I cannot find the evidence to push this claim any further, nor have I found in Rizal or in any of the other ilustrados more explicit references to Jews in their writings. From a different angle, Benedict Anderson makes an extended argument about the anarchist sources of Simoun's appearance and rhetoric. His plot to sow despair and discontent, culminating in the terrorist bombing of a party attended by the top officials and the

wealthiest members of Manila society, is consistent, Anderson argues, with the spread of anarchist acts to assassinate heads of state and sow fear among the bourgeoisie between the late 1880s through the early twentieth century. See Anderson, "In the World-Shadow of Bismarck and Nobel." In either case, one senses the power of Simoun to lie in his irreducible foreignness stemming from the mystery of his origins. He continues to haunt readers of Rizal to this day, as he doubtless did during Rizal's own time.

20. For this formulation of revenge, I am indebted to Siegel, *Fetish, Recognition, Revolution*, 169–70. For another explication of revenge in relation to nationalist consciousness, see Anderson, "Reading 'Revenge' by Pramoedya Ananta Toer."

21. See L. M. Guerrero, *The First Filipino*, 18–19.

22. See Cullinane, "Accounting for Souls." Governor General Claveria's 1849 decree is reproduced in *Catalogo alfabético de apellidos.*

23. Cited in L. M. Guerrero, *The First Filipino*, 38.

24. Ibid., 297 and 298.

25. Ibid., 299.

26. De la Costa, ed., *The Trial of Rizal*, 106.

27. L. M. Guerrero, *The First Filipino*, 421.

28. De la Costa, ed., *The Trial of Rizal*, 103.

29. L. M. Guerrero, *The First Filipino*, 425.

30. De la Costa, ed., *The Trial of Rizal*, 134.

3. THE CALL OF DEATH

1. Rizal, *Noli me tangere*. Here, I use the facsimile edition published by Instituto Nacional de Historia, Manila, in 1978. All page citations appear in the main text, and all translations are mine.

2. Benedict Anderson has pointed out the key significance of this phrase in identifying an abiding feature of nationalism as such: the tendency toward comparison. My discussion, however, moves in a somewhat different direction, since I am more concerned in this chapter with how the question of comparison is linked to telecommunication and endows the nation with a legacy of spectrality. See Anderson, *The Spectre of Comparisons*, 2.

3. See the translation by Lacson-Locsin.

4. For a more extended discussion of ilustrado photographs, see Rafael, "Nationalism, Imagery and the Filipino Intelligentsia of the Nineteenth Century." Thanks to the generosity of Ambeth Ocampo, I became aware of the extensive photographic remains of Rizal and his generation.

5. Rizal, quoted in Schumacher, *The Propaganda Movement*, rev. ed., 83–84.

6. I owe these ideas to Walter Benjamin's essays "The Work of Art in the Age of Mechanical Reproduction," "Some Motifs in Baudelaire," and "A Little History of Photography."

7. For two of the most illuminating studies of this link between technology at the origins of nationalism, see Siegel, *Fetish, Recognition, Revolution*, and Mrazek, *Engineers of Happy Land*. As is evident throughout this book, the general problematic of nationalism's

debt to technology comes out of my own engagement with the writings (in translation) of the philosophers Walter Benjamin, Martin Heidegger, and Jacques Derrida. For an incisive articulation of the relationship between technology and being, see Bernard Stiegler, *Technics and Time*, vol. 1. For an extended commentary on technology and translation in the works of Heidegger, see Weber, *Mass Mediauras*.

8. Cited in Schumacher, *The Propaganda Movement*, rev. ed., 89–91.

9. My formulation of the relationship between the photographic image and its meanings and referent is, of course, indebted to Barthes, *Camera Lucida*, as well as to the sources acknowledged in note 7.

10. See Rafael, *Contracting Colonialism*, especially the introduction and chapters 2 and 4.

11. For a history of the transformation of precolonial ideas about death and their reorganization around a colonial-Christian matrix from the later sixteenth to the early eighteenth century, see ibid., chapter 6.

12. For example, see Schumacher, *The Propaganda Movement*, rev. ed., 89–90; and L. M. Guerrero, *The First Filipino*.

13. For histories of the reception of the *Noli*, see the essays in Reyes, *The* Noli me tangere *a Century After*; Hau, *Necessary Fictions*, 1–92; Schumacher, *The Propaganda Movement*, rev. ed., 83–104; Retana, *Vida y escritos de José Rizal*, 99–119; Palma, *Biografía de Rizal*, 79–88; L. M. Guerrero, *The First Filipino*, 119–53; Joaquin, *A Question of Heroes*, 51–74; and Ileto, "Rizal and the Underside of Philippine History," 29–78.

14. See Anderson, *Imagined Communities*, especially chapters 1–3.

15. See Rafael, *Contracting Colonialism*, especially chapter 1. The fate of Tagalog is the subject of the next three chapters. We see how, in order to stir popular support, the revolution resorted to supplementing Castilian with Tagalog, but a Tagalog that would have had to undergo transformation and encipherment into a secret, coded language outside of Spanish translation. That is, Tagalog had to be transformed into a language other than itself. Only when it became a language foreign to its own speakers did it appear new and thus invested with the promise of being able to replace Castilian. That is not, however, the end of the story. Tagalog under the American colonial period goes through a process of reinvention, this time under the auspices of colonial institutions such as the Institute of National Language and under the direction of writers such as Lope K. Santos. By the 1930s, Tagalog, now figured as the "basis" for a state-sponsored and elite-directed national language yet to be born, was well placed to be an instrument of counterrevolution.

16. For the most recent discussion of Spanish laws that constructed and organized racial identities in the interest of collecting taxes, regulating population movement, and restricting economic activities, see Bankoff, *Crime, Society and the State in the Nineteenth-Century Philippines*.

17. For other moments when death breaks through as the voice that recalls unmet obligations in the *Noli*, see also Rafael, "Language, Authority and Gender in Rizal's *Noli*."

18. A historical sociology of rumors in the Philippine has yet to be written. In any attempt, Rizal's novels would be important primary sources. As Schumacher, that most

erudite of nineteenth-century Philippine social historians, has noted, rumors filled the everyday lives of Spaniards and Filipinos, especially in the latter half of the nineteenth century. It was often on the basis of gossip that certain people in the colony were placed under surveillance by the colonial police. Surveillance itself, built on the speculation of the meaning of certain words and actions, would add to rumors. These were then entered as evidence in trials of suspected filibusteros and used as a basis for their exile or execution. Rizal, of course, had fallen victim to precisely this sort of rumor mongering. See Schumacher, *Revolutionary Clergy*.

Rumors also figured in the conflict among revolutionary factions in 1896–97. The "father" of the Katipunan, Andrés Bonifacio, for example, was arrested by the forces of Emilio Aguinaldo in part because he was said to have entertained a wish to impose himself as a king over the people, that he was secretly funded by the friars, that he had stolen money meant for the purchase of arms and so forth. Like Rizal, he, too, was subjected to a mock trial by the revolutionary government in Cavite and executed in March 1897. The literature on this event, perhaps the most contested one in nationalist historiography, is enormous. See, for example, Quirino, *Minutes of the Katipunan*; Agoncillo, *The Revolt of the Masses*; Alvarez, *The Katipunan and the Revolution*; May, *Inventing a Hero*; and Ocampo, *Bones of Contention*, among others. My own attempt to think through the role of rumor in the formation and failure of nationalist politics in the twentieth century appears in Rafael, *White Love and Other Events in Filipino History*, 103–21 and 204–27.

19. For a suggestive discussion of the performative aspects of torture sustained by a grammar of violence, see Scarry, *The Body in Pain*.

20. For more on the communicative linkages among rumor, secrecy, and death that point to what will become a revolutionary modality of address that exceeds the comprehension of colonial society, see chapter 7 and the afterword of this book.

21. Here, I am tempted to think of this moment in the *Noli* as resonating with Freud's remarks on the most disconcerting sort of jokes, the nonsense joke. Unlike other kinds of jokes, this type reveals no repressed desires but only sheer excess and so undercuts the very possibility of typologizing and interpreting jokes altogether. See Freud, *Jokes and Their Relation to the Unconscious*. For a suggestive commentary on this work, see Weber, "The Divaricator." See also Siegel, *Shadow and Sound*, 213–27, for a reworking of Freud's notion of jokes linked to the threat of writing in a Southeast Asian context.

4. THE COLONIAL UNCANNY

1. For detailed descriptions of Spanish reactions to the novel, both in the colony and in Spain, see Schumacher, *The Propaganda Movement*, rev. ed., 95–104.

2. Ibid., 96. *See* also Retana, *Vida y escritos de José Rizal*, 129–36.

3. Rodriguez, *¿Porque no los he de leer?*, 9–10, cited in Schumacher, *The Propaganda Movement*, rev. ed., 98.

4. For Rizal's comments on Vicente Barrantes, see Rizal, *Escritos politicos y historicos*, 182–93. Subsequent references to this essay will appear in the text.

5. Histories of the comedia are taken from Retana, *Noticias historico-bibliográficos del*

teatro en Filipinas; Barrantes, *El teatro tagalo*; and de los Santos, "Florante." In the 1960s and 1970s, nationalist scholars rediscovered the comedia at the moment of its near disappearance. See Lumbera, *Tagalog Poetry*; Tiongson, *Kasaysayn ng komedya* and *Philippine Theater*; Mojares, *The Origins and Rise of the Filipino Novel* and *Theater in Society, Society in Theater*; and Fernandez, *Palabas*. My own account is heavily indebted to these sources, although it differs in its interpretation of this genre.

6. I am grateful to Nicanor G. Tiongson for calling my attention to the history and typology of comedias and alerting me to their function for reproducing colonial-Christian ideology. However, it will become obvious in the discussion that follows that I have a somewhat different understanding of the historical roots and political effects of the comedia than Tiongson, one which necessarily builds on his earlier insights. See Tiongson, *Komedya*, 1–9. See also Laconico-Buenaventura, *The Theater in Manila*, 44–45, for a discussion of "Chinese comedias" performed among the Chinese community in Manila in the nineteenth century but which did not appear to spread to the provinces.

7. See Tiongson citing the titles of the late-eighteenth-century playwright Huseng Sisiw, *Kasaysayan*, 18. See also the titles listed in Retana, *Noticias historico-bibliográficos del teatro en Filipinas*, 122, such as "Historia y vida tristisima de los sietes Infantes de Lara y de su humilidismo padre en el Reino de España."

8. Retana, *Noticias historico-bibliográficos del teatro en Filipinas*; see also Fernandez, *Palabas*; Mojares, *The Origins and Rise of the Filipino Novel*; and Lumbera, *Tagalog Poetry*.

9. See Mojares, *Theater in Society, Society in Theater*; and Fernandez, *Palabas*.

10. De San Augustin, quoted in Mojares, *Theater in Society, Society in Theater*, 60.

11. Mojares, *Theater in Society, Society in Theater*, 59–60.

12. Retana, *Noticias historico-bibliográficos del teatro en Filipinas*, 122.

13. Ibid., 123.

14. Fernandez, *Palabas*, 64.

15. See Tiongson, *Kasaysayan*, 35.

16. Martínez de Zuñiga, *Estadismo de las islas Filipinas*, 1:76. Subsequent references appear in parentheses in the text.

17. Mojares, *Theater in Society, Society in Theater*, 85.

18. Tiongson, *Kasaysayan*, 53–54.

19. Guerra, cited in Tiongson, *Kasaysayan*, 62.

20. Fernandez, *Palabas*, 68.

21. One sees the persistence of this desire to evoke something beyond the everyday in the photographs of costumed actors during comedia performances in and around Manila in the 1950s found in Tiongson's books *Kasaysayan* and *Komedya*. The costumes come across as a pastiche of styles ranging from Hollywood costume romances and biblical epics to low-rent Las Vegas shows. In any case, they all seem intent on generating in the viewer a generalized sense of exoticism that had little to do with producing historically accurate scenes and costumes.

22. See Corpuz, *The Philippines* and *Roots of the Filipino Nation*; and Bankoff, *Crime, Society and the State in Nineteenth-Century Philippines*.

23. Guerra, *Viajes por Filipinas de Manila a Tayabas*, cited in Tiongson, *Kasaysayan*, 60–61.

24. Mojares, *Theater in Society, Society in Theater*, 84.

25. Ibid., 76. For comments on the absence of applause, see Tiongson, *Philippine Theater*, 64–65.

26. For a discussion of similar cases of the formation of audiences in Southeast Asia from which I have profited, see Siegel, *Solo in the New Order*.

27. Bowring, *Visit to the Philippine Islands*, cited in Tiongson, *Kasaysayan*, 64.

28. Lala, *The Philippine Islands*, 171–72, cited in Tiongson, *Kasaysayan*, 64.

29. See Rafael, *Contracting Colonialism*.

30. Guerra, cited in Tiongson, *Kasaysayan*, 61.

31. Tiongson, *Kasaysayan*, 61.

5. MAKING THE VERNACULAR FOREIGN

1. See for example, Retana, *Noticias historico-bibliográficos del teatro en Filipinas*; Barrantes, *El teatro tagalo*; and Martínez de Zuñiga, OSA, *Estadismo de las Islas Filipinas*. For a summary of these views, see Mojares, *Origins of the Novel*; and Fernandez, *Palabas*.

2. Minguella, *Ensayo de gramatica hispano-tagalo*, 2:872.

3. Guerra, *Viajes por Filipinas de Manila a Tayabas*, cited in Tiongson, *Kasaysayan ng komedya*, 71–73.

4. Barrantes, *El teatro tagalo*, 127–31; 136–38.

5. Retana, *Noticias historico-bibliograficos del teatro en Filipinas*, 177.

6. Ibid., 123.

7. For a concise summary of nationalist thinking about the comedia, see Tiongson, *Kasaysayan ng komedya*, 77–101.

8. Rizal, *Noli me tangere*, 224.

9. For the debates regarding the place of the comedia in nationalist literature, see the articles in the newspaper *Renacimiento filipino*. Much of these debates are summarized in Tiongson, *Kasaysayan ng komedya*, 77–101.

10. Ibid., 95. See also Cruz, *Kung sino ang kumatha ng "Florante,"* 3–4.

11. For de los Reyes's arguments, see Tiongson, *Kasaysayan ng komedya*, 86–87. As the most eminent contemporary scholar on the comedia, Tiongson himself echoes these ilustrado views regarding the colonial and therefore backward stigma of the comedia. See his book, *Philippine Theater*, 2:1–44.

12. Tiongson, *Kasaysayan ng komedya*, 88–89.

13. From an editorial of the Visayan newspaper *El tiempo*, 1903, cited in Tiongson, *Kasaysayan ng komedya*, 92.

14. For a recent and important discussion of the history and politics of nationalist notions of representation, particularly the manner by which they privilege the link between education and self-formation in the struggle for recognition and freedom, see Hau, *Necessary Fictions*. For the philosophical genealogy of the nationalism's investment in education as emancipation, see Cheah, *Spectral Nationality*.

15. See Lumbera, *Tagalog Poetry*; Mojares, *The Origins and Rise of the Filipino Novel*; and Tiongson, *Kasaysayan ng komedya*.

16. Information about Balagtas's life comes mostly from Cruz, *Kung sino ang kumatha ng "Florante."* Page numbers appear parenthetically in the text.

17. José Rizal, "Arte Metrica del Tagalog," 257–60.

18. Cruz, *Kung sino ang kumatha ng "Florante,"* 103–6; de los Santos, "Florante," 55–57.

19. De los Santos, "Florante," 57.

20. Rizal, quoted in ibid., 55.

21. Manuel Adriatico, quoted in ibid., 59.

22. Ibid.

23. Ibid.

24. Cruz, *Kung sino ang kumatha ng "Florante,"* 5.

25. Lope K. Santos, writing in the nationalist newspaper *Muling Pagsilang*, quoted in ibid., 121, 127.

6. PITY, RECOGNITION, AND THE RISKS OF LITERATURE IN BALAGTAS

1. Tiongson, *Kasaysayan ng komedya sa Pilipinas*, 40–41; Lumbera, *Tagalog Poetry*, 97–98; Mojares, *The Origins and Rise of the Filipino Novel*, 74–75.

2. For Rizal, see chapter 5; for Mabini, see Subido, *Apolinario Mabini's Hand-Written Version of Francisco Baltasar's "Florante at Laura."* For a note on how Balagtas is properly speaking not a nationalist writer but someone who is subsequently claimed to be one, see Anderson, *Imagined Communities*, 28–29.

3. Mojares, *The Origins and Rise of the Filipino Novel*, 78; Tiongson, *Kasaysayan ng komedya*, 40–41.

4. Mojares, *The Origins and Rise of the Filipino Novel*, 79.

5. See the Schumacher, *Father José Burgos*; *The Propaganda Movement*, rev. ed.; and *Revolutionary Clergy*.

6. For a discussion of Tomas Pinpin and ladino poetry, see Rafael, *Contracting Colonialism*, chapter 2.

7. Cited in Lumbera, *Tagalog Poetry*, 106. Lumbera has modernized the Tagalog orthography of Balagtas, and since I do not have access to the primary sources of the poetry, I follow Lumbera's postrevolutionary modernization of Tagalog spelling.

8. Ibid., 185.

9. Ibid.

10. See Cruz, *Kung sino ang kumatha nang "Florante,"* 39; and Mojares, *The Origins and Rise of the Filipino Novel*, 195. See also Almario, *Balagtasismo versus Modernismo*; and Sevilla, *Poet of the People*.

11. I use the text provided by Carlos Ronquillo, which according to him dates back to 1861, the last edition issued while Balagtas was still alive. Ronquillo's edition first appeared in 1921. It was edited and republished by Alberto Florentino in 1973. Many other editions exist, such as those in Cruz, de los Santos, and Mabini cited in chapter 5. More recently, Virgilio Almario has published an edition of *Florante* based on a copy of the 1875

edition found at the Newberry Library in Chicago with an insightful history of the different editions of the play, *Florante at Laura ni Balagtas.*

12. Lumbera, *Tagalog Poetry*, 226.

13. Heidegger, *Poetry, Language, Thought*, 226.

14. This process of being shocked by a call one did not expect to the point of drawing near to its source and responding to its appeal is analogous to the process of conversion detailed in chapters 2 and 3 of Rafael, *Contracting Colonialism.*

15. The Tagalog word for "mourning," *damayan* also connotes the act of working together, collaborating on a project, or going through a common experience marked by deprivation and hardship. For a wide-ranging discussion of the political implications of *damayan*, see Ileto, *Pasyon and Revolution.*

7. "FREEDOM = DEATH"

1. *Tribune*, December 31, 1937.

2. Indeed, Quezon was popularly known among Filipinos by the nickname "Kastila," or Spaniard, which is of course also derived from Castilian. Quezon literally was the "Castilian," the embodiment of an ineradicable foreign element within the nation.

3. For a sustained historical treatment of the dilemma of Filipino elites caught between the contradictory demands of official power and popular legitimacy, see Ileto, "The Orators and the Crowd: Philippine Independence Politics, 1910–1914," in *Filipinos and Their Revolution*, 135–64. See also Cullinane, *Ilustrado Politics.*

4. See Gonzalez, *Language and Nationalism*; Santos, *Balarila ng wikang pambansa.*

5. The most penetrating study of popular uprisings during the early twentieth century is Ileto, *Pasyon and Revolution.* See also Sturtevant, *Popular Uprisings in the Philippines*; and Kerkvliet, *The Huk Rebellion.*

6. It is worth noting here that the call for separation among Filipinos was not universal. A number of ilustrados and nonilustrados opposed separation, and only when the revolutionary forces were poised to succeed in 1898 did they join with the emergent government led by Emilio Aguinaldo. Before that, there were always Filipinos from all social classes ready to collaborate with the Spaniards, especially as members of the colonial army. See McCoy, "The Colonial Origins of Philippine Military Traditions." See also M. Guerrero, "Luzon at War," for an instructive account of the counterrevolutionary forces within Aguinaldo's own government.

7. Rizal, *El filibusterismo*, 201–6.

8. For details, see Schumacher, *Revolutionary Clergy*, 16–17. According to Schumacher, Felipe Buencamino was believed to have been the student leader responsible for these leaflets.

9. For an account of the Cavite mutiny and the secularization controversy, see Schumacher, *Father José Burgos* and *Revolutionary Clergy*, chapters 1–2. See also Joaquin, *A Question of Heroes.*

10. Schumacher, *Revolutionary Clergy*, 26–27.

11. Real Academia de la Lengua Española, *Diccionario de la lengua española*; *Velazquez Spanish-English Dictionary.*

12. I am of course thinking of promises as an example of performative speech acts, and much of what follows in my discussion of conspiracies and oaths as performative utterances productive of magical effects is indebted to the work of Jacques Derrida, such as "Signature Event Context" and "Faith and Knowledge." See also Siegel, *Fetish, Recognition, Revolution*, 183–230, and "The Truth of Sorcery," 135–55.

13. The standard account of Philippine Masonry is Kalaw, *Philippine Masonry*. See also Schumacher, "Philippine Masonry to 1890," and "Philippine Masonry in Madrid, 1889–1896," both in *The Making of a Nation*. A more recent and insightful discussion of "Masonic power" is Aguilar, *The Clash of Spirits*. Jacobs, *Living the Enlightenment*, usefully situates masonry within the context of Enlightenment notions of civil society and the shaping of a bourgeois public sphere. I have also profited from the illuminating discussion of the sociology of secrecy and secret societies by Georg Simmel in "The Secret and Secret Societies." See also Derrida and Ferraris, *A Taste for the Secret*.

14. See Castillo y Jímenez, *El Katipunan*, 52.

15. Quoted in Kalaw, *Philippine Masonry*, 126–26.

16. See Retana, *Archivo del bibliofilo filipino*, 3:159–64. A creole, Sityar fought on the Spanish side against the revolution until 1898. During the second phase of the revolution, however, he switched sides and joined the Filipino forces.

17. Sastrón, *La insurreción en Filipinas y guerra hispano-americana en el archipielago*, 56–57.

18. Ibid., 57–58.

19. Ibid., 59. For similar sentiments, see Castillo y Jímenez, *El Katipunan*, 14–16.

20. Retana, *Archivo del bibliofilo filipino*, vol. 3, no. 17, 150–51.

21. Retana, *Archivo del bibliofilo filipino*, vol. 3, no. 54, June 12, 1896, 156–58.

22. Castillo y Jímenez, *El Katipunan*, 115.

23. Ibid., 113–17.

24. See Schumacher, *Revolutionary Clergy*; and Fuertes, "The Franciscans and the Philippine Revolution in Central Luzon."

25. Castillo y Jímenez, *El Katipunan*, 212–13.

26. See Sastrón, *La insurreción en Filipinas y guerra hispano-americana en el archipielago*, 5–16, 158–59; Castillo y Jímenez, *El Katipunan*, 7–10; and Caro y Mora, *La situación del país*, 11.

27. Castillo y Jímenez, *El Katipunan*, 125.

28. Sastrón, *La insurreción en Filipinas y guerra hispano-americana en el archipielago*, 82.

29. Ibid., 124.

30. Sixteenth-century Spanish missionary accounts of the Visayan areas note that the practice of blood compacts, known then as *sandugo*, literally "of one blood," were commonly performed among men (but not women) to establish a pact of mutual protection. Such was necessary given the absence of a translocal state structure in the precolonial Philippines and constant warfare among various villages. The ritual involved, as William Henry Scott summarizes it, "the imbibing of a few drops of each other's blood in wine or betel nut," followed by an oath "to support and defend one another until death." These

were most likely the same missionary accounts that Filipino ilustrados drew from in their understanding of the pacto de sangre. See Scott, *Barangay*, 136; and Schumacher, *The Propaganda Movement*, 2nd ed., 228–30.

31. Ibid., 228.

32. Ibid.

33. See, for example, Zaide, *History of the Katipunan*, 5–10; Agoncillo, *The Revolt of the Masses*, 49–50; and Ileto, *Pasyon and Revolution*, 116–20.

34. Agoncillo, *The Revolt of the Masses*, 49–50. See also Scott, *Ilocano Resistance to American Rule*, 118–19.

35. Castillo y Jímenez, *El Katipunan*, 37, 15–16.

36. Ibid., 35–36.

37. The term is from Mauss, *A General Theory of Magic*.

38. See Retana, *Archivo del bibliofilo filipino*, vol. 3.

39. Scott, *Ilocano Resistance*, 119.

40. Martin Luengo, "Algo sobre los sucesos en Filipinas," in Retana, *Archivo del bibliofilo filipino*, 3:331.

41. See Scott, *Ilocano Resistance*, 119. Copies of signed oaths from 1900, some in Tagalog, others in Spanish and English translation, can be found among the records collected in the Philippine Insurgent Records. See especially reels 8, 31, and 38 at the Philippine National Archives.

42. See, among other writings, Derrida, "Signature Event Context."

43. For an example of this calling and the unexpected hearings it spawned in recent Philippine history, see Rafael, "The Cell Phone and the Crowd: Messianic Politics in the Contemporary Philippines."

AFTERWORD

1. The main source for information on the sole issue of *Kalayaan* are the memoirs of a Katipunero, Pio Valenzuela. See also Agoncillo, *Revolt of the Masses*, 96; Ileto, *Pasyon and Revolution*, 82–91; and O. D. Corpuz, *Saga and Triumph*, 39–40.

2. Retana, *Archivo del bibliofilo filipino*. The translated excerpts from *Kalayaan* are found in 3:134–45. References to this book appear in the main text.

3. See for example, Agoncillo, *The Writings and Trial of Andres Bonifacio*; and Ileto, *Pasyon and Revolution*, 82–91.

4. Pio Valenzuela's memoirs, written after the revolution, claim that it was his idea to start a newspaper, which the Katipunan leader Andres Bonifacio approved. The press was located in his house in Manila and was acquired with the money provided by two Katipuneros, Francisco del Castillo and Candido Iban, who had won an Australian lottery while working as sea divers there. Valenzuela further claims that the articles in the paper were written by him under an assumed name, as well as by Emilio Jacinto and Bonifacio. See O. D. Corpuz, *Saga and Triumph*. The veracity of Valenzuela's memoirs has been questioned by historians like Agoncillo, in *Revolt of the Masses*, and May, in *Inventing a Hero*. Given the physical absence of the original paper, both Retana's and Valenzuela's

accounts do not so much give definitive evidence of the origin of *Kalayaan* as testify to the enduring mystery which surrounds its genesis.

5. Again, Jacinto's authorship of this "Manifiesto" remains uncertain. As Ileto points out, this article is not found among Jacinto's collected works. See Ileto, *Pasyon and Revolution*, 88 n.23. To say that authorship in this case remains uncertain is to confront once again the inaccessible origins of revolutionary writing.

6. Once again, the voice of Kalayaan echoes Rizal, who writes in a letter in Castilian to a friend in 1892, a year after the publication of the *Fili*: "I prefer to risk death and willingly give my life to free so many innocent people from such unjust persecution. . . . I also want to show those who deny our patriotism that we know how to die for our duty and our convictions" (quoted in L. M. Guerrero's English translation of *Noli me tangere*, xiii).

7. Here I must acknowledge yet again my debt to Reynaldo Ileto, whose astute analysis of the texts in *Kalayaan* led me to think about the language of the revolution (see *Pasyon and Revolution*). However, it should be clear to any alert reader of Ileto that my own treatment and emphasis of these texts varies significantly. While Ileto is concerned with asking how the powerful yearning for freedom in the guise of Kalayaan was domesticated and understood in terms of vernacular Christian traditions, principally the epic story of Christ's suffering related in the *pasyon*, I have been more concerned with the technics of transmission and the terrible logic that conjoins freedom to death, allowing for the conversion of the Filipino fighter into a medium for murder and sacrifice. That is, I have been concerned precisely with Kalayaan's resistance to any mode or language of domestication and its defiance of any master trope.

WORKS CITED

Agoncillo, Teodoro. *The Revolt of the Masses: The Story of Bonifacio and the Katipunan.* Quezon City: University of the Philippines Press, 1959.

———, ed. *The Writings and Trial of Andres Bonifacio.* Manila: Bonifacio Centennial Commission, 1963.

Aguilar, Filomeno, Jr. *The Clash of Spirits: The History of Sugar Planter Hegemony on a Visayan Island.* Quezon City: Ateneo de Manila University Press, 1998.

———. "Tracing Origins: Ilustrado Nationalism and the Racial Science of Migration Waves." *Journal of Asian Studies,* forthcoming.

Almario, Virgilio. *Balagtasismo versus Modernismo: Panulaang Tagalog sa ika-20 siglo.* Quezon City: Ateneo de Manila University Press, 1984.

———. *Florante at Laura ni Balagtas.* Quezon City: Adarna House, 2003.

Alvarez, Santiago. *The Katipunan and the Revolution: Memoirs of a General,* translated by Paula Carolina Malay. Quezon City: Ateneo de Manila University Press, 1992.

Alzona, Encarnación. *A History of Education in the Philippines, 1565–1930.* Manila: University of the Philippines Press, 1932.

Anderson, Benedict. "Hard to Imagine." In *The Spectre of Comparisons: Nationalism, Southeast Asia, and the World,* 235–62. London: Verso, 1998.

———. "In the World-Shadow of Bismarck and Nobel: José Rizal: Paris, Havana, Barcelona, Berlin—2." *New Left Review* 28 (2004): 85–128.

———. *Imagined Communities: Reflections on the Origins and Spread of Nationalism.* Rev. ed. London: Verso, 1991.

———. *Language and Power: Exploring Political Cultures in Indonesia.* Ithaca, N.Y.: Cornell University Press, 1990.

———. "The Languages of Indonesian Politics." In *Language and Power: Exploring Political Cultures in Indonesia,* 123–51. Ithaca, N.Y.: Cornell University Press, 1990.

———. "Nitroglycerine in the Pomegranate: José Rizal: Paris, Havana, Barcelona, Berlin—1." *New Left Review* 27 (2004): 99–118.

———. "Reading 'Revenge' by Pramoedya Ananta Toer (1978–1982)." In *Writing on the Tongue,* edited by A. L. Becker. *Michigan Papers on South and Southeast Asia,* no. 33 (1989): 13–94.

———. "Republic, Aura, and Late Nationalist Imaginings." *Qui Parle* 7 (1993): 1–21.

———. *The Spectre of Comparisons: Nationalism, Southeast Asia and the World.* London: Verso 1998.

Anderson, Gerald, ed. *Studies in Philippine Church History.* Ithaca, N.Y.: Cornell University Press, 1969.

Arcilla, José, sj, "Ateneo de Manila: Problems and Policies, 1859–1939." *Philippine Studies* 32 (1984): 377–98.

Avestruz, Paulita C. "Building the Monument." *Business World*, December 28–29, 2002.

Balakrishnan, Gopal, ed. *Mapping the Nation*. London: Verso, 1996.

Baliza, R. J. C. "The Monument in Our Midst." *Starweek*, December 29, 1996, 10–12.

Balthazar, Francisco (Balagtas). *Pinagdaanang Buhay ni Florante at Laura sa Cahariang Albania. Quinuha sa madlang cuadro Historico o pinturang nagsasabi sa manga nangyayari nang unang panahon sa Imperio nang Grecia at tinula nang isang matouain sa versong tagalog*. Manila: Imprenta de Ramirez y Giraudier, 1861. With notes and an introduction by Carlos Ronquillo, 1921; republished and edited by Alberto Florentino, Mandaluyong: Cacho Hermanos, 1973.

Bankoff, Gregg. *Crime, Society and the State in the Nineteenth Century-Philippines*. Quezon City: Ateneo de Manila University Press, 1996.

Barrantes, Vicente. *El teatro tagalo*. Madrid: Tipografía de Manuel G. Hernandez, 1889.

Barthes, Roland. *Camera Lucida: Reflections on Photography*. Translated by Richard Howard. New York: Hill and Wang, 1981.

Benjamin, Walter. "A Little History of Photography." In *Walter Benjamin: Selected Writings, Vol. 2*, translated by Edmund Jephcott, et al., edited by Michael W. Jennings, 507–30. Cambridge, Mass.: Harvard University Press, 2002.

———. "Some Motifs in Baudelaire." In *Illuminations*, edited and translated by Harry Zohn, 155–200. New York: Schocken Books, 1969.

———. "The Task of the Translator." In *Illuminations*, edited and translated by Harry Zohn, 69–82. New York: Schocken Books, 1969.

———. "The Work of Art in the Age of Mechanical Reproduction." In *Illuminations*, edited and translated by Harry Zohn, 217–51. New York: Schocken Books, 1969.

Bhabha, Homi K., ed. *Nation and Narration*. New York: Routledge, 1990.

Bowring, John. *A Visit to the Philippine Islands*. London: Smith and Elder, 1859.

Bustamante, Fray Lucio Miguel. *Si tandang basiong macunat*. Manila: Imprenta de Amigos del País, 1885.

Caro y Mora, Juan. *La situación del país*. Manila: Imprenta del País, 1897.

Carr, Raymond. *Spain, 1808–1975*. 2nd ed. Oxford: Oxford University Press, 1982.

Castillo y Jímenez, José M. del. *El Katipunan, o El filibusterismo en filipinas*. Madrid: Imprenta del Asilo de Huerfanos del S. C. de Jesus, 1897.

Catalogo alfabético de apellidos. Manila: Philippine National Archives, 1975.

Chatterjee, Partha. *Nationalist Thought and the Colonial World: A Derivative Discourse*. Minneapolis: University of Minnesota Press, 1986.

Cheah, Pheng. *Spectral Nationality: Passages of Freedom from Kant to Postcolonial Literatures of Liberation*. New York: Columbia University Press, 2003.

Cheah, Pheng, and Bruce Robbins, eds. *Cosmopolitics: Thinking and Feeling Beyond the Nation*. Minneapolis: University of Minnesota Press, 1998.

Constantino, Renato. *The Philippines: A Past Revisited*. Manila: Renato Constantino, 1975.

Cordero-Fernando, Gilda, and Nik Ricio, eds. *Turn of the Century*. Quezon City: CGF Books, 1978.

Corpuz, Arturo. *The Colonial Iron Horse: Railroads and Regional Developments in the Philippines, 1875–1935.* Quezon City: University of the Philippines Press, 1999.

Corpuz, Onofre D. *An Economic History of the Philippines.* Manila: University of the Philippine Press, 1997.

———. *Roots of the Filipino Nation.* 2 vols. Quezon City: Aklahi Foundation, 1989.

———. *Saga and Triumph: The Filipino Revolution against Spain.* Quezon City: University of the Philippines Press, 2002.

———. *The Philippines.* Englewood Cliffs, NJ: Prentice Hall, 1965.

Covarrubias, Sebastian de. *Tesoro de la Lengua Castellana o Española,* Martin de Riquer, editor, Barcelona: S. A. Horta, 1943.

Craig, Austin. *Lineage, Life and Labors of José Rizal, Philippine Patriot: A Study in the Growth of Free Ideas in the Trans-Pacific America.* Manila: Philippine Education Company, 1913.

Cruz, Hermenigildo. *Kung sino ang kumatha ng "Florante."* Manila: Librería Filatelico, 1906.

Culler, Jonathan, and Pheng Cheah, eds. *Grounds of Comparison: Around the Work of Benedict Anderson.* New York: Routledge, 2003.

Cullinane, Michael. "Accounting for Souls: Ecclesiastical Sources for the Study of Philippine Demographic History." In *Population and History: The Demographic Origins of the Modern Philippines,* edited by Daniel F. Doeppers and Peter N. Xenos, 281–346. Quezon City: Ateneo de Manila University, 1998.

———. *Ilustrado Politics: Filipino Elite Responses to American Rule, 1898–1908.* Quezon City: Ateneo de Manila University Press, 2003.

———. "The Politics of Collaboration in Tayabas Province: The Early Political Career of Manuel Luis Quezon, 1903–1906." *Reappraising an Empire: New Perspectives in Philippine-American History,* in Peter Stanley, 59–84. Cambridge, Mass.: Harvard University Press, 1984.

Cushner, Nicolas, sj. *Spain in the Philippines: From Conquest to Revolution.* Quezon City: Ateneo de Manila University Press, 1971.

De Jesus, Ediberto C. *The Tobacco Monopoly: Bureaucratic Enterprise and Social Change, 1766–1880.* Quezon City: Ateneo de Manila University Press, 1980.

De la Costa, Horacio, sj. *Jesuits in the Philippines, 1581–1769.* Cambridge, Mass.: Harvard University Press, 1961.

———., ed. *The Trial of Rizal: W. E. Retana's Transcription of the Official Spanish Documents.* Manila: Ateneo de Manila University Press, 1961.

De los Santos, Epifanio. "Florante: Version Castellana del Poema Tagalo con un Ensayo Critico." *Philippine Review* 1.7–1.8 (1916). Reprinted as a pamphlet in Manila: Gregorio Nieva, n.d.

De Morga, Antonio. *Sucesos de las Islas Filipinas.* Edited by José Rizal. Paris: Libreria de Garnier Hermanos, 1890.

Derrida, Jacques. "Des tours de Babel." Translated by Joseph Graham. In *Acts of Religion,* edited by Gil Anidjar, 102–34. New York: Routledge, 2002.

———. "Faith and Knowledge: The Two Sources of 'Religion' at the Limits of Reason Alone." Translated by Samuel Weber. In *Acts of Religion*, edited by Gil Anidjar, 42–101. New York: Routledge, 2002.

———. *Memoires for Paul de Man*, revised edition, translated by Cecile Lindsay, Jonathan Culler, Eduardo Cadava, and Peggy Kamuf, New York: Columbia University Press, 1986.

———. "Signature Event Context." In *Margins of Philosophy*, translated by Alan Bass, 307–30. Chicago: University of Chicago Press, 1982.

Derrida, Jacques, and Maurizio Ferraris. *A Taste for the Secret*, edited by Giacomo Danis and David Webb. Cambridge: Polity Press, 2001.

Diaz-Trechuelo, Lourdes. "Spanish Politics and the Philippines in the Nineteenth Century." In *The Philippine Revolution and Beyond*, ed. Elmer A. Ordoñez, 1:141–59. Manila: Philippine Centennial Commission, 1998.

Fast, Jonathan, and Jim Richardson, *Roots of Dependency: Political and Economic Revolution in Nineteenth-Century Philippines*. Quezon City: Foundation for Nationalist Studies, 1979.

Fernandez, Doreen. *Palabas: Essays on Philippine Theater*. Quezon City: Ateneo de Manila University Press, 1996.

———. "The Philippine Press System, 1811–1989." *Philippine Studies* 37 (1989): 317–44.

Foronda, Marcelino. *Cults Honoring Rizal*. Manila: R. P. García, 1961.

Freud, Sigmund. *Jokes and Their Relation to the Unconscious*. Translated by James Strachey. New York: Norton, 1960.

Fuertes, Cayetano Sanchez, OFM. "The Franciscans and the Philippine Revolution in Central Luzon." Translated by B. F. Cadwallader. In *The Philippine Revolution of 1896: Ordinary Lives in Extraordinary Times*, ed. Florentino Rodao and Felice Noelle Rodriguez, 179–216. Quezon City: Ateneo de Manila University Press, 2001.

Gonzalez, Andrew B. *Language and Nationalism: the Philippine Experience Thus Far*. Quezon City: Ateneo de Manila University Press, 1980.

Grifol y Aliaga, Daniel. *La instrucción primaria en Filipinas*. Manila: Chofre, 1894.

Guerra, Juan Alvarez. *Viajes por Filipinas de Manila a Tayabas*. Madrid: Imprenta de Fortanet, 1887.

Guerrero, Leon María. *The First Filipino: A Biography of José Rizal*. Manila: National Historical Commission, 1963.

Guerrero, Milagros. "Luzon at War: Contradictions in Philippine Society, 1898–1902." PhD diss., University of Michigan, 1977.

Habermas, Jürgen. *The Structural Transformation of the Public Sphere: An Inquiry into a Category of Bourgeois Society*. Translated by Thomas Burger. Cambridge, Mass.: MIT Press, 1989.

Hau, Caroline S. *Necessary Fictions: Philippine Literature and the Nation, 1946–1980*. Quezon City: Ateneo de Manila University Press, 2000.

Heidegger, Martin. *Being and Time*. Translated by John Macquarrie and Edward Robinson, New York: Harper Collins, 1962.

——. *Poetry, Language, Thought*. Translated by Albert Hofstader. New York: Harper Collins, 1971.

Hertz, Neil. *The End of the Line: Essays on Psychoanalysis and the Sublime*. New York: Columbia University Press, 1985.

Ileto, Reynaldo. *Filipinos and Their Revolution: Event, Discourse and Historiography*. Quezon City: Ateneo de Manila University Press, 1998.

——. *Pasyon and Revolution: Popular Movements in the Philippines, 1840–1910*. Quezon City: Ateneo de Manila University Press, 1979.

——. "Rizal and the Underside of Philippine History." In *Filipinos and Their Revolution*, 29–78.

Jacobs, Margaret. *Living the Enlightenment: Freemasonry and Politics in Eighteenth-Century Europe*. New York: Oxford University Press, 1991.

Joaquin, Nick. *Culture as History: Occasional Notes on the Process of Philippine Becoming*. Manila: Solar, 1988.

——. *A Question of Heroes: Essays in the Criticism of Key Figures of Philippine History*. Philippines: Ayala Museum, 1977.

Kalaw, Teodoro M. *Philippine Masonry: Its Origins, Development and Vicissitudes up to the Present Time (1921)*. Translated by Frederic Stevens and Antonio Amechazura. Manila: McCullough, 1955.

Kerkvliet, Benedict. *The Huk Rebellion: A Study of Peasant Revolt in the Philippines*. Berkeley: University of California Press, 1977.

Laconico-Buenaventura, Cristina. *The Theater in Manila, 1846–1946*. Manila: De La Salle University Press, 1994.

Lala, Ramón. *The Philippine Islands*. New York: Continental Publishing, 1899.

Larkin, John. *The Pampangans: Colonial Society in a Philippine Province*. Berkeley: University of California Press, 1972.

Laurel, José B., Jr. "The Trials of the Rizal Bill." *Historical Bulletin* (Philippine Historical Association) 4.2 (1960): 130–39.

Legarda, Benito. *After the Galleons: Foreign Trade, Economic Change and Entrepreneurship in the Nineteenth-Century Philippines*. Quezon City: Ateneo de Manila University Press, 1999.

Lumbera, Bienvenido. *Tagalog Poetry, 1570–1898: Tradition and Influences in Its Development*. Quezon City: Ateneo de Manila University Press, 1986.

Lytle Shurtz, William. *The Manila Galleon*. New York: E. P. Dutton, 1959.

Maier, Hendrik J. "From Heteroglossia to Polyglossia: The Creation of Malay and Dutch in the Indies." *Indonesia* 56 (1993): 37–65.

Mar-Molinaro, Clare. *The Politics of Language in the Spanish-Speaking World*. New York: Routledge, 2000.

Martínez de Zuñiga, Fray Joaquin. *Estadismo de las islas filipinas, o mis viajes por este pais* (1800). Edited by Wenceslao E. Retana. 2 vols. Madrid: Imprenta de la Viuda de M. Minuesa de los Rios, 1893.

Marx, Karl. *Capital: A Critique of Political Economy, Vol. 1*. Translated by Ben Fowkes. New York: Vintage, 1977.

Marx, Karl, and Friedrich Engels, *The Communist Manifesto*. New York: Penguin Books, 2002.

Mauss, Marcel. *A General Theory of Magic*. Translated by Robert Brain. London: Kegan Paul, 1972.

May, Glenn. *Inventing a Hero: The Posthumous Re-Creation of Andres Bonifacio*. Madison: University of Wisconsin Center for Southeast Asian Studies, 1996.

McCoy, Alfred. "The Colonial Origins of Philippine Military Traditions." In *The Philippine Revolution of 1896: Ordinary Lives in Extraordinary Times*, edited by Florentino Rodao and Felice Noelle Rodriguez, 83–124. Quezon City: Ateneo de Manila University Press, 2001.

———. "Quezon's Commonwealth: The Emergence of Philippine Authoritarianism." In Ruby Paredes, ed., *Philippine Colonial Democracy*, 114–60. New Haven, Conn.: Yale University Southeast Asia Program, 1988.

McCoy, Alfred, and Ediberto C. de Jesus, eds. *Philippine Social History: Global Trade and Local Transformations*. Quezon City: Ateneo de Manila University Press, 1982.

Minguella, Fray Torribio. *Ensayo de gramatica Hispano-Tagalo* (1878). In *Aparato bibliografico de la historia general de Filipinas*, edited by Wenceslao E. Retana, 2:872. Madrid: Imprenta de la Sucesora de M. Minuesa de los Rios, 1906.

Mojares, Resil. *Origins and Rise of the Filipino Novel: A Generic Study of the Novel until 1940*. Quezon City: University of the Philippine Press, 1983.

———. *Theater in Society, Society in Theater: A Social History of a Cebuano Village, 1840–1940*. Quezon City: Ateneo de Manila University Press, 1985.

Mrazek, Rudolf. *Engineers of Happy Land: Technology and Nationalism in a Colony*. Princeton, N.J.: Princeton University Press, 2002.

Netzorg, Morton. *Backward, Turn Backward: A Study of Books for Children in the Philippines, 1866–1945*. Manila: National Bookstore, 1985.

Ocampo, Ambeth. *Bones of Contention: The Bonifacio Lectures*. Manila: Anvil Publishing, 2001.

———. *Rizal without an Overcoat*. Manila: Anvil Publishing, 1991.

Ongpin, Alfonso T. *La historia y fotografias del monumento al Dr. José Rizal en la Luneta*. Manila: n.p., 1942.

Owen, Norman. *Prosperity without Progress: Manila Hemp and Material Life in the Colonial Philippines*. Berkeley: University of California Press, 1984.

Palma, Rafael. *Biografia de Rizal*. Manila: Bureau of Printing, 1949.

Pecora, Vincent, ed. *Nations and Identities: Classic Readings*. Oxford: Blackwell Publishers, 2001.

Penny, Ralph. *The History of the Spanish Language*. 2nd ed. Cambridge: Cambridge University Press, 2000.

Philippine Insurgent Records, the Philippine National Archives.

Quezon, Manuel. *Messages of the President*. Manila: Bureau of Printing, 1937.

Quirino, Carlos, ed. *Minutes of the Katipunan*. Manila: National Heroes Commission, 1964.

Rafael, Vicente L. "The Cell Phone and the Crowd: Messianic Politics in the Contemporary Philippines." *Public Culture* 15 (2003): 399–425.

———. *Contracting Colonialism: Translation and Christian Conversion of Tagalog Society under Early Spanish Rule.* Durham, N.C.: Duke University Press, 1993.

———. "Language, Authority and Gender in Rizal's *Noli.*" *Review of Indonesian and Malaysian Affairs* (Winter 1984): 110–40.

———. "Nationalism, Imagery, and the Filipino Intelligentsia in the Nineteenth Century." In *Discrepant Histories: Translocal Essays in Filipino Cultures,* ed. Vicente L. Rafael, 133–58. Philadelphia: Temple University Press, 1995.

———. *White Love and Other Events in Filipino History.* Durham, N.C.: Duke University Press, 2000.

Real Academia de la Lengua Española, *Diccionario de la lengua española.* Madrid: 1984.

Renan, Ernest. "Que'est-ce qu'une nation?" In *Oeuvres Completes,* 1:887–906. Paris: Calmann-Levy, 1947–61.

Republic of the Philippines, Bureau of Commerce and Industry. "The Rizal Monument: Story of Its Erection." *Philippines International* 8.2 (1964): 4–9.

Retana, Wenceslao E. *Archivo del bibliofilo filipino: Recopilacion de documentos historicos, cientificos, literarios y politicos, y estudios bibliográficos.* 5 vols. Madrid: Viuda de M. Minuesa de los Rios, 1898–1905.

———. *Noticias historico-bibliográficos del teatro en Filipinas desde sus origenes hasta 1898.* Madrid: V. Suarez, 1909.

———. *El periodismo filipino: Noticias para su historia, 1811–1894: Apuntes bibliográficos, indicaciones biográficas, notas criticas, semblanzas anecdotas.* Madrid: Viuda de M. Minuesa de los Rios, 1895.

———. *Vida y escritos de José Rizal.* Madrid: Libreria General de Victoriano Suarez, 1907.

———, ed. *Aparato bibliográfico de la historia general de Filipinas.* 3 vols. Madrid: Imprenta de la Sucesora de M. Minuesa de los Rios, 1906.

Reyes, Soledad, ed. *The* Noli me tangere *a Century After: An Interdisciplinary Perspective.* Ateneo de Manila University, Budhi Papers No. 7. Quezon City: Phoenix Publishing House, 1987.

Rizal, José. "Arte metrica del Tagalog, 1887." In *Estudios Varios, 1873–1892,* 257–60. Manila: Comisión Nacional del Centenario de José Rizal, 1961.

———. *El filibusterismo: Novela filipina.* Ghent: F. Meyer-Van Loo, 1891. Facsimile edition published in Manila by the Comisión Nacional del Centenario de José Rizal, 1961.

———. *Escritos politicos y historicos, 1872–1896.* Manila: Comision Nacional del Centenario de José Rizal, 1961.

———. *Noli me tangere: Novela tagala.* Berlin: Berliner Buchdrukerei-Actien-Gesellschaft, 1887. Facsimile edition published by Instituto Nacional de Historia, Manila, 1978.

———. *Noli me tangere: Novela tagala.* Translated by María Soledad Lacson-Locsin. Manila: Bookmark, 1996.

———. "Sa mga kababayang dalaga sa malolos" (1889). In *Escritos politicos e historicos,* 55–75. Manila: Comisión Nacional del Centenario de José Rizal, 1961.

——. "Por Telefono." In *Prosa por José Rizal*, 85–91. Manila: Comisión Nacional del Centenario de José Rizal, 1961.

——. *The Rizal-Blumentritt Correspondence*, 2 vol. Manila: National Historical Institute, 1992.

——. "Los viajes." In *Prosa por José Rizal*, 18–23. Manila: Comisión Nacional del Centenario de José Rizal, 1961.

Robles, Eliodoro G. *The Philippines in the Nineteenth Century*. Quezon City: Malay Books, 1969.

Sánchez-Gómez, Luis Ángel. *Un imperio en la vitrina: El colonialismo Español en el Pacifico y la exposición de Filipinas de 1887*. Madrid: Consejo Superior de Investigaciones Cientificas, 2003.

Santos, Alfonso P., ed. *Rizal Miracle Tales*. Manila: National Bookstore, 1973.

Santos, Lope K. *Balarila ng wikang pambansa (ikalawang pagkalimbag)*. Maynila: Kawanihan ng Palimbagan, 1944.

Sastrón, Manuel. *La insurreción en Filipinas y guerra hispano-americana en el archipielago*. Madrid: Imprenta de la Sucesora de M. Minuesa de los Rios, 1901.

Scarry, Elaine. *The Body in Pain: The Making and Unmaking of the World*. New York: Oxford University Press, 1985.

Schumacher, John, SJ. *The Propaganda Movement, 1880–1895: The Creation of a Filipino Consciousness, the Making of a Revolution*. Rev. ed. Quezon City: Ateneo de Manila University Press, 1997.

——. *Father José Burgos: A Documentary History*. Quezon City: Ateneo de Manila University Press, 1999.

——. *Revolutionary Clergy: The Filipino Clergy and the Nationalist Movement, 1850–1903*. Quezon City: Ateneo de Manila University Press, 1981.

——. *The Making of a Nation: Essays in Nineteenth-Century Filipino Nationalism*. Quezon City: Ateneo de Manila University Press, 1991.

Scott, William Henry. *Barangay: Sixteenth-Century Philippine Culture and Society*. Quezon City: Ateneo de Manila University Press, 1994.

——. *Ilocano Resistance to American Rule*. Quezon City: New Day Press, 1986.

Sevilla, Fred. *Poet of the People: Francisco Balagtas and the Roots of Filipino Nationalism; Life and Times of the Great Filipino Poet and his Legacy of Literary Excellence and Political Activism*. Manila: Trademark, 1997.

Siegel, James T. *Fetish, Recognition, Revolution*. Princeton, N.J.: Princeton University Press, 1997.

——. *A New Criminal Type in Jakarta: Counter-Revolution Today*. Durham, N.C.: Duke University Press, 1998.

——. *Shadow and Sound: The Historical Thought of a Sumatran People*. Chicago: University of Chicago Press, 1979.

——. *Solo in the New Order: Language and Hierarchy in an Indonesian City*. Princeton, N.J.: Princeton University Press, 1986.

——. "The Truth of Sorcery." *Cultural Anthropology* 18.2 (2003): 135–55.

Simmel, Georg. "The Secret and Secret Societies." In *The Sociology of Georg Simmel*, translated and edited by Kurt H. Wolff, 306–95. New York: Free Press, 1964.

La solidaridad. Original Spanish texts with English translations by Guadalupe Fores-Guanzon and Luis Mañeru, 7 vols. Pasig City: Fundación Santiago, 1996.

Stiegler, Bernard. *Technics and Time*. Vol. 1: *The Fault of Epimetheus*. Translated by Richard Beardsworth and George Collins. Stanford, Calif.: Stanford University Press, 1998.

Sturtevant, David. *Popular Uprisings in the Philippines, 1840–1940*. Ithaca, N.Y.: Cornell University Press, 1976.

Subido, Tarrosa, ed. *Apolinario Mabini's Hand-Written Version of Francisco Baltasar's Florante at Laura*. Translated by Tarrosa Subido. Manila: National Historical Commission, 1972.

Tiongson, Nicanor G. *Kasaysayan ng komedya sa Pilipinas, 1766–1862*. Manila: De La Salle University Press, 1982.

——. *Philippine Theater: History and Anthology*. Vol. 2: *Komedya*. Quezon City: University of the Philippines Press, 1999.

Totanes, Stephen Henry. "The Historical Impact of the *Noli me tangere* and *El filibusterismo*." In *The Noli me tangere a Century After: An Interdisciplinary Perspective*, edited by Soledad S. Reyes, 17–28. Ateneo de Manila University, Budhi Papers No. 7. Quezon City: Phoenix Publishing House, 1987.

United States Bureau of Census. *Census of the Philippine Islands*. 5 vols. Washington, D.C.: Government Printing Office, 1905.

Valenzuela, Pio. "The Memoirs of Pio Valenzuela." In *Minutes of the Katipunan*, edited by Teodoro Agoncillo. Manila: National Heroes Commission, 1964.

Velazquez Spanish-English Dictionary. Chicago: Follett Publishing, 1974.

Weber, Samuel. "The Divaricator: Remarks on Freud's *Witz*." In *Glyph 1*, 1–27. Baltimore: Johns Hopkins University Press, 1977.

——. *Mass Mediauras: Forms, Technics, Media*. Stanford, Calif.: Stanford University Press, 1996.

Wickberg, Edgar. *The Chinese in Philippine Life, 1850–1898*. New Haven, Conn.: Yale University Press, 1965.

Zaide, Gregorio F. *History of the Katipunan*. Manila: Loyal Press, 1939.

INDEX

Bonifacio, Andrés, 168, 171, 204 n.18, 211 n.4

Bourbon reforms, 6, 133, 193 n.6

Bowring, John, 194 n.12, 207 n.27

British traders, in Manila, 7

Buencamino, Felipe, 209 n.8

Burgos, José, 41, 44, 62, 86, 166, 201 n.10

Bustamante, Lucio Miguel, 197 n.16

Caro y Mora, Juan, 184, 210 n.26

Carr, Raymond, 194 n.9

Castilian: as agency analogous to money, 13; in Balagtas's work, 134–36; in *comedia*, 12–13; demand to teach natives, 21–22, 25; in *Fili*, 58–59; in *Florante*, 144; foreignness of, 72; friars blocking the teaching of, 22, 26; as lingua franca, 17–35, 79; and literature, 96–102; and local languages, 13–14; as medium of transmission, 65; misappropriating, 43–54; nationalists' fascination with, xvii–xviii, 12–13, 28–29, 96–97; as official language, 161–62; political power of, 162–63; popular fascination with, 102; print, 20–21; promise of, 20–25; reasons for limited spread of, 21–22; reciting in classrooms, 46–47; and recognition, 27, 101; and Spanish identity, 34–35; symbolism of learning, 28; telecommunicative reach of, xviii; as term, 191 n.7; and translation, 14; vernacular theater in (see *Comedia* [vernacular theater]). *See also* Tagalog

Castillo y Jímenez, José M. del, 170–71, 175–77

Catholic Church: *comedia* as sanctioned by, 103–4; legitimizing colonization, 22–23. *See also* Christian discourse

Cavite mutiny, 165–66

Celia (character), 145

Censorship, colonial, 17–18

Cervantes, Miguel de, 130

Chatterjee, Partha, 191 n.5

Chinese people, 7–9

Christian discourse: address in, 14, 136–37, 139; and *Florante*, 142–43

Classroom: as extension of the church, 45–46; in *Fili*, 45; reciting Castilian in, 46–47. *See also* Education

Clavería, Narciso, 61–62

Colonial authority, 78, 81, 112–13

Colonial censorship, 17–18

Colonialism, and origins of nationhood, 2, 13, 163–64

Colonial society, 71–72, 109

Colonization, legitimization of, 22–23

Comedia (vernacular theater), 12; absence of Philippine references in, 107; address in, 109–10, 135–39; appearance of colonial society in, 109; audience of, 117, 139, 157; and Balagtas, 127–28; Castilian in, 12–14; characters in, 106–7; costumes in, 113–14; crowds watching, 110; "dangers" posed by, 120–21; described, 104; elites' attempt to curtail, 123–24; Europe in, 106–13; the foreign in, 105, 109, 119; history in, 109; identity in, 114; "lack of realism" in, 120–21; language in, 13–14, 103–5, 115–16; nationalists on, 125; natives sharing, 118; not regarded as *filibusterismo*, 119; as offerings, 116–17; origins of, 106; plots of, 104, 106–7; popularity of, 103–4, 110, 119, 121; preparing natives to encounter authority figures, 112; as products of translation, 117–18; responding to, 119–26; as sanctioned by Catholic Church, 103–4; as source of shame, 125; Spanish critique of, 121–22; telecommunicative effects of, 122, 137; and translation, 104–5; untranslated words in, 105,

Penitente, Placido (character), 49–52
Penny, Ralph, 191 n.7
Philippine Republic of 1899, 2
Philippines: control of, 6; daily life in, 8–9; economy of, 6–8; history of, 5–11; "indebtedness" to Spain, 1–4; notion of separating from Spain, 40; nineteenth-century economy of, 6
Photography, 70–71
Pinpin, Tomas, 134, 208 n.6
Pity, in *Florante*, 147–50, 153–55
Poblete, Pascual, 199 n.1
Prayers, address of, 136–39
Princesa Miramar at Principe Leandro (*comedia*), 108
Principalia (elites), 9
Print technology, and photography, 70–71
Propaganda Movement, 18

Quezon, Manuel L., 1–4, 159–64, 182, 193 nn.1–2, 209 n.2
Quirino, Carlos, 204 n.18

Recitations, Castilian, 46–47
Recognition: of actors, 116; in *Fili*, 46; in *Florante*, 142–43; in *Noli*, 84. *See also* Misrecognition
Recur, Carlos, 194 n.11
Renan, Ernest, xv–xvi, 191 nn.1–3, 4
Republic of the Philippines, 182
Retana, Wenceslao E., 103, 106, 121–22, 170, 183, 185
Revenge: in *Fili*, 41, 54, 58–60; gift of, 54–61; for misrecognition, 57–58, 66; as speaking for the dead, 59; and violence, 59
Revolution: and Castilian in *comedia*, 12–13; Spanish accounts of, 171–73
Reyes, Severino, 123
Richardson, Jim, 193 n.6
Rivera, María Ascunción, 127

Rizal, José, 35, 192 n.8, 201 nn.11, 13, 212 n.6; authorial voice of, 60–61; on Balagtas, 128, 132; charges of *filibusterismo*, 96; on *comedia*, 124–25; on the crowd, 82–90; death of, 77; dedications of, 68; on experience of travel, 196 n.6; and *filibustero*, 40–43, 55; foreignness of, 36, 38–39, 65; frustration with Spain, 200 n.9; interest in publishing *Noli*, 71; and the Katipunans, 63–64; language of works of, 163; and Liga Filipina, 168; life of, 65; on lingua franca, 79–80; linguistic skills of, 38, 54; meaning of being an author for, 61–65; on *mi Patria*, 68, 78; misrecognition of, 97; monuments of, 36–39, 70, 199 nn.1, 3; name of, 54–55, 61–65, 67; on protagonist of *Noli*, 100; pseudonym used by, 185; recognition of, 101; on rumors, 90, 93, 204 n.18; as Simoun, 60–61, 64; strangeness of, 36–40; women characters of, 201 n.18. *See also El filibusterismo* (Rizal); *Noli me tangere* (Rizal)
Rizal, Paciano, 62, 199 n.1
Robbins, Bruce, 195 n.19
Robles, Eliodoro, 193 n.6, 194 n.14
Rodriguez, José, 97, 205 n.3
Ronquillo, Carlos, 208 n.11
Rosario, Tomas G. del, 199 n.1
Rumors: and images of the dead, 93; in *Noli*, 89–95; in Rizal's works, 90, 93, 204 n.18; social effects of, 90–91

Sa Babasa Nito (preface to *Florante*), 145–46
Sacrifice, notion of, xv–xvi
Salví, Padre, 74, 81–82
Sánchez-Gómez, Luis Ángel, 198–99 n.23
Santo (saint), and actors, 113–14
Santos, Lope K., 123, 130, 204 n.15
Sastrón, Manuel, 169, 171

VICENTE L. RAFAEL is
a professor of history at the
University of Washington.

Library of Congress
Cataloging-in-Publication Data
Rafael, Vicente L.
The promise of the foreign : nationalism
and the technics of translation in the
Spanish Philippines / Vicente L. Rafael.
p. cm.
Includes bibliographical references and
index.
ISBN 0-8223-3651-0 (cloth : alk. paper) —
ISBN 0-8223-3664-2 (pbk. : alk. paper)
1. Nationalism—Philippines—History—To
19th century. 2. Philippines—Politics and
government—19th century. 3. Language
and languages—Political aspects—
Philippines. 4. Spanish language—
Philippines. 5. Philippine literature
(Spanish)—History and criticism.
6. Translating and interpreting—
Philippines—History. I. Title.
DS675.R34 2005
320.54'09599'09034—dc22
2005011388